Feminisms, Technology and Depth Psychology

Feminisms, Technology and Depth Psychology explores the intersection of a variety of feminist thought with technology through the lens of depth psychology, and investigates how current approaches to technology impact female life globally – from internet use, to biotechnology, to how female creators imagine life.

This thought-provoking collection is a discussion on changing female capacities and creativity. It questions whether female oppression is becoming more easily enabled within the context of technology use, touching on topics of manipulation, ecological awareness, female decision making, and more. Part One is a three-chapter investigation on queer history, birthing, and reproductive technologies in science fiction novels. Part Two explores images of females and technology in a variety of cultural products ranging from science fiction films to contemporary TV dramas and novels. Part Three looks at the political impact of technology on female worlds, and Part Four examines perspectives on the creative process behind writing science fiction and fantasy.

Feminisms, Technology and Depth Psychology will appeal to Jungian analysts and psychotherapists, and analytical psychologists. It also offers insightful perspectives to academics and students of psychology, gender studies, and politics.

Leslie Gardner, PhD, is a fellow in the department of Psychosocial and Psychoanalytic Studies at the University of Essex; she has published articles on depth psychology and a book, *Rhetorical Investigations: CG Jung and GB Vico* (2014), as well as co-convened conferences and edited books of the conference feminisms and depth psychology, and classics and depth psychology. She heads up an international literary agency, Artellus Ltd in London, UK. She is assisting as co-editor on a new series of Jung and politics with Routledge. Her upcoming work is on ghostwriting, commissioned by Routledge.

Catriona Miller is a professor in Media at Glasgow Caledonian University and author of *Cult TV Heroines* (2020). She has also published on film theory, feminism, and mythology from a depth psychology perspective. She is Editor-in-Chief of the *Journal of Jungian Scholarly Studies* and a senior fellow of the Higher Education Academy.

Roula-Maria Dib, PhD, is an award-winning Jungian/literary scholar, poet, educator, and editor. She is the founding director of the London Arts-Based Research Centre, founding editor of literary and arts journal, *Indelible*, and creative producer of literary event series, Indelible Evenings, as well as Jungian virtual salon, Psychreative.

Feminisms, Technology and Depth Psychology

An Enquiry

Edited by
Leslie Gardner, Catriona Miller,
and Roula-Maria Dib

LONDON AND NEW YORK

Designed cover image: © Dr. Frances Gray

First published 2024
by Routledge
4 Park Square, Milton Park, Abingdon, Oxon OX14 4RN

and by Routledge
605 Third Avenue, New York, NY 10158

Routledge is an imprint of the Taylor & Francis Group, an informa business

© 2024 selection and editorial matter, Leslie Gardner, Catriona Miller and Roula-Maria Dib; individual chapters, the contributors.

The right of Leslie Gardner, Catriona Miller and Roula-Maria Dib to be identified as the authors of the editorial material, and of the authors for their individual chapters, has been asserted in accordance with sections 77 and 78 of the Copyright, Designs and Patents Act 1988.

All rights reserved. No part of this book may be reprinted or reproduced or utilised in any form or by any electronic, mechanical, or other means, now known or hereafter invented, including photocopying and recording, or in any information storage or retrieval system, without permission in writing from the publishers.

Trademark notice: Product or corporate names may be trademarks or registered trademarks, and are used only for identification and explanation without intent to infringe.

British Library Cataloguing-in-Publication Data
A catalogue record for this book is available from the British Library

ISBN: 9781032186818 (hbk)
ISBN: 9781032186795 (pbk)
ISBN: 9781003255727 (ebk)

DOI: 10.4324/9781003255727

Typeset in Times New Roman
by codeMantra

This collection is dedicated to firebrand philosopher Drucilla Cornell, supporter and inspiration for feminists and progressive people everywhere, whom we lost in 2022.

Contents

Notes on contributors   ix
Preface: Care as a Subversive Enterprise by Robin McCoy Brooks   xii

Introduction   1
LESLIE GARDNER

PART ONE
Technological Invasions: Reproduction and Regeneration in Time   5

1   Polydore Vergil and the Immortal Jellyfish (or, How to Read Queer History without Any Queers)   7
CLEO MADELEINE

2   The Rupture of the Sacred: Intrusion of Technology into the Birth Process   31
HEBA ZAPHIRIOU-ZARIFI

3   Speculative Reproduction: The Technology of 'Giving Birth'   54
LESLIE GARDNER

PART TWO
Cultural Product and Female Aspects   67

4   *Evolution* and Enigma: On the Origins of Obstetric Violence   69
EMMY VYE

5 Re-constellating the Great Mother: Images of the Gynoid in
   Contemporary SF TV Drama   83
   CATRIONA MILLER

6 *Quantum Fiction*: The Presentation of Eros in a World of Logos 103
   ROULA-MARIA DIB

PART THREE
Political Impact of Technology on Female Worlds   117

7 Zoom as the Cuckoo Bird   119
   RENÉE M. CUNNINGHAM

8 A Transcendent Future: A 'Discovery" of Nonbinary Stories'   130
   MARIEKE CAHILL

PART FOUR
Enactment: Performative Demonstrations   157

9 Wonder Vision (Adapted from a Talk Which Was Even More
   Chaotic Than This)   159
   JUSTINA ROBSON

10 *Eve and Ava at the Flaming Sword Café*: The Genesis of a
   Very Short Play   170
   ELIZABETH ÈOWYN NELSON

   Index   *187*

Contributors

Marieke Cahill is a transdisciplinary and multi-modal artist, author, speaker, and activist focusing on Jungian Arts Based Research that queers Jungian theories and explores vocal archetypes. They hold an M.A. in Engaged Humanities with Emphasis in Depth Psychology from Pacifica Graduate Institute and are currently pursuing a Ph.D. in Depth Psychology.

Renée M. Cunningham, MFT, is a Diplomate Jungian analyst in private practice in Phoenix, Arizona. She is a member of the Inter-Regional Society of Jungian Analysts-Texas Chapter, International Association of Jungian Studies and the Chinese American Psychoanalytic Alliance. She has been published in the Jungian journal, *Psychological Perspectives* (December, 2018), and recently published *Archetypal Nonviolence: Jung, King and Culture Through the Eyes of Selma* (Routledge, 2020).

Roula-Maria Dib, PhD, is the founding director of the London Arts-Based Research Centre, the founding editor of literary and arts journal, *Indelible*, and creative producer of literary event series, *Indelible Evenings*, as well as *Psychreative*, a virtual salon for researchers and creatives with a background in Jungian psychology. She is a holder of the UK Global Talent Visa as an award-winning literary scholar, poet, educator, and editor; she has authored *Jungian Metaphor in Modernist Literature* (Routledge, 2020) as well as a poetry collection, *Simply Being* (Chiron, 2021). Her MOOC, "Why Online Creative Communities Matter", is featured on Academia.edu.

Leslie Gardner, PhD, is the convenor of biannual feminisms conferences and classics and depth psychology conferences. She is a Fellow in the department of psychosocial and psychoanalytic studies at the University of Essex, and has published numerous chapters in collected volumes; as well as edited collections of essays with co-editors Frances Gray, Catriona Miller, Paul Bishop, Terence Dawson, Richard Seaford. She is author of *Rhetorical Investigations: GB Vico and CG Jung* (Routledge, 2014) based on her PhD. An upcoming commissioned volume on ghostwriting is due out next year, to be published by Routledge. Leslie also runs an international literary agency, Artellus Ltd.

Cleo Madeleine teaches at the University of East Anglia, where she completed her PhD in queer historiography. Her current research looks at queer visibility in contemporary liberation movements. She is also a spokesperson for the charity Gendered Intelligence, a poet, and an activist.

Robin McCoy Brooks is a Jungian Analyst, Trainer, Educator, and Practitioner of Group Psychotherapy and consultant living in Bellingham, WA, USA. She is the Co-Editor-in-Chief of the *International Journal of Jungian Studies* and the author of *Psychoanalysis, Catastrophe & Social Action* (Routledge, 2022) and a co-author along with Graham Harriman and Lusijah Marx of *The Healing Power of Community in Mutual Aid Cultures: Exploring how we may radicalize mental health today through our experiences during the AIDS crisis* (Routledge, 2024, in production).

Catriona Miller, Phd, is a Professor in Media at Glasgow Caledonian University, where she teaches on creativity and media content development. Her research interests include storytelling and the archetypal dimensions of science fiction, horror, and fantasy genres. She published a monograph *Cult TV Heroines* for Bloomsbury in 2020, and "What has the mistress of all the lands done?: Inanna's Descent Recontextualised" in *The Descent of the Soul and the Archaic: Katábasis and Depth Psychology* (2023), edited by L. Gardner, P. Bishop and T. Dawson. She also publishes on Jungian film theory and co-edited *Exploring Depth Psychology and the Female Self: Feminist Views from Somewhere* with Leslie Gardner for Routledge in 2021. She is a Senior Fellow of the Higher Education Academy.

Elizabeth Èowyn Nelson, faculty at Pacifica Graduate Institute, has been a professional writer and editor for more than thirty years. She specializes in research design, methodology, scholarly writing, and dissertation development. Dr Nelson bridged her professional experience in Silicon Valley with her background in literature and expertise in depth psychology to teach courses on the profound impact of digital technology. Her books include *Psyche's Knife: Archetypal Explorations of Love and Power* (Chiron, 2012) and *The Art of Inquiry: A Depth Psychological Perspective* (Spring Publications, 2017), co-authored with Joseph Coppin.

Justina Robson is from Leeds, UK and was born in 1968. She is the author of 11 published science fiction novels and many short stories. She was the winner of the 2000 Amazon Writers' Bursary, for her first two novels which explored AI and human engineering, respectively. Her third novel moved towards the far future – set in a transhuman solar system of political upheaval and personal change as humans encounter their first post-singularity aliens. After that, the launch of a series with *Quantum Gravity* playing with cyberpunk and bodily augmentations. Most recently she's written about further human engineering in the female-centric world featured in the novel *Glorious Angels*, and in the corporatised far future where people themselves are commodities.

Contributors xi

Emmy Vye is completing an arts-based PhD in feminist psychoanalysis at Goldsmiths, University of London. She is a lecturer in Jungian and Post-Jungian Studies at the University of Essex.

Heba Zaphiriou-Zarifi (GAP, UKCP, IAAP) is a Senior Jungian Analytical Psychologist, training analyst and supervisor, with a private practice in London. She is Leadership trained in BodySoul Rhythms® at the Marion Woodman Foundation and founder of The Central London Authentic Movement Practice. Heba integrates Philosophy, Body-psychotherapy, Embodied Active Imagination, and the creative arts into her clinical work. She consults on psychosocial projects in the Middle East, also working with victims of war. She is a speaker at international conferences and a published contributor to academic journals. Her alma mater is the Sorbonne, where she gained two master's degrees and wrote her doctoral thesis on Philosophy. She is mother to three children, all born at home and in their own time.

Preface
Care as a Subversive Enterprise

Robin McCoy Brooks

Leslie Gardner, Catriona Miller, and Roula-Maria Dib are to be celebrated for the thematic vision for this volume and for their selection of contributors. The essays share a capacity to push our frames of seeing, knowing and apperceiving to the very edge and then pushes us over. The disciplines referred to in the title of the book are depth psychology, feminism(s), and technology but the actual range of the perspectives contained exceed the promise of the title. The authors are concerned with the psychosocial effects of cultural *disindividuation* on the female, queer, and/or trans-gendered body/psyche in particular. The term psychosocial subverts a distinction between psyche and social by recognising that there is no firm division between them but becomes a meeting ground from which a critical study of how a self- and multi-faceted world integrated with technological developments may arise.

I am reminded of Gilbert Simondon's supposition over seventy years ago that viewed the human subject as both *constituting and being constituted* by multiple co-affective modalities including the natural world (science), psychical (being) collective, and mechanical (technics) processes involved in any and all constructions of individuation, including collective individuation (Simondon, 1992; and see also Saban, 2020). Simondon (as did Lacan and Jung as luminaries of the psychosocial) decentres our understanding of how we become from the individual into a conceptualization of multiple, distinct, and ontogenetically generated individuation processes. The late French philosopher Bernard Stiegler would find in Simondon a theoretical point of departure in support of his concern for *thinking's disindividuation*, a concept he borrows from Simondon that means a moving away from the conditions of individuation at any tier and particularly our ability to think critically into the world's wound as a means of returning to self-reflection *as a collective practice* (Brooks, 2022; Stiegler, 2019).

Extending this idea, we can feel how each author calls on the reader to personally engage their work by drawing on our minds, our corporeal intuitions, and subaltern knowledges that are social and relational and rooted from the multiple interpretive and trans-historical traditions each of us inhabits. The essays are thus conceived within a trans-disciplinary problematic. Lisa Baraitser has described trans-disciplinary practices as those research practices that allow a concept, text, or method to freely "roam, inserting itself like a foreign entity within an otherwise homogenous field" that opens an inquiry to a transformational component through its raw daring to go where others have not (Baraitser, 2015). To break away, in other words from what feminist Nadine Naber refers to as the "academic industrial complex: a pervasive structure that determines how and what kinds of knowledge may be produced within a power matrix that erases other ways of knowing".[1] (Nadine Naber is an academic and radical feminist scholar who teaches how to align research goals and other creative productions through authentic commitments to social transformation.) Thus, each essay powerfully critiques what is missing from dominating discourses.

We are asked to engage specific kinds of phenomena of our times: the subjugating polyvagal experience of ZOOM platforms, the juxtaposition of femininity and technology depicted in media, eros in a quantum universe of science fiction, profound confusion, or loss of mind regarding our fate as a culture mirrored back in contemporary film, the silencing of gender at the core of technology and medical interventions, vulnerability of teenage girls, subjective destitution reconfigured within a 360-degree film viewing experience, the deprogramming of impossible demands that quash desire, and autonomy of psychic life in the modern world.

Many of these essays are also concerned with the question of what can be expected, or what might happen if accepting our vulnerability or shared precarity as creatures (in Judith Butler's sense) might unleash a possibility of enabling new ways of knowing amidst accelerating disindividuating realities. We can discern a note of hope precisely because a truth of things (many ugly truths) is being carefully placed at our feet, possibly spawning a modest breakthrough for both author and reader. We can be inspired by the ways in which each author becomes de-invisibilized by writing about what each deeply cares about becoming a form of social activism that may pull us into some sort of somatic attunement and *to care with them.*

Care in today's world is a subversive enterprise. The call to care arises with and amongst others but is singularly apprehended – a transient truth about oneself, how to live, how to conduct oneself with others when confronted with our capacity for untruth. These essays have the potential to move each of us from a sort of mindless disengagement with the degree to which female and queer-trans bodies are ongoingly compromised across time. Let us consider the terrible loss not only to the disenfranchised but to humankind as a whole that limps along without a fullness of engagement in a world that desperately needs all of us at the helm.

Disclaimer

All names and places of clients/patients mentioned in case studies have been made anonymous and any similarity to living persons is completely inadvertent.

Note

1 Nadine Naber is an academic and radical feminist scholar who teaches how to align research goals and other creative productions through authentic commitments to social transformation. See her website for more information on her published and other works at https://nadinenaber.com/

References

Baraitser, L. (2015) Temporal drag: transdisciplinarity and the "case" of psychosocial studies. *Theory, Culture & Society*, 32(5–6), pp. 207–231.

Brooks, R. (2022) *Psychoanalysis, Catastrophe and Social Change*. New York and London, Routledge.

Naber, N. (2021) Liberate your research, in *Liberation Pedagogy Project*, episode 14, Spotify, https://anchor.fm/liberationpedagogypodcast/episodes/Episode-14---Liberate-Your-Research-erddcr (Accessed 1 August 23).

Saban, M. (2020) Simondon and Jung: rethinking individuation, in *Holism Possibilities and Problems*, in C. McMillian, R. Main, and D. Henderson (eds), London and New York: Routledge, pp. 91–97.

Simondon, G. (1992) The genesis of the individual, in J. Crary and S. Kwinter (eds), *Incorporations*. New York: Zone.

Stiegler, B. (2019) *The Age of Disruption Technology and Madness in Computational Capitalism*. Trans. by Daniel Ross, Medford, MA: Polity Press.

Introduction

Leslie Gardner

Embodied life for a female is both comprised of and compromised by the ways and means of giving birth, raising children, displaying and living out identities, and galvanised by the problematics of gender.

Closely intertwined to physiology is the psyche: and, for Jung, consciousness is a secondary phenomenon. We are born with pre-loaded instincts and habits (a personality) that we find response to in the world around us and which we interact with by picking up cultural and maternal indications in that world.

That inborn set of predispositions is the primary layer of human personality. Consciousness comes later. "Human consciousness created objective existence and meaning and man [sic] found his indispensable place in the process of being" as Jung wrote in Memories, Dreams, Reflections (1963/1977, p. 285). You might propose that this finding is the basis of his direct work on speculative fiction, the 'Flying Saucers' essay (see Jung and Hull, 1978). Those objects were projections formulated in the midst of an anxious search of the skies for meaning. UFOs are technological metaphors for the processes of psychic human life, affective and physiologically compromised.

In related ways, traditionally designated 'female' body parts no longer seem sufficiently to designate gender. Giving birth and performing intimacy are no longer conventionally so easy to describe or enact.

In this book inspired by a conference held in autumn 2020 (appropriately held online), entitled 'Feminisms and Technology' participants explored the issue of how feminist thought from a depth psychology aspect impacts on technical considerations of the body, on reproduction, on cultural product, on social media, fictional and dystopian future ways of living too within oppressed and colonised communications, and inhabitation of difficult terrains. We added chapters from interested people who didn't attend, too.

Feminist sf writer and literary commentator and professor, Joanna Russ, in her 1978 essay on technology wrote that thinking and writing about technology has become an addiction, particularly in academia – a rabbit hole of endless depths with twists and turns that engage us ferociously (see Russ, 1995). In her novel *The Female Man* (1977) she explores those adaptations wrought by cloning, which she deems faulty due to historical contexts, and despite the finesse of DNA matches.

DOI: 10.4324/9781003255727-1

The fourth clone of Jane orchestrates a world without males, and attempts to draw in the other clones from different cultures and times with her. The result is of middling success.

We learn from Donna Haraway about metaphors of cyborg life (2004), and 'situated knowing' (1988) – algorithms of life generated by performative requirements, recalling Judith Butler's earlier works, and by unconscious and unpredictable curves in agency.

Does the very use of technological means impact on the psyche, as Karan Barad (see 2003, for example) insists? Cultural life, including but not limited to the internet and AI, robotics, underpins contemporary living globally. Jung, among other depth psychologists, addressed ways these props impinged on life ... the geography of imagination that runs alongside the everyday world of an agreed common reality? ... either facilitating or quashing genuine human living – indeed, are the very technological tools themselves infused with conventional and continued restrictive ways; for example, of how we give birth in hospitals full of the imagery of animal behaviour? Are our screens setting us on paths of how to regard female warriors, home-makers, politicians?

Jungian psychology accommodates thinking and imagining that the psyche can take on multiple personalities (personae) successfully – in fact we all use these as weapons for survival. Jungian psychology looks to collective tropes and psychosocial cultural tools, legitimising the multiple faces of embodied life, especially for females.

Approaches to technology impact on female life globally – from internet use, to invasive and biologically altering medical technology, and science fiction as female writers imagine life. The facility of interaction on social media – is it blurring female capacities and creativity, or enabling oppression more easily? Is the manipulation of pain as a side effect in enhancing the body toward technologically enhanced 'looks' viable? The ecologically aware use of technology has a specific effect on females as they try to raise children in ways that will mean there is a habitable planet – in fact, decisions about having children are core to female reproductive themes. To what extents do we go to enhance our presentations of ourselves as females.

The essays are divided into four parts.

1. Technological invasions – impact on the body from feminist perspectives
2. Cultural product and female aspects
3. Political impact of technology on female worlds
4. Enactment – a script exploring Haraway's cyborg ideas

In Part One, Cleo Madeleine discusses how to read queer history in her recounting of the medievalist, Polydore Vergil, who talked about transformation as immortality as she explores what transformation is. Heba Zaphiriou-Zarifi takes on the problematics of medicalised pregnancy and birth: the rupture of the sacred and the sealed; and Leslie Gardner explores female intelligences in the history of automata, robots, and clones – among other technological creations, focusing too on themes of reproduction.

In Part Two, Emmy Vye delves into the work of film director and writer Lucile Hadžihalilović on evolution and the enigmas of controlled development, while Catriona Miller explores whether contemporary images of manufactured females (gynoid characters in TV sf drama) might be a fresh constellation of the Great Mother Archetype and what they might be trying to tell us. Roula-Maria Dib susses out quantum fiction and the presentation of Eros in a world of logos typically masculine through the work of sf novelist Justina Robson.

In Part Three, Renée Cunningham sets out the anomalies of communication for feminists on the platform of virtual talk: Zoom. The personality alliances and modes of talking for transsexual feminists is beleaguered by algorithms of language embedded in collective consciousness as Marieke Cahill explores highlighting her own non-binary experience.

In Part Four, teacher and scholar Elizabeth Èowyn Nelson presents a dramatic talk, a presentation of ecological and feminist issues, alluding to Haraway.

Our conclusions perhaps respond to Russ's complaint.

References

Barad, K. (2003) Posthumanist performativity: Toward an understanding of how matter comes to matter, *Signs*, 28(3), pp. 801–831.
Haraway, D. (1988) Situated knowledges: The science question in feminism and the privilege of partial perspective, *Feminist Studies*, 14(3), pp. 575–599.
Haraway, D. (2004) A manifesto for cyborgs: Science, technology and socialist feminism in the 1980s, in *The Haraway Reader*, New York: Routledge, pp. 7–45.
Jung, C.G. (1963/1977) *Memories, Dreams, Reflections*. London: Fontana Paperbacks.
Jung, C.G. and Hull, R.F.C. (1978) *Flying Saucers: A Modern Myth of Things Seen in the Sky* (from Vols. 10 and 18, *Collected Works*), Princeton, NJ: Princeton University Press.
Russ, J. (1995) SF technology as mystification, in *To Write Like a Woman: Essays in Feminism and Science Fiction*, Bloomington, IN: Indiana University Press, pp. 26–40.
Russ, J. (1977) *The Female Man*, Boston, MA: Gregg Press.

Part One

Technological Invasions
Reproduction and Regeneration in Time

1

Polydore Vergil and the Immortal Jellyfish (or, How to Read Queer History without Any Queers)

Cleo Madeleine

Notes on the text

References follow MHRA standards, excepting the works of Polydore Vergil as contained in the University of Birmingham's Philological Museum, which are embedded in the text in brackets with the initials of the work in question, the number of the book, and the number of the section. For instance, a reference to section 1 of book 1 of *Anglica historia* would be marked (AH 1.1).

All translations are my own, unless otherwise specified. My translations of the printed *Anglica Historia* owe a great deal to Prof. Dana Sutton, from whose work in many cases I have found no cause to deviate or elaborate. Manuscript abbreviations and elisions have been expanded and marked with *italics*. Marginal notes in both manuscripts and printed books are underlined. Superscript and interlinear insertions are in [superscript].

Manuscripts are referred to by shelfmark and folio number. For instance, 'BAV, vat. urb. lat. 497, fol. 1r' would refer to the recto side of the first folio of record 497 in the Urbino collection of the Biblioteca Apostolica Vaticana.

There are a few particular choices of phrasing that warrant a little pre-emptive explanation. The first, and most important, is the conscious choice not to use the word 'Anglo-Saxon' to refer to the early medieval period or its peoples. Although accurate in certain specific contexts, in its general sense this word has become inextricably bound up with modern white supremacist identitarian discourses. In the rare occasions where I might have had cause to use it (as, for instance, many older works on Gildas do) I have preferred 'early medieval'. A few words occur with specific uses in this thesis that differ somewhat from their most common readings. *Organise, organising* and so on (and its opposite) I typically use to mean processes and vectors which proceed towards the formation of an *organism*, in the Deleuzian sense. *Synthetic* I use to refer to historiographies, temporalities, and so on that are the product of plural strands under singularising pressure. This is not to say that I have completely abjured the conventional meanings, *disorganised* can still mean disordered and confused; *synthetic* can still mean artificial. *Reading* is perhaps the worst offender. Reading and readership have an exorbitant polysemy that I am neither willing nor able to constrain. Suffice to say: *reading* is a reciprocal, mutual

DOI: 10.4324/9781003255727-3

act of interpretation conducted between bodies; it is transtemporal and, invariably, anachronistic – it always leaves a mark.

This chapter began as a paper of the same name presented at the Feminism and Technology Conference 2020 and largely draws from the introduction to my PhD thesis, *ego qui scriptum est scribo: finding a new queer historiography with Polydore Vergil* (2022). I would like to give special thanks to Leslie Gardner, Roula-Maria Dib, and Catriona Miller, whose support has not only allowed this chapter to be published, but also shaped the course of my research as a whole. I am greatly indebted to them.

Turritopsis dohrnii is immortal. If this jellyfish is injured or stressed, old or sick, it can revert from its adult form, the medusa, to its juvenile form, the polyp, and begin its life cycle again. Most multicellular life, including humans, develops from simple cells into more complex, specialised types. The immortal jellyfish undergoes a process called transdifferentiation, in which these developments are altered. Older, fully developed cells effectively become younger. To the human observer it travels against the flow of time. We cannot even begin to presume the perspective of the jellyfish. If we did, we might imagine they see us as hopelessly adrift, borne in just one direction by the current of time.

They are spreading around the world on ocean currents and carried in the ballast tanks of ships and submersibles. Indomitably adaptable, each new environment provokes a new mutation and the shooting of a new branch of the cnidarian family. They are carnivores but not predators, feeding on plankton, molluscs, and other microorganisms. More often they are prey, being eaten by an exhaustive range of ocean dwellers including sea anemones, sharks, and sea turtles. And always they are regenerating: "a worldwide silent invasion" (Than, 2009). Resistant by their very nature to human conceptions of both embodiment and time, they offer a model for both that doesn't just deconstruct linearity but attempts to entirely abdicate it.

This chapter seeks to explore (or perhaps explores to seek) alternative queer methodologies of reading history. That said: Polydore Vergil's *Anglica historia* does not present readily or immediately as a subject for queer analysis, however radical. Begun around 1504, completed around 1513, and not published until 1534, its composition spanned one of the greatest periods of turbulence in English history. Despite this, it has been largely remembered for its contentious "denial of the historicity of Arthur," which kept Polydore's name in ill graces for centuries to come, and for its furnishing of the figure of Richard III that Shakespeare would make infamous (Connell, 2004). Otherwise it is little talked about. There is, at least nominally, no queer content to speak of. But neither the visible presence of queer figures nor the apparent opportunity for their recuperation are necessary preconditions for queer reading. In fact, I would argue that the search for queer identity in the past has, to a certain extent, been a foil to queer readings, bringing with it the baggage of the contemporary struggle for recognition and understanding of our own identities. That is not to say that we should call off the search entirely, rather, that a series of "anti-normative historicist investments" in historiographical methodology is necessary to pursue a sincere and fruitful queer investigation of the past (Wiegman, 2011, p. 209). If we model our approach to historiography not on the human organism but on the immortal jellyfish, if we reconceive our most steadfast ideas of linearity and chronology, if we embody fluidity, plurality, and anachronism, then we might cast off the yoke of conventional interpretative norms and invest in a novel queer historiography.

It can certainly be levelled at this study that, like so much of the canon it seeks to rebel against, its principal subject is straight, white, cisgender, and male and as such is an agent of straight, white, cisgender male history. This is a fair challenge, and one that I support as a paradigmatic line of questioning for historiographical scholarship in general, but what does it mean in this case? These things seem self-evident and mutually contingent. It makes sense to imagine Polydore as a heterosexual, cisgender man because there are no intimations to the contrary in his works or his biography. Had he had, for instance, in lieu of his bitter professional rivalry with Andrea Ammonio, a homoerotic poetic correspondence like Erasmus' then we might have cause to trouble our assumptions. But he didn't, and so we don't.

This is precisely my problem, and what has (along a rather winding path) led me to this theoretical approach. Literary criticism and queer theory have long been acquainted with Judith Butler's theory of gender performativity, and yet the penetration of its conceptual framework into broader historiographical thought feels inconsistent. (Gender performativity is a common enough concept that I don't think bears explaining at length here, but for further reference see Butler, 1990.) The understanding that gender is not innate but socially constructed based on sets of norms is widely accepted. So too is the historicist assessment that the past is governed by alien social and cultural mores that produce occasionally recognisable, but often different or strange norms to the present. And yet our norms for historical identity continue, by and large, to be rooted in contemporary ideas of presentation of gender, sexuality, and so on. This is not to make the argument that Polydore Vergil could be ascribed any particular queer identity, so much as that one doesn't need to, and shouldn't have to do so in order to facilitate a queer reading. Historiographical norms are thus limiting in two ways: they prescribe contemporary heteronormativity as default when contradictory evidence does not present, and they proscribe certain kinds of readings based on those norms. My research did not begin from a queer theoretical perspective. Rather, it emerged from collision with the boundaries of these norms; a set of beliefs and ideas that have grown over the course of my interactions with this text and my own development and reflection as a queer historiographer. *Anglica historia* attempts to produce a complete English history with attention to both historicity and comprehensiveness. But the more I tried to bring this project – mine and Polydore's – into focus, the more such an endeavour seemed hopelessly complicated and messy.

This *mess* is my preferred conceptual framework and methodological model. It articulates the simultaneous possible presence and absence of agency in 'making a mess'; it suggests both accident and incident. Although there may be evidence of causal and/or chronological order (that is, in the *res gestae*, the sequence of events by which the mess was made) it may have little or no identifiable correlation with the organisation of the present state. My claim is not quite that all historiographical practice is pattern-recognition in an essentially meaningless scribble of events, but I might go so far as to suggest that historiographical frameworks – ways and modes of reading history – work by prioritising certain patterns and excluding others. Nor is this to suggest that robust historiographical practice should, or could, be reduced to baseless imaginative leaps or flights of fancy (at least, reduced any further than it always has been). Reading history is the province of the aporiac, who delights in seeing something in nothing. To relate to the very recent past, let alone the distant, some blanks must be filled in. Rather, this is to say that with imaginative investment we can look past or suspend prominent interpretations of the cosmic mess of history and bring into focus the dim, the unusual, the forgotten. We are always imposing order on history, whether we intend to or not, but by acknowledging mess we can retroactively trace the patterns and mechanisms of ordination. "In a book, as in all things", write Gilles Deleuze and Felix Guattari,

> there are lines of articulation or segmentarity, but also lines of flight, movements of deterritorialization and destratification. Comparative rates of flow on these lines produce phenomena of relative slowness and viscosity, or, on the contrary, of acceleration and rupture.
> (Deleuze and Guattari, 2005, pp. 3–4)

Deleuze and Guattari argue (and I massively oversimplify here) that in the condition of modernity these movements, flows, and connections are stifled or dissociated, limited by their articulation as organic ('arboreal') structures. Polydore's project, then, is appealing because of its messiness. It tugs on the threads of articulation. It de- and re-territorialises land and nation, it runs in parallel chronologies of varying speeds. Like *T. dohrnii*, it pulls apart in its drawing together. And here, I am reminded of the Japanese word 挨拶 (*aisatsu*), which means 'greeting' but is composed of the kanji 'push open' and 'draw together'. It embodies the salutary nature of this chapter, introduction without a conclusion as it is, and the contradictory nature shared by both bodily contact and reading history: an opening that must close.

This "fractured and fragmentary" reading is visible in Polydore's historiography (Cox Jensen, 2012, p. 91). In *Anglica historia* he frequently lists his sources, particularly when they contradict each other, but also lifts large chunks of his history wholesale without acknowledgement. Boundaries are blurred between stylistic influence, reference, and imitation. But it is also underwritten by and preoccupied with the pursuit of historical truth and the "unanswerable question of origins" (Hodgen, 1966, p. 316). Polydore expresses this anxiety over origins – and introduces his history as a salve for it – in the proem to *Anglica historia*, where he writes "nulla ferme extaret historia qua cognoscere liceret [...] quae gentis origi" [No history has stood out by which [the Britons] might discover the origin of their people] (*AH* 1.proem). However, Polydore's claim here belies a more substantial problem to the recuperation of England's past. *Extaret* could also, indeed, might well be translated as "exists", "is extant", "is visible". The use of the imperfect subjunctive emphasises the presence, breadth, and tantalising seeming proximity of the historical lacuna, pointing towards that which might have preserved the continuity of English history for some time but has since become unavailable to the historiographer.

Worse than English antiquity having lain fallow and in need of recuperation or having not been recorded in the first place and lost to time, there is a feeling of irrecoverability from the space where its archives once were. Polydore particularly refers to the absence of a native classical tradition to convey the acts and deeds of the nation's early inhabitants, as in the historiographies of Italy and Greece, and this absence is felt first and foremost in the land. There is no internal record of England's earliest history to give it form. It must be defined externally, whether extraneously by the extant accounts of other national narratives or anachronistically by the projection of forms from other times. For instance, the opening of *Anglica historia* is (and, as far as we can tell, has been since its inception) modelled on Caesar's *De bello gallico*. The surviving 1513 MS begins:

> BRITANNIA omnes quae hodie Anglia est insula in oceano contra gallicum littus [illegible] in quattuor partes ᵈⁱᵛⁱᵈⁱᵗᵘʳ quarum unam incolunt Angli alia*m* [illegible] Scoti, Walli, quarta*m* Cornubienses. Ii omnes aut lingua vel moribus seu institutis inter se differunt.

> [Britain, which all today call England, is an island in the ocean facing the Gallic shore, divided into four parts of which one is called England, another Scotland, Wales, and the fourth Cornwall. These all in both language, customs and institutions differ among themselves.]
> (Biblioteca Apostolica Vaticana (BAV), vat. urb. lat. 497, fol. 8ᵛ)

Compare this with the 1504 Filippo Beroaldo edition of *De bello gallico*, which reads:

> Gallia est omnis divisa in partes tris: quarum unam incolunt belgae: aliam aquitani: tertiam qui ipsorum lingua celtae: nostra galli appella*n*tur. Ii omnes lingua institutis legibus inter se differunt.

> [Gaul is all divided into three parts, of which one is called Belgae, another Aquitaine, a third which in its own language is called Celtae and in ours Gaul. These all differ among themselves in institutions and laws.]
> (BSB, 2 A.lat.b.51, fol. f5ʳ)

The similarities indicate not just a stylistic influence but a "conscious imitation" (Momigliano, 1990, p. 81). Nor is this the only example of this kind of imitation in Polydore's construction of the land. For instance, on the shape of the island he writes, "Forma*m* totius Britanniae triquetram hoc est triangularem esse liquido constat: quippe quae tres habet angulos triaq*ue* latera contra G[alliam] est: et usq*ue* in Cantium" [It is agreed that the whole of Britain is triangular, this is clear, of course, it has three corners and three sides [one side of which] faces Gaul and runs all the way to Kent] (BAV, vat. urb. lat. 497, fol. 14ᵛ), while *De bello gallico* gives the similar "Insula natura triquetra: cuius unum latus est contra galliam. huius lateris alter angulus qui est ad cantium" [The island is a natural triangle, of which one side faces Gaul. Of this side the far corner is towards Kent] (BSB, 2 A.lat.b.51, fol. 30ʳ). *De bello gallico* made familiar to a Roman audience the *terra incognita* of transalpine Gaul. Polydore inverts this dynamic, utilising a foreign voice to re-establish for an ostensibly English audience what ought already to be familiar: the bounds of their country.

The need for a whole body is satisfied in this fashion, although not unproblematically. Polydore is not just using the information imparted by *De bello gallico*, but directly modelling its structure in a way that invited comparison by the early modern reader. A tension precipitates between comprehensive critical historiography from origin to present – and the attempt at authentic historical synthesis such a thing entails – and the essential messiness. This tension exposes a normative process by which assumed properties of history are constructed. Continuity, linearity, singularity; the properties necessary for historical truth to exist, are established at the expense of alterity. Not only that, but constructed to a design, a set of norms agreed by convention and only partially articulated in the modern notions of cisheteropatriarchy, binarity, and so on.

Polydore is at once illustrative of, subject to, and deviant from these norms. The properties mentioned above – continuity et al. – are limited examples of an unlimited category that might be expressed in *monolith* or *synthesis*. Although referring to distinct bodies and processes, both these terms embody the supposedly necessary criteria of history, that is, that there are certain events that have happened in a certain way at certain times, that these events have happened in a particular sequence, that that sequence proceeds in a particular direction at a particular pace, and that all these systems cohere in time and space. Disputes over the dating of events or even the psychologies underpinning them are subordinate to these axioms; even without a satisfying resolution they are still understood to be processes occurring with a certain spatio-temporal congruence. Uncertainty over the date and manner of the fall of Troy does not trouble the philosophical conviction that it happened in a particular place at a particular time, and that it is happening at that time and in that place proscribes it is happening anywhere else or at any other time. I am not sure whether it is too bold or too basic to stake the claim that historiography is conventionally understood in these frameworks, but I am going to stake it anyway.

Walter Ong identifies 'synthesis' as a loaded term, "itself a visualist construct, meaning at root a putting together – that is, an operation conceived of as local motion in a spatial field" (Ong, 1967, p. 127). Synthesis describes Polydore's history in the general sense that it attempts to reconcile diverse historiographies, but also in this particular sense that in its putting together of these threads it localises them. The machine operations we witness in his work are those that facilitate synchrony and synchory of disparate time and place, extending beyond the boundaries of event history to epiphenomena like chronology, nation, readership. But this synthesis, like the norms that prompt it, has a kind of formal existence that fails in execution. The internal conflicts and ruptures provoked by this process of reconciliation are suppressed or sublimated by *chrononormativity*.

Chrononormativity is described by Elizabeth Freeman as "the use of time to organize individual human bodies toward maximum productivity", one consequence of which is the continuity and linearity of normative time (Freeman, 2010, p. 3). For instance, in the example of the historicisation of myth, distinct and irreconcilable temporal schema – the theological and the mythological – are unified under the aegis of chrononormativity, because the alternative would be to countenance the difference and produce a profound historical rupture of one form or another. Freeman's example of chrononormativity is taken from Thomas Paine's critique of Burkean historicism:

> because it animated and depended on feelings that were historically derived rather than spontaneous, on codes of conduct that were appropriated from the past rather than inborn [...] of bringing the living too close to the dead, and so ruining the living body's constitution.
> (Freeman, 2010, p. 14)

The necromantic rupture threatened by Burke's historiography is present, too, in *Anglica historia*. What appears to be an error in Polydore's geography is in fact an intersection of temporal and geographical bodies that runs together chronologies and leaves them entangled. The issue is the identification of the Isle of Man with Anglesey. This not only persists from the initial fair copy into later editions of the text, but in fact becomes more inaccurate in later versions. The manuscript reads:

> Altera est Mona insula nominatissima: quam hodie vocant angleseyam. Adiacet a septentrionem Walliae: a quae vix duobus milibus passuum distat: immo quotiens decrescit marem: [...] magna fiunt aestus: adeo tenui ficto ab Wallia disiecta [illegible]: ut sine navigiis homines eam adiri posseret
>
> [Another most famous island is Mona, which today they call Anglesey. It lies by the North of Wales, from which it is hardly two miles distant. Indeed, when the sea ebbs [...] it becomes a great tide, to such an extent that, made separate from Wales by a slight distance, men might be able to reach it without boats].
> (BAV, vat. urb. lat. 497, fols. 15^r-15^v)

Despite his established use of *De bello gallico* as a source, Polydore's description seems only loosely based on Caesar's, which simply offers the following: "in hoc medio cursu est insula: quae appellatur mona" [in this middle course is the island, which is named Man] (i.e. in the middle of the voyage between Gaul, Ireland, and Britain) (BSB, 2 A.lat.b.51, fol. 30^r). This is quite clearly a description of the Isle of Man as opposed to Anglesey to anyone even vaguely familiar with British geography. Where in his introduction of the land Polydore embodies Britain with Caesar's Gaul, here he uses neither the structure nor the content.

The 1555 edition has the following revised description:

> Altera est Mona insula nominatissima, quam mutatione unius literae Manam vocant, quae ab aquilone Scotiam, ab ortu aestivo Angliam, ab occasu mare Hybernicum habet propinquum. Haec olim mari disiuncta angusto, quoties decrescebat oceanus, cuius magni fiunt omni tempore aestus, adeo prope terram erat ut sine navigiis adiri posset (*AH* 1.12)

> [Another most famous island is Mona, which with a single letter changed they call Man, which has nearby Scotland to the South, England by the sun's rising in the East, and the Irish sea by its setting. This once was separated from the sea by a narrow strait, whose tides become great in all seasons, and whenever the ocean ebbed it came so near that land could be reached without boats]

Here the syntax is more closely modelled on the description of the Isle of Man as equidistant from the constituent parts of the British Isles. The name of Anglesey has been removed, and an original etymology for Man has been added. Andrew Escobedo describes how the unification of England and Scotland under James "represented for some English writers both the *restoration* of an ancient heritage and a fictive *novelty*, the artificial yoking together of the disparate traditional cultures of England" (Escobedo, 2004, p. 149). This conceptual framework could also be applied to this kind of etymology and the syncretist historiography it figures in *Anglica historia*. We have already seen how imitation of Caesar might perform a recuperative function, albeit one that produces a problematic historical rupture.

Classicising etymologies perform a similar address of the lacuna of England's origins. Ferguson describes how, at the hard limits of history where contemporary witnesses are all but absent and the distinction between poet and historian collapses, the early modern historian is left with "the historical imagination" as their only tool of historical criticism (Ferguson, 1993, p. 114). Although problematic, this also facilitates the perception of historical continuity. By following classical models, Polydore superimposes imagined (or at least anachronistically *inferred*) topographies onto England, causing the distinct chronologies of classical authority and etymological record to messily intersect. *Anglica historia* is studded with these originary classicisations. Elsewhere, *Nordovicum* is derived from *ordo* (AH 2.6), and then justified with the fabrication of a historical anecdote about an order of monks who once lived on the spot. The recuperative and fictive elements yoke together the disparate temporalities (absent and present, historic and contemporary) and, overlapping, the disparate topographies of Anglesey and Mona. Perhaps both these bodies are, like the greater land that both contains them and defines them in relief, particularly susceptible to collapsing the opposition between the temporal and the spatial that generically, if superficially, presents in chorography (Helgerson, 1992, p. 132). Insularity affords a variability of conceptual geography not available to the mainland, facilitating the "unexpected … connection, conjunction and construction of unusual interfaces" that produces an intensification of "the alien, otherness, the disparate in its extremes" (Grosz, 1995, p. 198). The flux of intervening bodies of water and the imaginative, mysterious potential of insular position, relative to other fixed bodies but seemingly unmoored, invites a correspondingly fluid, flexible, and porous corporeality. Indeed, it is the language of islands that Grosz uses to describe the body in a state of disruption through sexual interactions: "The interruption and interaction of a surface with another, its disengagement from the circuit of organic functioning [...] so that it realigns itself in different networks and linkages" and becomes "the site of intensive disruptions" (Grosz, 1995, p. 198).

The effect of this strange confluence is that, rather than updating the topography of earlier versions of the text by substituting the Isle of Man for Anglesey, the two locations are uncomfortably combined. Their physical properties, ostensibly incompatible, overlap, producing an island that is at once equidistant from England, Scotland, and Ireland and so close to the mainland that it can be crossed without boats. It calls to mind Prospero's island, at once off the coast of Italy and somewhere in the Bermudas, exact geographical location subsumed by magical and fluid insularity. We know that Polydore is particularly keen on reconciling the authority of the ancient with critical concern for historicity. But here the very reconciliation that should subordinate chronology, topography, and geography to chrononormativity has an abnormative effect. Dead names and places are, as Freeman describes, swept back piecemeal across the Styx and bound up with the living present, resurrected as something new – or undead.

When multiple historical strands present as equally valid, or valid in various but distinctly legitimate ways, then any exercise of critical thought also requires an exercise of ignorance – or else a restructuring of historical thought to selectively resist established models of authority. I think that one of the great self-deceptions of progressivism is the idea that modernity has furnished us, as historiographers, with the appropriate critical apparatus to determine what should be ignored and what should be admitted to the canon, when in fact it has simply made us more comfortable that ignorance and selectivity are the right answer. It is the unwillingness of early modern thought to so easily resolve that makes this kind of elucidation possible. Thus in *Anglica historia* we find both systems of chrononormativity and the historiographical modalities that allow liberation from it. In the push for synthesis we find syncresis, for monolith integument; something of a piece but fragmented, collocated but disparate in time and place. And thus mess.

The impulse toward locus and norm can be described by the closet. What Eve Kosofsky Sedgwick describes as "the defining structure of gay oppression this century" has an anachronistic historiographical function, describing the spatialisation and temporalisation of bodies on a much wider historical scale (this is both the retroactive closeting of modernity and the pseudo-closet projected onto our construction of the premodern, arbitration between which is impossible past a certain point) (Sedgwick, 1990, p. 97). Bodies are presented as whole, continuous, catholic. They are presented as diachronic. But this is only achieved through the obfuscation of those bodies or parts thereof that resist these archetypes. In historiography, this suppression of bodies can progress to abnegation and even obliteration from time itself if they are confined outside of diachronic historiography. This is what Jonathan Goldberg calls the "definitional impasse" of the closet, which secures sexual difference by rendering functionally invisible anything that disagrees (Goldberg, 1992, p. 10).

Following Cesare Casarino's model of fully incorporated time, we can fully embody historiography, both through its physical agents, like readers and books, and by corporealising the incorporeal, like nations and texts. My approach vector to Polydore, to *Anglica historia*, and to historiography in general is therefore one of embodiment – bodies *of* history and *in* time, but not human bodies, or not *entirely* human bodies. In *Volatile Bodies* Elizabeth Grosz recentres the body and its morphologies in feminist theory and displaces the self as the sole agent of subjectivity. I should clarify sooner rather than later that I do not agree with some of the implications of Grosz' critical work, least of all the potential narrowings of womanhood that might emerge from her reduction of properties of gender to physical morphology. (I want to stress that this is a note of caution, and absolutely *not* an accusation of trans-exclusionary writing or anything similar. One of the underrepresented casualties of the culture war is the ease with which the queer community has ceded radical feminism to so-called trans-exclusionary radical feminists (TERFs), a moniker I am extremely hesitant to use because of the pointlessly divisive mentality it encourages and because of the voluntary abdication of feminism it represents. I do not know exactly how it is that we came to willingly abandon those women who pioneered modern criticism of gender and sexuality, but I suspect it is partially because the memetic online spread of highly developed twenty-first-century taxonomies of identity have created a series of shibboleths in the popular queer consciousness that the feminist writers of the '70s, '80s, and '90s simply cannot pass. We cannot expect Andrea Dworkin, or, for that matter, Elizabeth Grosz, to satisfy our needs for things like trans-inclusivity when they were writing in a very different scholarly and cultural atmosphere. Conversely, I do not think that this makes their work any less useful to contemporary scholarship or, for that matter, any less inclusive. We cannot afford to cut these ties; we have an obligation as feminists not to.) However, I do believe that the contested, often caustic state of the current critical field around bodies, particularly in the contexts of gender and sexuality, has obfuscated the extreme usefulness of a "refiguring of the body so that it moves from the periphery to the centre of analysis" (Grosz, 1994, p. x). As Paul B. Preciado has demonstrated, the somatic narrative or "body-essay" is both imaginatively fictive and inherently political, to which I would add historical (Preciado, 2013, p. 11). And Donna Haraway illustrates the importance of extending our notions of historical bodies beyond the human, insisting that "History must give way to geostories, to Gaia stories, to symchthonic stories; terrans do webbed, braided, and tentacular living and dying in sympoietic multispecies string figures; they do not do History" (Haraway, 2016).

Naturally, bodies conceived of, circumscribed, and constructed in human terms or through a human lens (as, try as I might, my work is wont to be) are subject to the same limitations and abnegations as their human referents. (This is why, to us, the immortal jellyfish seems to reject the mandate of time.) These somatic narratives can explore various kinds of embodiment without decentring the contexts and conceptual frameworks that make such narratives intelligible. We might say they are the *res* to the *gestae*. Human bodies, of course, have a particular specificity. This project is, in senses both literal and metaphysical, predicated on my human body in the first order, and on many other human bodies thereafter (not least Polydore Vergil). The effect our inescapable role as human historiographers has on the way we experience, interact with, and record bodies is important enough to merit a privileged position in historiography (although not necessarily a positive one). But this is still not human history. It is body history.

Although the semiotic promiscuity of bodies lends empowers, rather than problematises this analysis – bodies must be endlessly diverse to be so harshly subjected to norms – it is still worth sketching a brief definition. A body is composed of parts (which may themselves be other bodies) over time and in space. It is capable of possessing identity characteristics (of which I will largely focus on gender and sexuality). A body is not necessarily a person but is ascribed traits of personhood, it lacks senses but can possess experiences, it is not alive per se but it is, to invoke Mary Shelley, animated. I will not be creating bodies (although all bodies are imaginatively invested to some degree), and the body is not a metaphor. The body here is a subject of history and an object of chrononormativity (to which choronormativity is subordinate, if only in the sense that of all the organising principles of history time is the most fundamental; as Freeman says, "the body is a temporal rather than spatial phenomenon") (Freeman, 2010, p. 46). As well as human bodies this includes other corporeal entities, texts, chronologies, and various organic systems. A body may or may not be any of these things. It is easier not to be specific; the notion that the existence of bodies demands a taxonomy of bodies is itself a product of the time-travelling closet. Embodiment under chrononormativity can therefore help us conceive of what is excluded from history, what has been permitted to persist, and the mechanisms that enact this process. And, in showing us the lacunae and tensions where bodies are suppressed, it can help us locate queer historiography.

Deleuze and Guattari offer a helpful way of thinking about this: "A book itself is a little machine; what is the relation (also measurable) of this literary machine to a war machine, love machine, revolutionary machine, etc." (Deleuze and Guattari, 2005, p. 4). As Grosz notes, Deleuze and Guattari do not have a "systematic account" of embodiment, but I do not think it misappropriates their work to apply it to bodies in historiography (Grosz, 1995, p. 167). Is a body not itself a little machine, existing in relation to other machines? What kinds of bodies are here? And are they in turn components in a history machine? In this way we can understand that not just historical subjects and objects, but the elemental components of historiography themselves are organised into bodies, both in how they are organised and in how the functions and processes of their organs are determined and understood. Again we feel the shadow of the closet. Bodies are imagined as synthetic because the organs are subordinated to the whole. They are imagined as monolithic because the processes are hierarchised and unified in singular function.

But the bodies of *Anglica historia* are complicated. This results partially from the troubles of historiographical plurality, as we have seen above, but also from its particular condition of spatio-temporal crisis. Polydore Vergil is an Italian émigré living in London in the first half of the sixteenth century. Over the course of the composition of *Anglica historia* (and, indeed, most of his works, but it is the history that takes longest) he becomes a naturalised citizen, becomes a successful member of the clergy, rises to popularity at court. He is charged with producing the history of his new nation. He witnesses the xenophobic Ill May Day riots of 1515, the ignition of which occurs almost outside his window over St Paul's Churchyard. The death of the king brings a fall from favour, he is imprisoned, he fears for his life. He flees the country and returns. He writes and re-writes his history. Ultimately it is printed in 1534, amid the uncertainty of the English Reformation. This is not to say he is remarkable in a way that privileges him over other historiographers, but that as a historiographer he has a particular relationship to time and place and is writing on the very point of a cataclysmic restructuring of history, "a time whose violence offers up queer possibilities despite itself" (Freeman, 2010, p. xii). Polydore reminds me of the angel of history, debris piling up before him while behind, time races towards the unknown.

Let us return to the proem: "quod nulla ferme extaret historia qua cognoscere liceret quae Britanniae, quae nunc Angliae est soli natura, quae gentis origi" [Because hardly any history exists from which might be learned the nature of Britain, which is now England, and the origin of its people] (AH 1.proem). The response to temporal crisis is a mitigating move towards universalisation that ultimately propels *Anglica historia* towards a transtemporal synthesis that, when it encounters the impossibility of such a task, exposes the machinery of chrononormativity. And this shows in the history. Time and place are fatigued, stress fractured. As we can see in the above example, the system of historical roots is broken down, and the consequent overlap and interaction of these fragments produces precisely the rupture that is the apparent inception of the collapse. This is not to repeat wholesale the argument of the particular historical rupture caused by early modern relation to the classical past. If anything, there is a kind of permissibility to this rupture, as if the historical identities of the present are shored up and defined by the recognition of a certain kind of dead past. The extent to which (not just in early modern European historiography but in the present day) a break from an ancient but relatable past can fuel national(ist) identities suggests that even rupture can be organised under chrononormativity.

Rather, this is to express "anxiety about heterogeneity in England's past" as a recognisable example of a much wider phenomenon (Escobado, 2004, p. 5). *Anglica historia* is a mammoth text and to make an exhaustive, or even a detailed assay of its various intersecting bodies would overflow the banks of this book. However, a brief but rich example can be found at the very beginning of the history, in the first book of *Anglica historia*, when Polydore discusses the origin of the Britons. He begins:

> Caius itaque Iulius Caesar, antiquissimus rerum scriptor [...] tradit Brittaniae partem interiorem ab iis incoli quos natos in insula memoriae proditum esset, et maritimam partem ab iis qui praedae ac belli inferendi causa ex Belgio in

insulam transissent, ac eos ubi illuc pervenerunt, bello illato, ibi permansisse atque agros colere coepisse.

[Thus Caius Julius Caesar, writer of the most ancient matters [...] hands down that the interior part of Britain was inhabited by those who were remembered to have been born there, but the maritime part by those who had crossed over out of Belgium to make war, and when they arrived, having borne out their war, they remained and began to farm the fields]

(AH 1.18)

This is fairly straightforward. The grounds for use of *De bello gallico* as a source are clearly stated: classical authority, primacy of age, and ancient memory. So far, so good. But Polydore continues, "Huic opinioni Cornelius Tacitus [...] pene [This is, as much as I wish it wasn't, a typographical error for *paene*] assentitur" [To this opinion Cornelius Tacitus [...] hardly agrees] (AH 1.8). He goes on to describe Tacitus' proposed ethnography of Britain in which he posits a Germanic origin and cites ethnic similarities with the Silures. A detailed exploration of British ethnography and its ramifications in *Anglica historia* will be made in *bodies of land*; for now, suffice to say that Polydore finds disagreement in his most ancient sources for the history of England and elects to juxtapose them. He goes on to find further disagreement in the early medieval writers ("vero homo Anglus" [true Englishmen] (AH 1.18)) Bede and Gildas and the more contemporary fourteenth-century antiquarian Pomponio Leto ("recentium autorum gravissimus favet" [of recent authors considered the most serious] (AH 1.18)). And these all have their own substantiating criteria of authority. Notwithstanding Polydore's sustained praise of Gildas' honesty and moral rectitude, there is the implicit indigeneity of Gildas and Bede relative to the history of England, and the suggestion that Leto is most valued by the standards and/or practices of contemporary historiography. The use of indigeneity in this context is deeply problematic, and I intend to fully explore and critique my use of it in bodies of land. The idea of British, and particularly English indigeneity in modern discourses has been appropriated by white supremacist organisations with widespread success. Indigeneity is a specific terminology that carries with it specific structures of power and prejudice, and I do not, by using the term here, suggest that there is any worth to historicising the ancient Britons in such a way. I do, however, believe that sixteenth-century historical imaginings of a semi-mythic indigenous past (including but by no means limited to *Anglica historia*) are part of the historiographical fabric of ethnonationalism, and that understanding these conceptions of the past on their own terms can help us understand how they have become a fundamental part of the weft of 'Englishness'.

Polydore sets before us a problem of historiographical methodology. It is advanced in a critical sense, demonstrating sensitivity to the breadth of possible, often oppositional approaches to history, but it does not appear to capitalise on this by proffering a methodological solution. Although he criticises Geoffrey of Monmouth for mingling history and fiction, of those whose historicity he trusts he says only "pollicitus sum me neque de unius neque de alterius sententia [...] iudicio legentium subiecturum" [I have promised neither one opinion nor the other [...] I would subject to the judgement of my readers] (AH 1.20). *Sententia* is a difficult word to translate in this context. It refers literally to the separate sentences and phrases that distinguish the various historical authorities, but also carries a sense of an opinion, of the proverb, of received wisdom. These proposed origins are ascribed both the weight of historicity and the affective rhetorical sense of sententiae. And while Polydore does set out his personal critical reasoning it is conducted entirely in terms of his reflections as a reader. That is, his judgement is not privileged over that of the reader of *Anglica historia* or demonstrated for use as a model. The component parts of historiography are clearly laid out along with the tools for assembly, but no instruction manual is provided.

Arthur Ferguson characterises the development of early modern attitudes toward the mythic past as "a subtly pervasive skepticism that was the product not so much of philosophical inquiry as of a rising conflict between the will to believe and a stirring discontent with explanations that did not square with reason and experience" (Ferguson, 1993, p. 2). In the same breath, however, he acknowledges "the ability of Renaissance minds to half-believe or believe in contradictory things"(Ferguson, 1993, p. 2). Polydore's model is defined by these oppositional vortices, developing an evolving historical criticism and concern for authenticity even as it embraces the palimpsestible. The reassuring linearity of chrononormativity is present, but always frustrated by the permissibility of conflict. It is not unrelated, I think, that this is also the first history of England to be printed with an index, complete with usage instructions *tibi lector*. Indeed, Polydore was instrumental in the introduction of index use in other kinds of works – compilations, adagia, and so on – with the inclusion of an early one in his 1496 edition of Niccolò Perotti's *Cornucopiae* (Hay, 1954, p. 102). There is a groping anticipation of later sixteenth-century chronology, like Scaliger's *De emendatione temporum* with its "obsession with computation" (Ott, 2010) caught between the impulse towards organisation and the awareness of fragmentation. The tool is provided that, although it ostensibly *organises* the body, in fact offers the means of dissection through non-serial reading. The same book that codifies the mass reproduction of English history through print also introduces reading strategies that infinitesimally individuate readership.

In this brief example we see in turn the land, the nation, and even the text itself at once corporealised, individuated, and drawn together. "The nation refuses to fit neatly in time, but rather remains a community that emphasizes the impression of historical difference" (Escobedo, 2004, p. 7). Even the first step towards synthesis lays open the machine; exposes the body for dissection. The sensitivity to chronological variation and the guided index assist the reader in exposing these historical differences, working into the cracks and breaking down the historiographical bodies. In this sense they are less the Deleuzian Body without Organs than the *disiecta membra*, time and place, reader and book, historiographer and history embodied and transected.

This body trouble is a product of chrononormativity. Freeman draws on Robert Graves' poem *It's A Queer Time* to introduce the schema, extant and potential, of queer temporality. Although she does not reject the deconstructive approach of queer theory outright she describes the limitations of both nostalgia and "queer antiformalism" and offers instead "ways of living aslant to dominant forms [...] inventing possibilities for moving through and with time, encountering pasts, speculating futures, and interpenetrating the two in ways the counter the common sense of the present tense" (Freeman, 2010, p. xv). Karma Lochrie describes a similar problem in her introduction to *The Lesbian Premodern* when she negotiates the problem of the historicity of (cis)heteronormativity. "The role normativity plays in establishing modern sexualities" is historicised, leading us to persistently locate premodern queerness in the imagined shadow of heteronormativity (see Lochrie in Giffney, Sauer and Watt, 2011, p. xiii). Not only is this a historicist problem, it artificially narrows the liberatory and recuperative queer readings of history, excluding perceived presentations of heterosexuality or cisgender identity on anachronistic grounds. I don't know what the noun form of xgender should be, that is, whatever word for *cisgender* or *transgender* etc. corresponds to *heterosexuality*, *homosexuality*, etc. I don't know if this is a product of my own ignorance or a genuine linguistic problem in queer theory. xgenderedness implies an adjectival form xgendered which is inaccurate, xgenderism evokes problematic parallels with the ideological and pathological, and xgender identity involves the baggage of contemporaryidentitarian discourses. I have gone with the latter in this case, if solely because it is a less loaded term as regards the *cis*.

Grosz argues that "the preferred body was one under control" (Grosz, 1995, p. 1). It is relatively easy to understand that there is a set of historical norms roughly analogous to modern cisheteropatriarchy to which historiography conventionally inheres and by which bodies are therefore controlled. It is harder, and perhaps more personally distressing, to accept that queer historical imagination can enforce these norms in much the same way. That even structures of empowerment inhabit structures of power. I am reminded of Umberto Eco's *Baudolino*, in which the bodies of the three magi seized by Barbarossa at Constantinople are stripped of their Byzantine dress and reclothed like bishops so that they might seem more holy (Eco, 2003). If we imagine the queer past as lost but whole and continuous with our present then whatever fragments we find will become part of that continuity and their essential fragmentariness is annihilated: "You want/don't want this self-knowledge" (Shields, 2010). This work does not use page numbers, rather, it is organised into a series of fragments, of which this is the 464th. This way of doing things is an excellent elucidation of the principles of my argument, if not very bibliographically helpful). The process by which temporal bodies (and thus all bodies that interact with time) appear as whole, continuous, and catholic is an aspect of chrononormativity. It can be the progressivist assumption that the past is less liberal than the present as regards attitudes towards queerness, or the persistence of the idea that straight and cisgender are human default settings, or the suggestion, however anachronistic, that particular queer identities did or did not exist at any given point in time.

I feel I must stress that I am not invalidating any of the excellent recuperative work on queer history! Of course, there have always been men who both conceived of themselves as and performed the gender of men and who romantically and/or sexually loved other men, and women who loved women, and every other (im)possible permutation. Robyn Wiegman movingly argues for love as the paradigmatic plane of queer historiography and I am inclined to agree (Wiegman, 2011, p. 206). All I mean to say, really, is that our understanding of these material queernesses is constantly normativised. Furthermore, it is inevitable that even in this brief chapter I, too, will fall prey to the dictum of chrononormativity – we all will, how could we not, when it underwrites our own desire for recuperation and embodiment. In her reading of *A Thousand Plateaus* Grosz articulates the post-critique address of Deleuze and Guattari, of all philosophers really, that their theory falls prey to its own criticisms (Grosz, 1994, p. 182). Rhizomatic methodology is in and of itself a system, the conceptual frameworks necessary to interpret it reorganise it, the shadow of the conventional will always be inevitable even in the most poetic modality. However, accepting the impossibility of total abandonment of norms opens the way for the reincorporation of the conventional *into* the rhizomatic. Hierarchies can be nominally dispensed with but their material existence and the inadmissibly infinite systems they have propagated cannot be avoided, only imaginatively erased. Indeed, Grosz responds that

> Deleuze and Guattari will readily acknowledge that one must pass by way of or through binaries, not in order to reproduce them but to find terms and modes that befuddle their operations, connections that demonstrate the impossibility of their binarization, terms, relations and practices that link the binarily opposed terms.
> (Grosz, 1994, p. 181)

We might describe this approach as 'soft' historicism; the attempted negotiation of a temporal problem couched in the foreknowledge of the impossibility of its execution. If I am compromised, I will try to be so in such a way that it at least illustrates the problem.

Freyja Cox Jensen describes early modern humanist receptions of Caesar and his tradition as a "disintegrative interpretive strategy" (Cox Jensen, 2012, p. 99). Caesar's works, and Caesar as an individual both internal and paraphernal to those works, are read selectively to produce certain figurations. Take, for instance, illustrations of Caesar in republican Florentine codices, which depict him not as "a medieval universal ruler holding a globe … but rather as the author of the Commentaries" (McLaughlin in Griffin, 2009, p. 838). The tradition is disintegrated and interpreted, recombined. And the combination of this with a boom in both demand for and technological capacity to produce texts like *De bello gallico* from the last quarter of the fifteenth century and consequent critical conversation "regarding the authorship of the Gallic War" (Brown, 1979, p. 111) rendered figurations of Caesar that were simultaneously individually valid and contradictory. The disintegration of the unilateral body reveals those bodies or body parts of Caesar that have been marginalised, although, of course, recombination naturally returns to the individual, the cohesive, so that when one body or aspect thereof is demarginalised another is remarginalised, shunted into the shadows by chrononormativity's demands for integrity.

Even if the disintegrative practice Jensen describes ultimately turns toward synthesis, it nevertheless accepts as a condition, indeed, demands as a method of historiography, acceptance of fragmentary temporalities and spatialities. It thus lends itself willingly and effectively to negotiation of chrononormativity. And, likewise, as a mirror to myself as historiographer it offers critique of both my argument, in which I selectively read texts to try and produce understanding of the past, and my relation to the past, which I am compelled to disintegrate and recombine that I might understand myself. Is there not, then, a danger of anachronistically furnishing history with imaginative potential? Or of trying, through the diffusive aspect of queer time, to vainly conceal or project the uncertainties of the queer self? Yes and no. In *Phaedrus*, Plato describes the over-zealous seeker of historical truth who attempts to explain centaurs and chimeras and such things (and what are these creatures but *impermissible* disintegrations and recombinations). Impermissible isn't quite what I mean here, but forbidden even less so. *Haram* is closer but feels like it belongs too much to a different set of discourses. Centaurs and chimeras (and indeed manticores, blemmyes, and the rest of the fantastical bestiary who have percolated into *Dungeons & Dragons*) have the sense of the illegal move in a board game, the (im)possible. Plato, Ferguson notes, "suggests that those who are accustomed to devising such explanations are wasting their time, adding that such efforts will in any case be never-ending" (Ferguson, 1993 p. 42). Demonstrating the historicity of these abnormalities requires that they be admitted into a chronology that resists their existence by nature; even addressing them with sincere scepticism requires that they be subjected to the kind of probabilistic analysis ordinarily reserved for the real.

The monstrous body is, like the cartographer's customary warning on untravelled oceans and *terra incognita*, confined to the margins (Sanford, 2002, p. 10). Jeffrey J. Cohen describes this "affront to natural proportion" as encoding an excess that confines it beyond "the realm of the human, outside the possibility of desire" (Cohen, 1999, p. xi). Robyn Wiegman's 'economies of visibility' offers a useful way of thinking about these particular kinds of bodies. Wiegman describes how ostensibly liberal demands for visibility of marginalised groups are appropriated by conservative political actors to produce a visibility that "replaces, at the popular level, historical invisibility" but in fact effects "the profound transformations that underlie both the form and structure" of contemporary prejudice. She gives the example of civil rights movements in the Bush–Reagan era being co-opted in support of white supremacy (Wiegman, 1995, p. 5). This constructed, sanctioned visibility creates an illusion of the liberation of history while sustaining the marginalisations that mandated the impulse to liberality.

I am cautious not to imply that twentieth-century racism exists within a homogenous framework of marginalisation that can simply be translated to any historical incidence thereof; that would be to desperately trivialise and departicularise the historical moment, causality, and trajectory of the prejudice Wiegman describes and that persists today. However, I do believe that the conceptual framework of visibility applies to bodies beyond the twentieth century and that visibility can be used as a generic term to describe interactions with margins without obviating the understanding that different marginalisations are differently particular. This terminology of visibility and marginalisation is a helpful descriptor of chrononormativity insofar as it articulates a process by which reality is determined by consensus (*consensus* here useful in its literal sense, but also to describe a coming-together and compromising of the sensible, what Freeman calls "an amalgam of the incommensurate" (Freeman, 2010, p. xvii)). It is an unhelpful descriptor of chrononormativity insofar as it contains either one or two binaries, depending on whether you read it as visible/marginalised or visible/invisible and marginalised/normalised. One must allow for the barely visible and the edge case (or the nowhere at all); grey areas and saccades.

What I am proposing is half in agreement with and half in opposition to Plato's point, that is, that we do indeed admit the far-fetched monsters of the past into chronology, but that we do not waste our valuable time and breath exhaustively scepticising them, or indeed that we tie ourselves up in knots attempting to establish ontology as some kind of precondition for historical recognition or historicity as a criterion of reality. Scott F. Gilbert points out that this monstrosity is present in our own bodies at the most fundamental levels: "We are genomic chimeras: nearly 50% of the human genome consists of transposable DNA sequences acquired exogenously" (Gilbert et al., 2012, p. 334). The immortal jellyfish travels up and down its timeline in vagabondish rejection of the constraints of the telomere. Elsewhere in nature we find carcinization, the process by which distinct genomic strands have branched out through time along diverse paths and returned, unprompted and uncoordinated, to crabs. Queer historiography is likewise chimeric, not belonging to history but built from a series of disintegratively and anachronistically read historical moments. In place of synthesis it performs symbiosis, which by its very nature disorganises as it integrates. By reintroducing these moments, de-insularising them, we can reflect and see ourselves reflected fully, all our fragments present at once, history chimericised.

So what is the point of this approach? What does it benefit us to take apart Polydore Vergil and his works like this? I believe that through this case study we can both productively advance queer theoretical approaches in historiography and work towards breaking down the arbitrary barriers that distinguish the queer reading from the rest of literary theory, that peculiar imagined fortress of solitude. First, there is the liberation of the margins. Not in terms of social justice, at least not entirely, but in terms of restructuring our understanding of margins as conditional on and ancillary to the whole. Rhonda Lemke Sanford describes London's Elizabethan Liberties as "a place fraught with ambiguity: the place of the leper, the traitor, the prostitute, and the player, the place relegated to all those people and activities that do not fit into the city's social scheme [...] what Michel Foucault has termed 'heterotopias'" (Sanford, 2002, p. 102). And yet they are not ideologically or ritually contingent on the city, they are part of a circulatory process in which "the contradictions of the community – its incontinent hopes, fears, and desires – were prominently and dramatically set on stage" (Mullaney in Sanford, 2002, p. 102). The continence of history, control of its body, is conditional on the understanding that it is monolithic, that the relationship between the canonical and the marginal is hierarchical. Much like the Liberties of early modern England suppression is a pretext for the power that sustains the hierarchy; intrinsic difference is a lie told to enforce hierarchical organisation. By upsetting this the body can be made incontinent, that is, it can be made to flow in unpredictable and unexpected directions.

This can be compared to Grosz' critique of progressive medicalisation of the body, which demonstrates "a body pliable to power, a *machinic* structure in which 'components' can be altered, adjusted, removed or replaced" (Grosz, 1995, p. 35). But while for Grosz this is categorically an instrumentalisation of discipline to normalise bodies under control, I think that more nuanced reading can locate sites of resistance and circulation within these structures. I agree absolutely that increased medicalisation effects control on bodies in a way that particularly targets female bodies, trans bodies, disabled bodies, bodies of colour; and that historically these bodies have been and continue to be medicalised as a function of oppression (e.g. sterilisation as a punishment for deviant sexuality or state-mandated population control, or the modern application of mandatory DNR protocols for people with certain disabilities). That said, I would argue that progressive medicalisation (i.e. developing with time, not necessarily improving over time) can provide within its structures of regulation and discipline opportunities for queer embodiment. Grosz' description particularly evokes reproductive health and (it is implied, elective) cosmetic surgery, both conventional sites of oppression for certain kinds of body. But – and we have the advantage of twenty-five years here on Grosz' writing – these procedures can also affirm and recuperate.

In fact, I would argue this paradoxical response is an inevitable outcome of the surgical trauma effected by chrononormativity over time. Amputation has for so long been a condition of the continued existence of the abnormative body that the dysmorphic body must now be wounded to be healed. Indeed, the very existence of dysmorphia and dysfunction is predicated on monolithic notions of shape and purpose. These bodies are all one or another corporealisation of time, just as in the post-industrial disjunction of linear–national and cyclical–domestic time "history appears as damaged time; time appears as the plenitude that heals the historical subject. Time [...] appears to 'bind' history's wounds" (Freeman, 2010, p. 7). Bodies that appear disfigured in chrononormativity, or else disrupted or lost as they stray beyond its bounds, are 'healed' in such a way. The transition, the underground scene, and the self-forgetting; the struggles of identification by taxonomy, limitation by legislature, and obliteration by historiography – these are all modes of reassimilation. My personal experience as a trans woman and my wider sense of the relationship between bodies and time, both historical and contemporary, sometimes leads me to a rather gloomy conclusion about the possibility of meaningfully reconciling ourselves with chrononormativity in a way that doesn't simply reaffirm it. Even the increasing popularity of the 'Glow Up' in online communities, proposing radical reconnection with the queer body as a historical subject, often erases those whose bodies are marginalised in such a way that they cannot access affirming resources or procedures, or those who do not wish to. It also presumes, for the most part, the abnormative queer body as a purely contemporary being, or at least a product of postmodernity. The parameters of 'acceptable' embodiment may be troubled, or redrawn, but ultimately not to any lasting effect. I take some heart at the small emergent, insurgent online communities of various genders who have taken this discourse to its (il)logical extreme (e.g. "I'm transitioning to AFAB"), something I think would sit well with Margery Kempe and her restored virginity. I think that this kind of conversation offers a much more productive challenge to norms of queer identity. There is, of course, a non-intrusive but much harder way to 'fix' the dysfunctional machine, and that is to relinquish our preconceptions of function. Until then we will continue to cut ourselves to fit.

I believe that the liberation that can be found for queer bodies, both within the carceral structures of medicalisation and *despite* the historic trauma perpetuated by those structures and their analogues, can serve as a model for the liberation of bodies from chrononormativity. And, like the uncomfortable feeling this prolonged discussion of surgery awakens in all but the most hardened medical fetishist, the affect of this liberation is discomfort. Jonathan Sawday reflects on this kind of masochistic, anatomised desire in sixteenth-century romance, in which "physical disintegration at the hands of the beloved" is a consummation through suffering. We might paraphrase Sawday's "beloved object" as the impossible perfect/complete body, which maims and destroys in its acquisition (Sawday, 1995). In another embodiment, Freeman describes the corporealising effect of Hamlet's time "out of joint": "time has, indeed *is*, a body" (Freeman, 2010, p14). In the same breath time is given a body and that body is wrenched, dislocated. It hurts for the immaterial to become material; "we gain the understanding that hurt is what morphologises" (Freeman, 2010, p. 14). This same affect is present in the realisation of anachronism or plurality, and in the coincidence and flattening of bodies in conflict. As with the Freudian libido, the insistent ache of the repressed feeling manifests in local sensations of discomfort. It does not sit well with us to have a thing happen two ways, or out of sequence, or for time to flow any way but forwards. I have already mentioned the *disiecta membra*, and it is no coincidence that crises of temporality are embodied and sustained by metaphors of corporeal disintegrity.

The tempting conclusion to make is that this discomfort is an incipient property of bodies that are incomplete or internally conflicted or compromised, or even that the feeling is a masochistic resolution of the abnormative body's pain and restriction, but I suspect that both of these outcomes pathologise queer pain in disappointingly conventional ways. We might ask why "even in queer theory, only pain seems so socially and theoretically generative?" (Freeman, 2010, p. 12). This discomfort, not unlike the encounter with the *unheimlich*, belongs to queer bodies but is not inherent to them; rather, it adheres to them from the constraints of norms. Perhaps the best description of this relationship with discomfort is the apartment on Uranus described by Paul B. Preciado, in which impossible living conditions take the form of a liberatory dream (Preciado, 2020). The best, most precise expression of this feeling is found in from Jean Genet's *The Thief's Journal*:

> The atmosphere of the planet Uranus appears to be so heavy that the ferns there are creepers; the animals drag along, crushed by the weight of the gases. I want to mingle with these humiliated creatures which are always on their bellies. If metempsychosis should grant me a new dwelling place, I choose that forlorn planet, I inhabit it with the convicts of my race. Amidst hideous reptiles, I pursue an eternal, miserable death in the darkness where the leaves will be black, the waters of the marshes thick and cold. Sleep will be denied me. On the contrary, I recognize, with increasing lucidity, the unclean fraternity of the smiling alligators.
>
> (1954/2004, p. 47)

Examples of this body that seeks comfort in discomfort and wholeness through monstrosity are strewn throughout history. There are Plato's hermaphrodites, forever searching for reunion in a body that is physically monstrous, socially excluded, and politically suppressed. There is Milton's 'darkness visible', in which a body composed of an impossible contradiction is doomed to suffer for the gambit of self-actualisation.

Furthermore, despite my aforementioned concerns about the ossifying effect of locating queer identities in the past there *is* a recuperative and reparative outcome to be gained. It would be a slightly tired restatement of established queer theorists and historians like Freeman, Lochrie et al. to say that queerness cannot simply be written into history (although one has to read very little history to discover that it can be written out). However, it would also not be groundbreaking, I think, to suggest that the lack of queer readings of, for instance, Bede, is primarily because Bede is not coded as queer-available. A quick search finds mostly results regarding a queer-coded character from the latest *Pokémon* game who is indeed inspired by the venerable sage, although the resemblance is nominal at best. And however sensible the assumption that the *Historia ecclesiastica* does not offer much to the queer historiographer it cannot be denied that that assumption has its basis in modern projections of heteronormativity, and therefore in chrononormativity. It is not impulsive queer antiformalism or radicalism for radicality's sake to make a queer reading of Bede (or rather, a reading that presumes queerness in Bede, which is categorically different from a reading that argues Bede is gay). Rather, it is to "seize anachronisms" and in doing so "bring out the latent dreams and lost power that dwell within" (Freeman, 2010, p. xvii). This has a restorative effect, both allowing for the possibility of persistent queer identity in the past, even in a fashion at least cognate with our own, and disrupting the vectors through which chrononormativity is enforced. That *Anglica historia* has an apparent dearth of queer content *and yet* is particularly susceptible to this kind of disintegrative reading is evidence enough that there are conduits and permeations of queer historiography that remain untapped.

It is profitable, even necessary for capitalist history that these margins remain excluded. In early modern biological classification "Complexity of animal organization is accompanied by the increasing division of labor among organs", with an increasingly individualistic understanding of nature feeding into an increasingly individualistic organisation of society, and vice versa (Gilbert theorises that ultimately this leads to a mutual developmental relationship between Linnaean classification and libertarian capitalist socioeconomic ideology (Gilbert et al., 2012, p. 239)). Just as capitalism relies on the subdivision of labour under the class system, so chrononormativity demands that history exist in a condition of binarity. And, just as the very existence of the immortal jellyfish challenges seemingly natural assumptions about biological organisation, so fully realised queer historiography rejects the most routinely accepted assumptions of binarity. Binarity is what closes off historiography to these particular ways of reading – it is the antithesis of the membrane and the aquifer. Even the most fundamental binaries – is/is not – must come under question in this theoretical approach, because to accept this binary is to comply with the chrononormative state of history, that is, that there is history that did happen and history that did not happen. I'm a little concerned that this sounds like dangerous relativism or revisionism. In the former case it should go without saying that any sincere queer historiography must be guided by a firm moral sense, that is, both the knowledge that a monolithic historical canon demands suppression of the Other and an understanding of *why* it is right that the margins be liberated. In the latter case I agree: all *serious* history is revisionist. Deleuze and Guattari describe the fundamental image of the Tree as an endless binary, one becoming two, always directional and destinational (Deleuze and Guattari, 2005, p. 5). The (im)possibilities exiled by this structure are like Haraway's not-yet-existent worlds that we must "bring into being in alliance with other critters, for still possible recuperating pasts, presents, and futures" (Haraway, 2016). By exploring the tensions and cracks in Polydore Vergil's historiography and realising their overlaps, articulating their interstices, and fully embodying their contradictions, the impossible transtemporal synthesis that precipitates his methodological crisis can be achieved, in the sense that it will no longer demand resolution. I will not be so bold as to claim to be able to dispel chrononormativity (or even to declare myself especially abnormative). I will tentatively venture this hope: that in attempting to imagine the anorganism of history we might glean a sense of what it would be like if the impossible body, however briefly, was.

References

Brown, V. (1979) Latin manuscripts of Caesar's *Gallic War*", in *Paleographica Diplomatica et Archivistica. Studi in onore di Giulio Battelli*, Rome: Storia e Letteratura.

Butler, J. (1990) *Gender Trouble: Feminism and the Subversion of Identity*, London: Routledge.

Cohen, J.J. (1999) *Of Giants: Sex, Monsters, and the Middle Ages*, Minneapolis, MN: University of Minnesota Press.

Connell, W. (2004, September 23). Vergil, Polydore [Polidoro Virgili] (*c*.1470–1555), historian. *Oxford Dictionary of National Biography*, www.oxforddnb.com/view/10.1093/ref:odnb/9780198614128.001.0001/odnb-9780198614128-e-28224 (Accessed 2 August 2023).

Cox Jensen, F. (2012) *Reading the Roman Republic in Early Modern England*, Leiden: Brill.

Deleuze, G. and Guattari, F. (2005) *A Thousand Plateaus: Capitalism and Schizophrenia*, trans. by Brian Massumi, Minneapolis, MN: University of Minnesota Press.

Eco, U. (2003) *Baudolino*, London: Vintage.

Escobedo, A. (2004) *Nationalism and Historical Loss in Renaissance England*, Ithaca, NY: Cornell University Press.

Ferguson, A.B. (1993) *Utter Antiquity*, Durham, NC: Duke University Press.

Freeman, E. (2010) *Time Binds: Queer Temporalities, Queer Histories*, Durham, NC: Duke University Press.

Genet, J. (1954/2004) *The Thief's Journal*, Paris: The Olympia Press.

Giffney, N., Sauer, M., and Watt, D. (eds) (2011) *The Lesbian Premodern*, New York: Palgrave McMillan.

Gilbert, S.F., Sapp, J., Tauber, A.I. (2012) A symbiotic view of life: We have never been individuals, *The Quarterly Review of Biology*, 87(4), pp. 325–341.

Goldberg, J. (1992) *Sodometries: Renaissance Texts, Modern Sexualities*, Redwood City, CA: Stanford University Press.

Griffin, M. (ed.) (2009) *Companion to Julius Caesar*, Chichester: Wiley-Blackwell.

Grosz, E. (1994), *Volatile Bodies*, London: Routledge.

Grosz, E. (1995) *Space, Time and Perversion: Essays on the Politics of Bodies*, New York: Routledge.

Haraway, D. (2016) Tentacular thinking: Anthropocene, Capitalocene, Chthulucene, *E-Flux*, Issue 75, www.e-flux.com/journal/75/67125/tentacular-thinking-anthropocene-capitalocene-chthulucene/ (Accessed 2 August 2023).

Hay, D. (1954) *Polydore Vergil: Renaissance Man of Letters*, London: Routledge & Kegan Paul.

Helgerson, R. (1992) *Forms of Nationhood: The Elizabethan Writing of England*, Chicago, IL: University of Chicago Press.

Hodgen, M.T. (1966) Ethnology in 1500: Polydore Vergil's Collection of Customs, *Isis*, 57(3), pp. 315–324.

Momigliano, A. (1990) *The Classical Foundations of Modern Historiography*, Berkeley, CA: University of California Press, p. 81.

Ong, W. (1967) *The Presence of the Word*, New Haven, CT: Yale University Press.

Ott, E. (2010) Of time and type: Joseph Scaliger's De Emendatione Temporum, *The Chapel Hill Rare Book Blog*, https://blogs.lib.unc.edu/rbc/2012/08/29/of-time-and-type-joseph-scaligers-de-emendatione-temporum/ (Accessed 2 August 2023).

Preciado, P.B. (2013) *Testo Junkie*, New York: The Feminist Press.

Preciado, P.B. (2020) *An Apartment on Uranus*, London: Fitzcarraldo Editions.

Sanford, R. L., (2002) *Maps and Memory in Early Modern England*, Mew York and Basingstoke: Palgrave MacMillan.

Sawday, J. (1995) *The Body Emblazoned: Dissection and the Human Body in Renaissance Culture*, London: Routledge.

Sedgwick, E.K. (1990) *The Epistemology of the Closet*, Berkeley, CA: University of California Press.

Shields, D. (2010) *Reality Hunger: A Manifesto*, New York: Knopf.

Than, K. (2009) Immortal jellyfish swarm world's oceans, *National Geographic News*, www.nationalgeographic.com/animals/article/immortal-jellyfish-swarm-oceans-animals (Accessed 31 January 2021).

Wiegman, R. (1995) *American Anatomies: Theorizing Race and Gender*, Durham, NC and London: Duke University Press.

Wiegman, R. (2011) The lesbian premodern meets the lesbian postmodern, in N. Giffney, M.M. Sauer, D. Watt, and P.D. Watt (eds), *The Lesbian Premodern*, New York: Palgrave MacMillan.

2

The Rupture of the Sacred
Intrusion of Technology into the Birth Process

Heba Zaphiriou-Zarifi

The level of maternal mortality had been generally high across the whole of Europe up to the eighteenth century, and it was only during the nineteenth century that it started to decline, though not continuously, in most parts of the West (Manfredini et al., 2020). This is not the case in the developing world, where pregnant women face high risks of disease and death due to malnourishment and poverty, untreated basic health issues and infections, lack of education, environmental crises, and socioeconomic and political hazards (Tinker, 2000). Their children also face these risks, with 30–40% infant morbidity (Tinker, 1997). This loss of lives could be averted with adequate general health interventions such as the introduction of antisepsis techniques in hospitals and maternal institutes and adequate cures for bacterial infections. Addressing pre-existent conditions such as malaria, viral hepatitis, poor diet, or severe anaemia, exacerbated during pregnancy (World Health Organization, 1999), is basic to promoting healthy maternity. Medicine and science have secured sanitation and brought rampant diseases to a halt and alleviated unnecessary suffering. By the twentieth century, science-backed practices as well as technology saw the levels of mortality decrease in proportion to the increase of global life expectancy at an unprecedented rate. The arrival of penicillin, antiviral drugs, insulin, and immunotherapy, to name but a few, provided unparalleled breakthroughs in medical practice. Agriculture, energy, electronics, and robotics brought medicine and its achievements altogether to another level of accomplishment.

These excellent advancements have come with a gain but also a loss, at least in the estrangement from nature and a splitting of the nature of the body from its essence. It is worth noting that deaths in maternity and infancy directly correlate to malnutrition, poor hygiene and sanitary conditions, contaminated water and scarce electricity supply and are not in fact caused by pregnancy or childbirth *per se*. Insalubrious conditions, socioeconomic deprivation, and political upheavals, as mentioned above, make an unmitigated impact on maternity and childbirth, causing complications that are otherwise preventable.

In this short chapter I will attempt to discuss some presumptions that reflections on technology and its successes, in relation to pregnancy and childbirth, have evaded. Like science or medicine, technology is not a perfect instrument and, when overused, appears as an end in itself. "I value science extraordinarily highly: But there are actually moments in life where science also leaves us empty and sick" (Jung, 2009, p. 329). It is this loss of meaning if not loss of soul in modern maternity wards, as well as the dismissal of the female body, treated with a technological attitude, that I wish to consider in relation to pregnancy and parturition in the Western paradigm of technological success.

Certainly, technology has its place in the advancement of comfort and convenience. Its labour-saving has freed further spaces for women to inhabit as they continue reclaiming and exploring more comprehensively their embodied identity. It brought progress to our modes of communication, to the development of assisted knowledge, and provided devices and tools for the best possible state-of-the-art practice of medicine. When used in tandem with the latest scientific research, it recoups its original purpose and, like an art, it develops into a life-enhancing instrument. Technology has become an inevitable, if not indispensable, fact of life. Its influence is indisputable. Technology is a double-edged sword and must be wielded carefully: *in extremis* it can terminate the civilisation that invented it. But the question I would like to raise here is specifically concerning the impact of technology on women's pregnancy, parturiency, and childbirth.

Technology fascinates. The underlying assumption is that it will improve pregnancy, labour, and protect life. Its overestimation will produce an illusionary belief that it can resolve everything it may be used for. Using technology with an overinflated sense of its power over the natural world bespeaks a contrived investment in technology to do more and better, rather than questioning our narcissism in deluding ourselves that we will master technology and resolve the problems it poses. This attitude begs the question: in whose hands does technology fall, what is the underpinning mindset that upholds its administration, and to whose benefit is it produced and used?

Technology may be an advance in many aspects of our working lives, yet it carries the inherent risk of disconnecting us from soul, from our instinctual nature and metaphysical ground. Our deepest nature is to create more consciousness, but modern technology, Jung realised, "actively thwarts the main aim of our existence" (Jung, 2015, p. 537) with feminine consciousness more readily sacrificed. The feminine values of receptivity, flexibility, and resonance are undervalued despite the need for women to re-own them as core empowering qualities. Relying solely on technology without *presence*, the lynchpin of the feminine, feeds into the disembodiment of women. Body-awareness is already undermined in the modern era of electronics which has convinced everyone that, without electronics, it is impossible to be productive or to communicate; but technology in birthing units further accentuates the disappearance of the body. It limits the range of women's creative abilities, shutting down expressions of their nature, robbing them of their vitality, their imagination, and connection with their instinctual–spiritual integrity. Jung argues that technology "give[s] us no answer to our spiritual dissatisfaction and restlessness, on account of which we are threatened from within as from without" (Jung, 2015, p. 537).

When asked, midwives have listed about ten popular technological innovations that made their work easier (Wickham, 2020). The mobile phone came first in the list for the speedier communication with labouring mothers, compared to hospital pagers; cars did too. Washing machines brought handwashing nappies to an end, and comfortable machine-washable clothes saved time and trouble, as did the clothes-dryer. The internet provided wider access to women's cumulative knowledge, to databased research underpinned by scientific evidence, thus empowering women with up-to-date information to examine. The midwives listed the handheld doppler as a non-interfering tool – when used sparingly – as it allows monitoring of the baby's heartbeat whilst the mother is mobile. Like any technological equipment, it has a downside and may heat tissues and transmit energy to the baby if used frequently. Common sense gets it right: the tool is only as effective as the skilled hands that wield it; in the *wrong hands* or with the wrong mindset it becomes a weapon. Perinatal Technology must be constantly reviewed in the light of the latest scientific research based on women's experiences.

Midwives warned about the excessive, if not addictive, use of technology, and women caution against the prevailing dominant current of contrived modernity by reclaiming childbirth, maternity, and lactation among central issues of feminine identity and the feminist movement. The Feminine is not seen here in terms of gender but as a principle of being-ness. In Marion Woodman's words: "It is the courage to Be and the flexibility to be always Becoming" (1985, p.78). The feminine in our modern world has become unknown, estranged, and outcast, and because of that repression it evokes fear. Yet women who suffer consciousness in their bodies bring the feminine home to the womb, where it belongs.

Technology becomes a liability when used routinely, without considered rationale or appraisal for its implications. Misused, technology can lead to harmful side-effects with inescapable cascades of further technical interventions which could otherwise have been avoided. Overused, it becomes an unwelcome intruder into the female body, disrupting her bodily rhythms, upsetting the complex hormonal system that regulates her stages of labour and delivery. Technology disconnects her from her natural mothering instinct and disturbs her female sexuality. Sex after forceps is not attractive, and routine episiotomy – a cut artificially incised between the vagina and anus to enlarge the opening for delivery – deforms the tissues and muscles with bulges, and causes lacerations and unusual dryness, painful during intercourse. Women reported having poorer body image and less satisfying sex after surgical cuts and sutures than women who tear – and heal – along the lines of the muscles' natural formation. Verena Schmid's study on the pelvic floor muscles in "About physiology in pregnancy and childbirth" (2005) shows how muscles, like rose petals, retract petal after petal as the baby's head emerges. A dynamic peristatic movement of the muscles around the crown of the head are triggered in accord with the mother's push down the birth canal. A spontaneous tear is organically different to a cut that rips the perineal muscle fibres, causing unnecessary trauma to sensitive intimate tissues. The impact of these artificial cuts wound women emotionally with scars that interfere with breastfeeding and early mother–child bonding (Kitzinger and Walters, 1981). Moreover, the risks of stress incontinence and sexual dysfunction are not to be dismissed as transient.

Needless to say, exporting unscientific technology to Third World countries has increased its use to extremely high rates among practitioners, which is particularly undermining to indigenous knowledge, disruptive to transgenerational know-how. To paraphrase birth anthropologist Brigitte Jordan (Jordan and Davis-Floyd, 1993, p. 196), to legitimate a form of knowledge as authoritative it is necessary to devalue all other forms of knowledge. Colonialism presents itself as a harbinger of 'civilising' culture to the natives, and, whilst it pursues incremental improvements, it tampers with women's traditional practices that have endured time. Aline, a French midwife who'd been posted to Algiers, told me of her struggle to let go of her need to obsessively sanitise everything yet maintain safe hygiene practices. To her surprise, she discovered the ease with which native women gave birth naturally. She recalled an incident whereby dilation, not running its normal course, was progressed by the parturient squatting over burning herbs that women of her family had prepared, and which released a thick smoke. She remembered these women's soft voices supporting, encouraging the parturient, with mysterious incantations following each contraction as though they were the foetus sliding down the birth canal. Humming in the body's sounds whilst rubbing the belly in a circular movement brought comfort and ease. The birth was an ecstatic experience. The parturient was fed honey-glazed grains to stop the bleeding. Aline was personally transformed by this experience, and it likewise transformed her practice as a midwife. She learned from Algerian women many natural techniques, such as specific caresses and massages accompanied by sounds to ease off contractions and help women through the first and second stages of labour. These techniques, which were closer to an *art* than to a *skill*, she confided were extremely useful also in helping European women give birth more easily. She explained: "Like the Algerian women, I 'talked' to the uterus, inviting it to open. Contractions became bearable then, and a deeper relaxation was initiated." She recalled tapping into the indigenous female way of birthing for a European woman threatened with a possible caesarean section: "I felt under my fingers a relaxation, then a sudden change in the quality of the contractions. The dilation accelerated and became regular, gradually leading to birthing a serene babe."

Exporting Westernised systems of tool usage not only jars with local, more down-to-earth, natural birthing traditions; it is another form of erasure of the natural by the artificial, the indigenous by the 'civilised'. The misuse of technical 'tools' has affected women's health worldwide but has estranged the indigenous from their ground of being. There are very few attempts to straighten the bent rod, or studies to elucidate the damage on the psychosocial structures these artificially imposed practices have impacted on the spiritual tenet and its body-image counterpart. Medical care for optimum health during pregnancy and childbirth is an undeniable right for every mother and child, especially when the life of either is endangered, but the over-medicalisation of interferences, overwrought with technology too readily enforced on the expectant woman as inevitable, causes disquiet concern and the neglect of its consequences a feminist issue.

Denounced by the World Medical Association, excessive medicalisation of childbirth undermines women's agency, their autonomy, and sense of dignity. Constant monitoring of heartbeats, vaginal fingering, shaving-off of pubic hair, enema imposition, systematic use of forceps, surgical episiotomy, amniotomy with its artificial rupture of the membranes, and induction are but some of the debilitating complaints women bring to the privacy of the therapeutic *temenos*, in contrast with the abuse of their privacy during labour and childbirth. The personal and intimate is vulnerable exposed to the advantage of the collective and impersonal, with psychological consequences that complicate attunement in the processes of bonding and attachment. The overuse of pharmacology for induction or augmentation of labour, placenta-expelling drugs, and systematic pre-labour caesarean sections are added wounds incised into the flesh of birthing women, also affecting her psychologically due to injuries too shaming to be named. In a technologically controlled environment, the expectant mother is more likely to be treated as a 'patient' and labour viewed as an 'illness' to be overseen in hospitals, leaving the future mother feeling undermined, dispossessed of her volition and violated, as though she is but a transient passenger in her own journey of delivery and imminent motherhood.

Women often experience long-term fear following repeated echographies. In her twenty-second week of pregnancy, Amalia was told her 'foetus' was not the 'right' size according to the number of gestation weeks. However much she attempted to explain that her husband is 'petit' compared to Western criteria, no heed was given. Amalia lived with chronic fear of giving birth to an unviable or deformed child, feeling "unfit and inadequate" for what lay ahead of her. "Something is wrong with me, and my baby is not growing as he *should* be," she cried in the therapeutic session. At week thirty-six, she was told: "The size of the foetus is okay after all – it is genetically determined." This prognosis was thrown at her with the same contempt for her capacity to understand it as the initial (erroneous) diagnosis had been. Her pregnancy was not viewed as 'mother with child', but as a transactional event, and her child not seen as a 'baby' but tagged as a 'foetus', Amalia concluded, with the retort that her baby was "a thing to be measured and diagnosed".

Fear triggers a general increase in brain arousal and may result in altered threat-processing with an increase in anxiety levels. The consequences of chronic fear on general health are comprehensively recorded, and studies on its effect on brain development are well under way. Clinicians announcing worrying news based on technology, ignoring the context and identity of the parent(s), induce unnecessary, harmful effects and countereffects. The HPA (hypothalamic-pituitary-adrenal) axis and the autonomic nervous system get activated when a threat is perceived (Rosenberg, 2017). Primary stress hormones such as cortisol and adrenaline are released. From observation, Amalia and I noticed a decrease in her natural defences: her habitual vigour had dwindled, and her usual energy levels had dropped. Amalia described "unusual fatigue, feeling overloaded". At times, she felt depressed, "burnout, unable to meet the demands" made on her. Singing lullabies to her, and with her, as well as voice-work *in simili* to sound-vibration patterns, fundamental to the formation of our developing brain, were intoned during our weekly meetings. Amalia gradually self-regulated to homeostasis. Her sleep pattern returned to its habitual curve. There was a risk of adrenal dysfunction, her GP warned, which increased her determination to reduce echography to a strict minimum. The Eurocentric appraisal of her and her baby's health posed a conflict whereby difference and differentiation were not part of the diagnosis. Amalia sensed the racial biases that stood in the way of her pregnancy. Together, we read Foucault's words: "There are times in life when the question of knowing if one can think differently than one thinks, and perceive differently than one sees, is absolutely necessary if one is to go on looking and reflecting at all" (Foucault, 1990, p. 8).

We agreed with his insight that there is always something ludicrous in (medical) discourse "when it tries, from the outside, to dictate to others, to tell them where their truth is and how to find it" (Foucault, 1990, p. 9).

Technology, despite its ever-increasing variety of procedures, is in fact repetitive, estranging women from their natural versatility and creative adaptiveness. It aims at managing pregnancy whilst penetrating the paradigm of confinement and birth. Desacralising birth renders the female womb a public arena, a theatre put on display with the intention of gaining control over the female instinctual body and the woman's freedom to express it. Squatting, walking, remaining upright, or moving at all are impossible, and moaning, breathing, singing, or going into deep silence are inhibited, when she is observed and her body confined to a bed, her legs in stirrups. The altered state of mind that a birthing woman travels through is, in the flesh, a pathway to free womanhood. To inflict on her a technical state of mind is fraught with traumatising incidences. To control her birthing body is to control an archetypal power set in motion in the service of life. Diverted from its *telos*, the archetypal energy, which needs to be expanded outwards, turns negatively inwards, pulling a woman not toward a broader development and maturity of the personality needed for the *becoming* of motherhood, but toward a negative vortex into darkness or depression. Postnatal depression is often correlated with the disempowerment of women during labour and degrading treatment at parturition.

The use of evidence is essential for guiding women toward a well-informed choice regarding their delivery. Clinicians need to share evidence with expectant parents as an ethical duty to facilitate informed consent. Yet we discover that even when mounting databased research has proven certain procedures, such as CEFM (Continuous Electronic Foetal Monitoring), are critically disruptive to the natural flow of labour, they remain obsessively imposed even in low-risk pregnancies (Alfirevic et al., 2017). Being strapped to a monitoring machine to constantly check her baby's heartbeat disrupted Emma's flow of contractions. Her labour was tampered with on the rationale of reducing the (very rare) risk of neonatal seizure. Trapped in fear, and unprepared to counter-argue whilst in on–off labour, Emma succumbed to having instrumental delivery with a ventouse suction cup. Her baby was scarred by cuts on face and scalp, and Emma by vaginal laceration. Emma's Stage 2 of labour was continually disrupted by technology and the incessant exits and entrances of the obstetrician and midwife. She needed to actively give birth, as would any other mammal, in the dark and in her familiar locus, privately, away from sight and noise, letting go of neocortical cognitive activities. All she needed to do was to dig deep, breathe, and surrender. Instead she had to comply with an enforced passivity neither she nor her baby enjoyed. Wireless telemetry is a more adaptive technology when needs must in critical pregnancies, but Emma's experience highlighted medical teams' mistrust in women's independent agency, the power of their uterus to contract and expel – the process to which they've surrendered – as well as disregarding an infant's survival instinct. It is the baby's body that releases a tiny amount of a substance that signals to the mother's hormones to begin labour (Amis, 2007; Condon et al., 2004). In most cases, labour will begin only when both a woman's body and that of her baby are ready. Pregnancy and delivery are a twosome, unique and personal to the mother–child mysterious dyad. Women need to be widely informed, empowered, and supported, not pathologised, fixed, or rescued. Reducing the risk of loss of life does not need to come at the detriment of natural processes forfeited for 'modernity'.

Managing a 'perfect' conception, birth, or motherhood technologically indicates that, in this frame of mind, nature is fundamentally corrupt and in need of salvation. Nature as 'shadow' drops "into hell and becomes the devil" to be feared (Jung, 2019, p. 569). But what 'we resist, persists' as in the psychotherapeutic motto; and in Jungian Psychology not only does shadow material persist – it gains momentum in the underworld and erupts in all kinds of ways, including in symptoms during pregnancy, uncontrollable pain during contractions, interruption of labour and many other debilitating outcomes, whilst all along it seeks redemption. Nature and the natural are the feared in a culture of domination that aims at correcting nature's 'faulty' processes. First, we alter the natural, deemed flawed, then intrude further to 'repair' and 'improve' whilst inflicting additional injuries; a phenomenon anthropologist Peter C. Reynolds defines as "one-two punch" (1991, p. 3ff). The culture of nature domination subverts the natural birth processes with technology, then employs added technology to undo the initial hurt. Technology blunders with additional technological blunders.

Natural birth, like nature itself, is misunderstood. It is not perceived in its cyclical, rhythmic balancing of creation and destruction. Instead, it is feared, mistrusted as a source of evil suffering that must be controlled. Fear is an age-old, deeply wired brain reaction to real or perceived threat. It bypasses cortical thinking and reroutes energy to the amygdala. Activated, the latter triggers speedy reactions for fight, flight, freeze, or fawn. Although it starts in the brain, the chemical reaction spreads throughout the body, releasing stress hormones detrimental to parturiency. Heart rate and blood pressure rise, breathing accelerates – all detrimental to safety in birthing. Fear of fear itself, fear of deformity, fear of the unknown and of what may be coming, is ultimately an attempt to control the fear of death. Death in this model is dislocated from life as a natural continuum; it is to be barred at all costs. The female body becomes the seat where control of death whilst giving life is played out. To control the mystery of the female body is to attempt to control the fear of the numinous, experienced in the flesh. Life bursting out of a human body is numinous like no other, inducing a spiritually transforming experience. Across cultures and throughout history, pregnancy and childbirth have been perceived as spiritual events because of the miraculous processes involved. The numinous is a viscerally felt phenomenon, impacting first and foremost the feeling–sensing body, where it is rooted. Controlling birth is controlling death, and by doing so we become a 'dissociated' culture.

> Through the act of controlling birth, we disassociate ourselves with its raw power. Disassociation makes it easier to identify with our "civilised" nature, deny our "savage" roots and connection with indigenous cultures. Birth simultaneously encompasses the three events that civilised societies fear: birth, death, and sexuality.
>
> (Richards, 1993, p. 28)

To learn to re-inhabit the body where the numinous dwells is to mark a conscious new beginning: the birth of the new god-image as 'experience' in the personal body–psyche, as Jung elaborated in *The Red Book* (2009), transformative of the human and cosmological levels. It is a continuous birth, a *continuing incarnation*, whereby the body is the bridge between the personal and the transpersonal: "spirit is the living body seen from within, and the body the outer manifestation of the living spirit – the two really being one" (Jung, 1933/2001, p. 224).

Darkness, the body, and sexuality are seen as the nexus of evil in patriarchal religions where the Divine Feminine is excluded, and the womb a sinful organ to be purged and cleansed. Is it the fear of natural femininity that hides behind the usurping of feminine power by technology? Or is it womb-envy that incites patriarchy to control the female organ as though to possess it? Or is it the fear of being sued by patients or their partners, helpless when facing the unfathomable, that incites obstetricians and the medical world at large to hand over their intuition and feeling to hard science and technology?

Women in therapy sessions grieve the disembodiment of their birthing experience under medical scrutiny: they yearn to develop a good-enough connection with themselves to learn to trust the wisdom of the body. They painstakingly struggle to re-own the intimate relationship with their bodily functions alongside the right to receive the care they choose. Having suffered the throes of 'unconscious' birth, by handing over their own power to technology and the person who wields it, they gradually pull the projection back and start to walk the untravelled path, the one to the 'left', recollecting what had been left behind. Pregnant and birthing women experience a boundary shift in consciousness. Technology is then free to be used both for what it is and what it is not: a tool that can help when needed but does not 'save' from the pain of *becoming*, nor does it 'protect' from the hurt of *unconsciously* stepping into the realm of the goddess. It only does what it is supposed to do, which is to measure. Overinvested with what technology is not, it can alienate the pregnant mother from her bodily experience (see Young, 1984).

By contrast, *conscious* suffering is like a sacred fire that brings women through to transcendence and to discovering a new feeling of ensoulment. The body is not a cloak, a thing, an object, the property of another, something to be tossed aside by dysregulated science; the body is who one is: it is the soul striving through the dark for the light.

Women who rely on technology or 'the doctor' do not know about transitioning into the maternal body. The challenges and shifts of the previous body–identity blur the boundary between self and other. Technology becomes the other that will save us from our self, splitting off the body from inner self, with a risk of dissociating the infant from the maternal body. Julia Kristeva emphasises women's connection to the maternal body, not reductively, as some feminists have criticised, but as the possible start of new beginnings, with pregnancy seen as the potential for change and transformation.

Like "fractured fairy tales" the shattering ignites "the emotional pathway women travel as they work to rediscover and redefine a new sense of self" (see Priddis et al., 2014). Kristeva reminds us of the relational intersubjectivity linked to birth-giving (1986: 182) and of the precultural maternal body "as bearing a set of meanings that are prior to culture itself". The mother–infant communication, she explains, is "underwater, trans-verbal communication between bodies" (1986: 182).

Lacking in bodily movement and autonomy whilst laid passively on their backs, a position suitable for the obstetrician but obstructive for birthing as it significantly narrows the passage through the pelvis (DiFranco and Curl, 2014), women are blamed if their physical body does not perform to the artificial protocol set out by the 'specialist' medical team, often without the women's knowledge or approval. Women's bodies are treated as objects, and, far from being the habitat of the personal and individual, their wombs become the scene of exposure and disclosure, a public showground for all to see. There is a tendency to opt for personal convenience when using technological tools, ignoring the imperceptible but real harm that may ensue on women's physical and psychological health.

Scientific databased research demonstrates that unnecessary intervention increases the risk to mother and infant health, whilst minimal use of intrusive technology decreases it. Outdated use of technology under the auspices of science must be screened and vetted as inefficacious and obsolete. In our modern world, where technology has a foothold in every aspect of our lives, we slip into believing that technology equates to science. Far from it; research has in fact shown the opposite in that "the most scientific birth is often the least technological birth" (Dreger, 2012).

Low-risk pregnancies with regular monitoring of weight gain, blood pressure, and urine, for example, need not be treated as high-risk, and hospitalisation does not necessarily improve mother–child dyadic physical or psychological health. Technology, used excessively or unnecessarily, reinforces patriarchal dualism, perpetrating false myths of mind over matter, hard science over art, intellect over body. Patriarchy as discussed here is not gender-based, but constructed on a power position that disconnects *logos* from *eros*. It devalues women as subordinate in the same way as it devalues vulnerability as irrelevant. It demonstrates male attitudes as well as organisations' rigidity in maintaining things as they are with no room for change or alternative methods of birth. If challenged, control-dominated deliveries render women helpless to voice their choices, setting their needs to one side, shaming them into complying with a system that has decided it knows best. Patriarchy appears to aim at taming the wild and the natural, the soft animal body, to dominate the instinctual and the chthonic for lack of connection to the body–self, and to sever relationship to the Feminine-Eros.

Bodily fluids, including sweat and blood, during childbirth are viewed as *dirty*, soiling, and uncivilised. They must be covered up, removed swiftly, and sanitised. The instinctual archetypal knowhow that women have stored in their genes and their somatic intelligence, passed down through the millennia from woman to woman, generation after generation, seems to dissipate in the face of *clean* technology. The wisdom of the body is denied, and generational knowledge undermined.

Discounting the psychological suffering of humiliating incidents following parturition, and the hampering effects they have on nascent mothering instincts, patriarchal attitudes reveal an underlying misogyny, with women treated as sexual objects. Sylvia came to see me after a post-partum depression which "hindered my bonding with my new-born". She complained that one of the depressive symptoms had led to an early interruption of breastfeeding. Sylvia talked about the wide range of psycho-physical benefits of breastfeeding for both child and mother, but the low self-esteem and loss of self-confidence following her birth experience meant she could no longer live by what she believed. She recalled a conversation held, whilst at her most vulnerable, after parturition, between the obstetrician and the nurse, who, winking at her husband, confided the doctor intended "to remodel my vagina with an extra stitch for my husband". Despite being half-drugged, she objected vehemently, to be told: "Now, be a good girl, and let the doctor do his job down there." She also remembered being slapped on the bottom to "snap me out of roaring and start to push" following the midwife's instructions.

Restricting the voice and the throat has a direct impact on the vaginal muscles and causes the cervix to tighten. An episiotomy was then exacted, when all her body wanted to do was to bear down and be allowed to do what it knows best to do. Sylvia was shamed for resisting the "progress of medicine" and was critiqued for behaving "like a primitive". The routine use of episiotomy and its negative effects have long been debunked. Yet nonmedical factors that benefit obstetricians and their corporations lead them to stubbornly continue to believe in technological transcendence in response to women's defectiveness (see Davis-Floyd, 1994).

We worked through this violent reminiscence stored in her body–memory, and reconnecting through earthbound movements and sounds to her sensual–sexual body, Sylvia went on reclaiming, re-owning, re-membering her parts that embody conscious femininity. We worked from the conscious standpoint of her being-ness, and with compassion nurtured values of conscious femininity by sensing her feet deeply rooted in the ground, her spine elongating, her neck supple and her head floating freely like an astral globe. This conscious body–work came as a response to a dream where she saw herself floating in mid-air, estranged from her body–sense, stranded, her legs strapped into stirrups and a surgical disposable cloth stuffed into her mouth. On all fours, however, she discovered that gravity was her agent and Mother Earth her sacred midwife.

Many years later, Sylvia developed her work in advocacy, highlighting the necessity to abolish violence in delivery and maternity wards and to humanise childbirth in hospital settings and in midwifery teaching. What women deserve is a "continuity of care" by doulas or midwives during pregnancy, labour, and postpartum. A new birth paradigm is to focus on the effectiveness of building trusting relationships rather than to focus on risk-aversion methodologies and their ensuing fear-provoking, control-dominated technologies. A shift from survival to life-giving patterns prioritises relational care, inviting women to be each other's guides and guardians in the 'sacred rite' of giving birth.

A few years ago, I ran a series of workshops for postpartum mothers who were experiencing what is commonly referred to as 'baby blues'. A kaleidoscope of dream images similar to Sylvia's was shared. A first-time mother had dreamt of technological gizmos strapped to her legs, depriving her of mobility; another had dreamt of stitched lips and a stitched vulva; another of suffocation; but what most women recalled as the most detrimental to their psychological wellness was their silencing during labour. Sonia felt let down by her partner's collusion with the obstetrician or the nurse in bartering her immediate bodily needs with what was presented as 'the best for her'. Allison had a dream of bloodied coins and banknotes dropping out of torn belly bandages. Her husband had insisted on booking her into 'the best' private clinic in London for reasons of snobbery and exceptionalism; she reflected: "*His* wife and *his* baby must receive the best treatment." And however she explained to him that the best for her was to have an experienced doula with whom she'd bonded for a home birth, or a homelike setting in a hospital birthing unit, he demanded that "*his* child will be born in a reputable clinic *he* trusts". Fathers-to-be taking over their partners' desires is infantilising, if not inferiorising, of women. Allison's suggestions, like many women's, were tagged 'irrational' and 'irresponsible'. What was irresponsible was the belief that birthing is a 'rational' event.

In *Birth Reborn* (1984) renowned obstetrician Michel Odent reframes birth as women's way of reclaiming their expertise when given the *space* to follow their instincts. The lack of privacy and the intrusiveness in hospital settings is considered by parturient mothers to be the most negative aspect of birth. Furthermore, fathers who co-labour with their partners play a capital role during pregnancy and childbirth that cannot be overlooked. It was found that partners' support was positive in decreasing the dosage of pain-relieving drugs and the length of labour. Their containing protective shield around the birthing unit of mother–child is the safest *temenos* for a labouring mother. Yet it remains essential to re-centre the woman, Odent insists, as autonomous subject, agent of free will, for this transformative familial adventure. The restitution of her active involvement by becoming her own birthing expert needs the support of positive masculinity disruptive of negative patriarchal norms.

Given adequate information, moral support, and respect, women's confidence in their DNA-inscribed instincts can be rekindled. The natural way the body births is free from drugs and medicalised technology. The latter have been increasingly recognised as bringing harm to mother and child, by disempowering women, muting their inspirational hopes and dreams with figures and numbers. Technological instruments are prized by husbands as human innovations responding to women's needs. Whilst there is some efficacy in these novelties, and truth in the need to respond to human suffering, what mothers-to-be need more than anything is knowledge, both acquired and experienced. They need to be reminded and reassured that as natural a pregnancy and birth as possible is within reach; that every woman is entitled to her own way of bringing her child into the world, even if this means confronting the power of the medical institution and relegating authoritative knowledge to the outskirts of helpful consultancy.

There is a seductive and enticing aspect to technology and to high-powered hospital settings. Yet in therapy, women reveal men's envy of the womb, as well as other women's envy of natural birth. This makes patriarchal wounding even more confusing. The life-force of a woman is envied for having 'more than', setting up a kind of rivalry between women, similar to that of Cain and Abel, making one's giving more valid than the other's in the eyes of the patriarchal father, in whichever mode of representation he may appear. Conditional valuing in patriarchal society forces women to act against the best interests of other women, to put them down or compete with them. Sylvia reflected on Marion Woodman's words about how "standing alone today demands even more courage and strength than it did in former cultures (1985, p. 16) setting women against each other. Some women confided they felt muted by other women, who competed by diminishing the experience of the newly birthing woman, pushing her nascent self-empowerment into the background. Patriarchy has poisoned our words and attitudes even when the intentions are good. Patriarchy is not always explicit in its domination of women; rather, it is an ongoing, longstanding systemised mechanism we partake in, mostly unconsciously. Born into it, we are misguided by it and, even with the best motives, unknowingly we perpetuate it. The parody of femininity is toxic femininity.

Whilst conception *in vitro* is rising in popularity like an epidemic, induction seems to be its counterpart. There was a time when gas and air were the ideal solution to pain, and episiotomy was another trick in the bag; now induction appears to be the lauded up-to-date technique for today's culture, no longer in touch with *kairos* time, the 'deep time' where linear time stops for a moment of a deep exhale. Linear thinking and timing propelling us forward is the only valued configuration of our society, which runs after time in a rush not to waste it. Rushing to cut the new-born's umbilical cord, or pulling on it to forcibly expel the placenta, then hurrying the baby away to wash off its (protective) vernix are but processes executed with a technological frame of mind rather than being *present* to the majesty of life bursting in. Kate, a woman in her thirties, described how the midwife on duty explained that "to save her from induction, [she] stuck her gloved fingers in my vagina for a membrane sweep. This broke the sac, and I felt in my confused state a terrible violation of my intimacy." A membrane sweep disconnects the amniotic sac from the wall of the uterus. The stripping of the membrane releases prostaglandins forcibly. This artificial technique, not in tune with the baby's time to be born or the mother's rhythmic contractions and labour arc, is used to soften the cervix and accelerate contractions. Kate's labour began, then stopped, then started again with sharper contractions as though to compensate for the automated way they were forced to kick-start. Kate noticed bleeding after the mucus plug was lost. Her labour lasted "too long", not knowing whether it was cramping or contractions. The pain was not a gradual build-up, but chaotic and difficult to track. "My body was no longer in tune with myself; I knew something had gone wrong. My body was overstimulated; at the end I was exhausted." The midwife noticed an irregular foetal heartrate, which threw Kate into panic. She was rushed to the operating theatre for a caesarean.

Neocortical activities interfere detrimentally during labour and birth. They are exacerbated by the administration of frequent testing and prodding, by being observed and bade to pay focused attention for precise responses. Light stimuli are another adverse component to the essential need that labouring women have for dark, warm, and quiet spaces. Silence is paramount for a labouring woman. Protected spaces are vital, and the sense of safety is utmost with a strictly minimal intrusion from the outside world. The womb is like a rose that opens with each contraction, if given time, petal after petal. Lacking that safe, protected space, neocortical stimulation represses the primal brain, inducing a splitting-off from the instinctual, thus inhibiting access to the mammalian strata of the brain that are fundamental for labour to proceed organically, followed by the foetal-ejection reflex, as well as the milk-ejection reflex. The earlier, instinctive brain is responsible by and large for the involuntary birth processes and the release of specific hormones at each particular stage of labour and parturition (Odent, 1984). For natural birth to proceed, neocortical stimulants must be inhibited, in the same way as for enjoying sexual orgasm (Thomson, 2015). This inhibition is conditional to opening a stairway to transcendence, giving access to another reality outside and beyond the confinement of space and time.

Technology alone is not enough to bring about the best outcome for women's birthing experiences. The non-dualistic, paradoxical feminine approach must be integrated. The integration of body–psyche energies rising from below – the cultivation of instincts, as Nietzsche says – is necessary for the individuation process. Nietzsche (1908/1979) suggested a plan for "becoming what one is" through the cultivation of instincts and various cognitive faculties, a plan that requires constant struggle with one's psychological and intellectual inheritances.

The body in this respect is essential for the process of becoming, aligning with what Jung advocates. In his active imaginations recounted in *The Red Book* Jung uncovers that individuals become whole only when the denied and repressed "primordial instincts" are integrated (2009, p. 308). A confrontation of preconceived ideas and inherited scientific knowledge with figures of the unconscious that arise to meet us when we descend downwardly and inwardly into matter, which the body holds for us, is required for the individuation of the human and the gods alike to occur. Inscribed in the individual's DNA conceived in the celestial womb of the gods at work, it is triggered at different stages of life, with birth being its prototype.

The four stages of physiological birth, with its first and second stages of labour morphing into transition, followed by the foetus-ejection reflex, and culminating with placental release, inform the individuation process psychologically, as though moving into transitional stages of life we move into the birth canal, with parallel patterns to the initial birthing process. Marion Woodman, speaking in an interview in 1987, said

> you can think about death and rebirth in terms of a birth canal: you are going to say good-bye to the womb and go into a new life. When people enter that "birth canal," they repeat the original birth trauma ... People who are born premature will try to go ahead of themselves: they'll always be two or three steps ahead of where they really are. Caesarean births are terrified of confrontation, usually. They've never confronted the initial struggle. People whose mothers were drugged are the ones most likely to fall into an addiction. They tend to be quite passive—waiting for someone to do something at a moment of difficulty.

Birth becomes the blueprint for symbolic births, at the crossroads of past and future, for the various stages of life aiming toward a constructive movement of the libido. Each birth retrieves past stored memories, each striving to form the ground of a new metabolised psyche-soma integration.

The mystery of birth can only be approached with humility, suggested yet not understood. Premature understanding, Jung often hinted, comes from the devil, and, by trying to perfect a rationale for surgically correct delivery, it excludes from possibility a value to non-rational understanding of the birth process as a natural set of facts that deserve at least equal attention. The emergence of a baby from the womb that has been containing that new life for the better part of a year is an opportunity to integrate the unexpected into the planned, as a chance for mother as well as baby to experience the possibility of a self with its own coherence in the face of what could not possibly be planned. It is a shame that Jung did not write of childbirth, because he could have applied his Taoist understanding of the value of being able to "let things happen" (Jung, 1967, p. 16). *Wu wei* as Master Lao Tzu clarifies enables "the Light to circulate according to its own law" (Jung, 1967, p. 16). It is action in non-action, the art of opening the door to the way of birthing, in accord with nature's law. At the crucial moment when a woman undergoes an initiation rite that transfigures her previous identity as nulliparous into becoming a mother, she finds herself battling with artificial constructs that disconnect her from the deeper layers of her psyche. Logic and objectivity are lopsided without the non-rational and personal subjectivity. They constrict one's own nature that in labour and birth reaches, if allowed, expansive altered spaces of consciousness, stretching into new maturity. "Technology ... is based on a specifically rationalistic differentiation of consciousness which tends to repress all irrational psychic factors" (Jung, 1958, p. 291). Wholeness, with its holistic approach to health, is contrived if not aborted in the minimised spaces of technology-assisted birth. Birthing women know they are traversing a third, in-between space, a paradoxical field of energy where heaven and hell, shadow and light meet at the zenith and the nadir of birth and death. Undiscerning confidence in technology implies a belief in its superiority over feminine nature, manipulating her body to serve unintegrated ends.

The mystery of the cosmic womb, the female womb, and the womb of the earth is not to be mined, but the seed of conception that grows in the woman, as if in the soil, is a cosmology pointing to other hidden realities. The cosmos and the human body mirror each other, and birth, like death, is a cosmological event. The pregnant body knows, if given the conditions to experience it, that the earth is the most reliable midwife of all. Moreover, the round belly of the pregnant woman needs the circular body of the moon and of planet Earth to attune to during birth, for there is an affinity between them, and whilst mirroring one another they also affect each other. Women who walk on the earth during their pregnancy will increase the chances of optimal birth. Likewise, women who open to the cosmic and drop down onto the earth, squatting during labour, will experience shorter labour. Their capacity to use breath to ride the wave of pain and glide with it closer to shore wards off the possibility of succumbing under its weight. Body–mind-oriented therapies as in Chinese medicine see the body as a microcosm of the universe, which is said to have its imprint in the body. But, as with nature, the female womb has become a 'field' for her internals to be observed and scrutinised, inspected and analysed to then produce a medical report. Nature in major parts of our contemporary world is no longer perceived as the pregnant womb, the living matrix of life, death and rebirth. She is consumed, disembowelled and, like the feminine body, objectified and exploited.

Archetypal initiation into birth-giving, motherhood and the deeper layers of embodying soul is dismissed from being experienced in the body; the unfathomable hovers unattained to preserve the legitimacy of the solely rational, civilising mind. The depreciation of the archetypal realm, nakedly experienced by women through their birthing instinct, renders women and their entourage spiritually depleted if not disabled. It aborts the opportunity to experience the immediacy of the life-force itself, together with the paradox of life and death as the sacred *temenos* to the burgeoning life on its way to death. The depreciation of *kairos* time, most appropriate for the creation of the *new*, alters *chronos* time whereby the specific and unique date and time of birth, as inscribed in the heavens and on earth, are irrevocably 'doctored'. This imbalance affects the mysterious timeline strung between the two ends of a wick. The arc of a lifespan from its beginning to its end is like a candle lit, in accordance with the dance of the planets, to burn a lifetime and wither at the end, only to light up again but on the other side. The question remains if the hour of death, as birth to another reality, is *in simili* affected by the time of birth and mirrors its pattern, even symbolically. The *way* of the woman is sacred, at all times, for "great is the power of the *way*. In it Heaven and Hell grow together, and in it the power of Below and the power of the Above unite" (Jung, 2009, p. 384). Conscious birth is the domain of the goddess who weaves the thread of time into destiny.

Introversion encourages the vertical axis of the libido, Jung explains (see 1971). By withdrawing from the horizontal movement invested in the outer reality, we are driven to explore the inner world. This becomes key to unlocking the energetically closed doors, be they psychological or physical, for nature to form a new instinctual–spiritual meaning, a new symbol of transformation. The introversion required for a natural birth during the nine months of pregnancy, culminating in a necessary pre-birth confinement period, is a time of slow and steady descent into the body. Connecting with the mammalian brain is basic for an optimal birth experience. Women's withdrawal from neocortical external activities favours a broader engagement with the personal, familial, even ancestral secrets carried on in the muted silence of the flesh. Wave after wave, each contraction washes to the surface a piece of the puzzling information to form a new consciousness and identity metamorphosis. "Consciousness arises through going into darkness, mining our leaden darkness, until we bring her silver out", writes Woodman (1985, p. 10). Labour takes a woman into *katabasis*, a descent into the underworld where the instinctual is the counterpart of the spiritual rising consciousness of the *anabasis*, both numinously encountered. If met with psychological resistance, the body will pull us into *katabasis* regardless, for a necessary conscious transformation on the personal and cosmic planes.

Pregnancy and birth are a *nekyia* (νέκυια) of sorts, a rite of passage through which the ghosts of the forgotten past are summoned and even questioned about the future. The forgotten and the repressed, be it personal or ancestral history, relegated to the unconscious underworld, transmits information with the chthonic through direct channels of ego–body–brain pathways. Womblike caverns and the birth canal are typical of such mysterious depths out of which the life-force is channelled. Yet a death of sorts is required in order to welcome the new life in the chrysalis. The archetype of birth, death, and rebirth underpins this experience at every stage of the birth from conception, some argue even from preconception to birth and beyond.

The goddess Eileithyia (Εἰλείθυια), connected to the Eleusinian mysteries, is the goddess of pregnancy and childbirth in Greek mythology. She relies on *techni* (τέχνη), the daemon of Technology that personifies the spirit of the art, crafts, and technical skills, or the art of weaving, in the appropriate time of *kairos*, an effective action: to produce, create, or give birth. To master a technique is to give way to the divine that resides in the human. It is to manifest the working and work of transformative intelligence common to every *techni*. If misused, *techni* binds women to necessity and to lack of inventive freedom, and in Ancient Greece it is often associated with slavery. The arts and crafts of midwifery, *magiki techni* (μαγική τέχνη), or magical knowhow, demonised as witchcraft, corrupted the nature of *techni*. No longer the art of production in the 'right time' with the 'right measure', technology lost its magic. "The practice of magic consists in making what is not understood understandable in an incomprehensible manner", Jung disclosed in *The Red Book*

(2009, p. 314). Psyche is not bound by time, space or causality which medicalised technology has befallen to, "psyche can function as though space did not exist …. This explains the possibility of magic" (Jensen and Mullen, 1982, p. 62).

Technology's best form is when it is practically applied, as an art, not to supplant but to support the goddess. *Eileithyia* means 'she who comes to aid' or 'to relieve' women in childbirth. She comes as a pair of *Eileithyiae*, a dual figure holding the polarities of childbirth together, with the pull of the earth and the push of the womb. She facilitates and retains, furthering birth or protracting it, thus balancing the intensity of contractions with the passive–active rhythms of labour and birth. Depicted as a woman wielding a torch to symbolise the burning pains of childbirth, her arms are raised in the air, in a typical gesture of a midwife, to guide the child to light. In my musing, I imagine her long black robe symbolising the necessary 'night-time' and isolation for natural birth to occur, and the embroidered stylised flowers representing the flowering of female sexuality into motherhood and to Kore-Persephone's (*Κόρη-Περσεφόνη*) transformative powers of nature. The red colour of her cloak and headband symbolises the blood and fire of the instinctual–spiritual energies needed to bring a protected birth to safe ground. Birthing energy requires an organic form of *katabasis*, like that of the maiden Kore pulled into Hades' underworld, to rise months later as Persephone: the goddess full of grace.

Primum non nocer, the Latin translation from the original Greek *Πρώτον, μην κάνετε κακό (próton, min kánete kakó)*, meaning '*first, do no harm*', is only part of the original Hippocratic Oath binding health professionals to abstain from "all intentional wrong-doing and harm". One translation of the original (Britannica, 2023) invites the pledger to commit thus: "I will follow that system of regimen which, according to my ability and judgment, I consider for the benefit of my patients, and abstain from whatever is deleterious and mischievous." The vow aims to ensure patients' health is prioritised over the professionals' financial ambitions, their institutions' goals, and the 'system' under which they practise. "The physician must be able to tell the antecedents, know the present, and foretell the future – must mediate these things, and have two special objects in view with regard to disease, namely, to do good or to do no harm" (Britannica, 2023) is an elaboration of the pledge as found in the *Hippocratic Corpus of the Epidemics*. In view of the not infrequent necessity for medicine to 'do harm' in order to 'do good', for example with a surgeon who must cut in order to operate, might we propose a more holistic attitude: to do good as much as one possibly can whilst keeping a vigilant connection to the founding principle of 'Nature Heals'.

In this connection, we have to ask how the pregnant female body became a scientific object, and how this fact of pregnancy has been internalised by women and men as the proper subject for scientific as well as moral inquiry. A well-prepared parturient, as she surrenders to her innate spontaneous movements and a free mindset, herself discovers that no less than a male Olympian athlete participating in a public feat, she too in the sacred temple of the Goddess is involved in a physical feat with a sacred dimension. She is not, innately, as willing to become a patient undergoing an ordeal from which she has to be rescued. When that happens, and the natural process becomes a surgical obstetric procedure, her body, even if as recently as when she got married was still seen as a sacred temple, is demoted to the profane as some-thing that needs to be cleaned up and anaesthetised so it won't get in the way.

To refrain from dropping into the delirious and the mischievous, or to link one's practice to past experiences and to those at present with a clear view of future consequences, calls on the practitioner's moral integrity. Like all aphorisms, this one opens a horizon of moral injunction and a reflection on its ethos. It also reveals its limitations within the uncontained freedom of practices 'on the make'. To become a moral agent for the amoral gods of Technology is to bind oneself to a 'religious attitude' – not to a creed or to blind faith, but to an attitude that binds one's actions to the bedrock of humanity. *Ahimsa* is one of the cardinal virtues in all Indian religions, based on the knowledge that all living beings have a spark of the divine within and that to hurt another is to hurt oneself. Ethics requires consciousness of that divine essence within. Health practitioners in all disciplines must grapple with this reality of "Do unto others as you would have them do unto you" (Luke 6:31). Like walking on a tightrope between good and evil, they are called upon to view the fine line that separates yet connects what 'doing good' or 'doing harm' means and entails. These valuation categories are not *absolutes* but belong to the realm of the *relative*. They cannot and should not be assessed without being weighed in the context in which they occur. Technocratic models devoid of scientific evidence and psycho-spiritual backdrop must give way to alternative knowledge more akin to integrative medicine which includes ethics at its heart.

Progress in technology, many would argue, has made us 'one world'; but it has been achieved without the required maturity to reflect on its ramifications. We fall short in assessing what this progress entails morally, ethically, and politically. The future of pre-emptive genetic testing, extra-uterine fertilisation, intra-uterine insemination, cryopreservation, matching of egg/sperm donor and recipient, surrogacy and commissioning parenting, and artificial procreation, push pregnancy onto the cusp of further major manipulations, most of which are programmed and produced under the cover of anonymity and secrecy. But for how long?

Beyond the Assisted Reproductive Technologies (ART), a world of experiments and new equipment is remodelling the female body, pregnancy, and childbirth. As always, the cutting-edge avant-garde research carries on the one hand an increase in medical research with unprecedented solutions and cures, and, on the other, if with the wrong frame of mind and the wrong ethics, a risk of out-of-control spiralling experimentations leading to commercial exploitation, as well as a threat to the futurity of natural pregnancy and birth.

More and more pregnancies are viewed as transactional contracts, where surrogacy, for example, not used in advertence of medical issues, is contracted for 'social' reasons; to avoid the pregnant body altogether. Women in high-powered positions, too busy to waste time in pregnancy, hire wombs to carry their fertilised egg, thus outsourcing labour, and childbirth in their stride. They live with the illusion of gaining time, not realising this is how they lose it: time is engendered in timelessness and the future in the present. Pregnancy stretches time beyond its confinement, and it is by losing that we gain. The losses that spiral us down elevate us to new fulfilments.

Women these days are swept up in a sort of Taylor Swift race for fame and thus, in the sought-after flashbulb glare of modelling and showbiz, are frightened that if they lose their looks, they will lose their jobs. People did murmur that having a baby ruined Beyoncé. Women have started to avoid sacrificing a year out of their careers and a longer season of subsequent stretchmarks by turning to surrogacy even when they have the biological capacity to carry a child to term. For fear of 'disfiguring' their appearance, they contrive to disfigure their deepest nature. The rationale is that it's okay to use another woman's body to get what she needs for herself. But does she really know what she wants? This new fashion highlights only too glaringly how patriarchy reinvents itself anew at the expense of the woman's own desires, even when she imagines she is freeing herself from all that. The granddaughters of women who were once locked out of careers by patriarchy are now advancing their own agency by falling in line with patriarchal norms for the shape and look of a female body and getting paid well for it. Needless to say, this engenders a new market for hefty profit-making. "If you are open to using other people's eggs, sperm or uteruses and are prepared to pay, anything is possible" … we do this "to make people happy" is posited as the latest technological positivism (Kleeman, 2019).

But is the 'happiness' that comes from being a success so primary a goal in life that it is worth a woman's chance to experience the wisdom of her own body? The body is the casualty when 'having' a baby becomes a mode of shopping, and the child itself another acquisition. Not only has the baby become a medicalised 'foetus'; even the foetus has become a commodity. Has surrogacy become a trade because adoption, due to its notoriously difficult route, is not? Another difference is that surrogacy pays, and adoption does not. And money talks. If you have money, you'll likely decide to 'have' a baby. Its proponents believe in this type of science, in its ability to offer family balancing, gender selection, using egg donors and sperm donors. The ultimate goal is to provide what a client feels would complete their lifestyle. It's all about goal achievement, but with no process involved, for women who do not realise that it takes an authentic metamorphosis, both inner and outer, to grow oneself into becoming a mother. This brand of feminism is anti-feminist, another patriarchal twist bending feminism to serve fame and fortune, power, and prestige – the Faustian virtues.

We are led to ask, what kind of children do we expect to raise, with this number of 'parents' carrying it down the contemporary assembly line: genetic (egg-donor), carrier (antibodies donor), and at least one intended parent who purchased the right to have the child delivered? Surely, we already know how strong the drive is in us all to know our generators whose very genes are carried in us. Those who learn they have been adopted will most probably track down their biological parents. How will future children, born in surrogacy from artificial insemination, cope with the anonymity of their actual mothers or fathers? What effects will multiple biological and non-biological parents have on the identity and psychological equilibrium of the children of such mix and match genetic combinations?

Meeting some of these women in clinical practice is like visiting a grand manor without a tenant: laden with glittering luxuries yet heavy with an inner emptiness. Tragically, some of their stories disclose how by risking pregnancy they would risk their jobs. They bear the weight of strenuous careers and, instead of receiving from their employers the necessary support during pregnancy, a new money-spinning industry has been born to hire carriers for their pregnancies rather than supporting them to bear their child themselves. These women hire so as not to be fired. Unable to feel the stream of love that pours into and through them when trust is poured out, they shut their body from being the doorway to transcendence yet exploit another woman's body to do the job. Are we witnessing the start of technocratic imperialism – the appropriation of the uterus for mechanised procreation? Will women with financial insecurity succumb to the pressures of renting their bodies for nine months, go through labour and give away the child that knows every sound of their voice, every beat of their heart, every sway in their walk, has shared their food, their mood, the language they speak?

The real phantom narrative behind all this uncertainty is technology, which has an uncanny fascination nowadays. To be sure, the use of gestational carriers and surrogacy is a debatable expedient option. It is legal in the UK and in most US states. But is 'medical surrogacy', needed for health issues, morally more palatable than 'recreational surrogacy', by which I mean hiring a uterus for aesthetic reasons, or out of sheer rejection of pregnancy per se, or for simply not being willing to give up time to becoming a mother? And isn't there somewhere a valorisation of the spectator sport involved in seeing the technology now open to women, but not only, work in this way? Some women confided that commercialising the world of medicine for some spurious 'social' pressures, by extorting from another woman's body a nine-month gestation, is ditching medicine and doctors, as well as patients, for practitioners who, on the back of genuine suffering, make a killing. "What a wonder is man! He is Lord of all things living ... There is nothing beyond his power", Sophocles exclaimed, and what can he not do? "He swings to good or evil ways without thinking of the consequences". But it is *techne*, not man, that is driving our contemporary wonder.

The natural wisdom of the body, like wildlife, is nowadays rendered an endangered species. But there are pressing concerns about children born within the frame of our contemporary technology enabling new family formations with multiple parents, both biological and non-biological. While advancing new solutions for new pressures, technology is in fact subverting 'process' for the sake of achieving a fixed goal. The psychological sanity of children born to unknown biological and multiple parents has to take precedence. We cannot resign ourselves to passivity, nor can we "rebel helplessly against [technology] and curse it as the work of the devil" (Heidegger, 1977, p. 26). How can we nurture an alternative way of working with technology to benefit from its advantages but evade some of its horrific inherent dangers? The feminine made conscious is a principle that can give birth to a different thinking process to patriarchy. This calls for a reorientation of our attitude toward technology, free from projection, realigning its relation to nature, respectful of her essence and the essence of the female body.

Women birth women into the feminine principle to love and cherish their womb as sacred, to educate other women on the use and misuse of technology, and to support them in claiming their right to healthy medicine backed by database research regarding the pros and cons of technological procedures. Women's attainment of the joyful and the ecstatic experienced through as natural a birth as possible relies on a harmonious partnership between technology and the feminine physical and psychological structure. Technology is not meant to supersede the feminine way, or to replace transcendence, but to serve and support it. It must be used specifically for what it is: a tool to enhance the woman's way of birthing, rather than a replacement for or subordination of her instinctive–spiritual knowledge. It can be transformational, as an art, when used in aid of the feminine way of birthing, respecting the natural processes with minimum interference. Reconnecting technology with its roots as *techni* is to redefine it not just as a tool but also as art, less concerned with measuring, classifying, and exploiting the resources of the world than with taking part in the process of coming-to-being (Heidegger, 1977). By doing so, we enter into a free – constantly critical, constantly *questioning* – relationship with the technology that is perpetually making new incursions into our lives. The convergence of unintrusive technology as art and the body's wisdom may develop a fruitful source of further innovation in full awareness of women's needs and natural processes.

Every birth is an embodied spiritual experience, but that fact is rapidly becoming relegated to the unconscious shadow with consequences for the soul as well. In 'developed' countries where technology is obtainable, availing oneself of it has been made sacrosanct. In more traditional societies, birth remains a sacrament that has little to do with what *techne* wants to prove. Babies recognise their mother's voice from birth. They decipher among other scents the smell of their mother's milk. When a child is born, the whole universe trembles with joy at the miracle of spirit and body coming together for a new spark to incarnate and dance. The womb is the chalice of the sacred emergence of a new centre of individual choice, a voice calling for life longing for itself. Birth is the vessel for the continuous creative act of renewal. Why start life in hospital, and indeed why end it in hospital? The secret of death is in the birth, for birth and death are one. As the flower withers, the seed is planted: a promise from the sealed mystery to the sacredness of life.

References

Alfirevic, Z., Gyte, G.M.L., Cuthbert, A., and Devane, D. (2017) Continuous cardiography (CTG) as a form of electronic fetal monitoring (EFM) for fetal assessment during labour, *Cochrane Database of Systematic Reviews*, 2, https://cochrane.org/CD006066/PREG_continuous-cardiotocography-ctg-form-electronic-fetal-monitor-ing-efm-fetal-assessment-during-labour (Accessed 7th August 2023).

Amis, D. (2007) Labor begins on its own, *Journal of Perinatal Education*, 16(3), pp. 16–20.

Britannica Editors (2023) Hippocratic oath, *Encyclopedia Britannica*, www.britannica.com/topic/Hippocratic-oath (Accessed 9 August 2023).

Condon, J.C., Jevasuria, P., Faust, J.M., and Mendelson, C.R. (2004) Surfactant protein secreted by the maturing mouse fetal lung acts as a hormone that signals the initiation of parturition, *Proceedings of the National Academy of Sciences of the United States of America*, 101(14), pp. 4978–4983.

davis-floyd, r. (1994) culture and birth: the technocratic Imperative, *International Journal of Childbirth Education*, 9(2), pp. 6–7.

DiFranco, J.T. and Curl, M. (2014) Healthy birth practice #5: Avoid giving birth on your back and follow your body's urge to push, *The Journal of Perinatal Education*, 23(4), pp. 207–210.

Dreger, A. (2012) The most scientific birth is often the least technological birth, *The Atlantic*, www.theatlantic.com/health/archive/2012/03/the-most-scientific-birth-is-often-the-least-technological-birth/254420/#.T2jRnoJUeog.email (Accessed 7 August 2023).

Foucault, M. (1990) *The Use of Pleasure: Volume 2 the History of Sexuality*, New York: Random House.

Heidegger, M. (1977) *The Question Concerning Technology and Other Essays*, New York: Harper & Row.

Jensen, F. and Mullen, S. (eds) (1982) *Jung, C.G., Jung, Emma Jung and Toni Wolff: A Collection of Remembrances*, San Francisco, CA: The Analytical Psychology Club of San Francisco.

Jordan, B. and Davis-Floyd, R. (1993) *Birth in Four Cultures: A Crosscultural Investigation of Childbirth in Yucatan, Holland, Sweden, and the United States*, Long Grove, IL: Waveland Press.

Jung, C.G. (1933/2001). *Modern Man in Search of a Soul*, London: Routledge Classics.

Jung, C.G. (1958) *Psychology and Religion: West and East*, London: Routledge & Kegan Paul.

Jung, C.G. (1967) *Alchemical Studies*, Hove: Routledge & Kegan Paul.

Jung, C.G. (1971) *Psychological Types*, London: Routledge & Kegan Paul.

Jung, C.G. (2009) *The Red Book: Liber Novus*, New York: W.W. Norton.

Jung, C.G. (2015) *Letters of C. G. Jung: Volume I, 1906–1950*, London: Routledge.

Jung, C. (2019) *Visions: Notes on the Seminar Given in 1930–1934*, London: Routledge.

Kitzinger, S. and Walters, R. (1981) *Some Women's Experiences of Episiotomy*, National Childbirth Trust. Pamphlet.

Kleeman, J. (2019) Having a child doesn't fit into these women's schedule: Is this the future of surrogacy? *The Guardian*. www.theguardian.com/lifeandstyle/2019/may/25/having-a-child-doesnt-fit-womens-schedule-the-future-of-surrogacy (Accessed 9 August 2023).

Kristeva, J. (1986) Stabat Mater, in T. Moi (ed.), *The Kristeva Reader*, trans. S. Hand and L. S. Roudiez, Oxford: Blackwell, pp. 160–186.

Manfredini, M., Breschi, M., Fornasin, A., Mazzoni, S., De Lasio, S., and Coppa, A. (2020) Maternal mortality in 19th- and early 20th-century Italy, *Social History of Medicine*, 33(3), pp. 860–880.

Nietzsche, F. (1908/1979) *Ecce Homo*, London: Penguin.

Odent, M. (1984) *Birth Reborn: What Childbirth Should Be*, New York: Pantheon Books.

Priddis, H., Schmied, V., and Dahlen, H. (2014) Women's experiences following severe perineal trauma: A qualitative study, *BMC Women's Health*, 14(1), https://bmcwomenshealth.biomedcentral.com/articles/10.1186/1472-6874-14-32 (Accessed 9 August 2023).

Reynolds, Peter C. (1991). *Stealing Fire: The Atomic Bomb as Symbolic Body*, Palo Alto, CA: Iconic Anthropology Press.

Richards, H. (1993) Cultural messages of childbirth ... the perpetuation of fear, *The International Journal of Childbirth Education*, 7(3), pp. 27–29.

Rosenberg, J. (2017) The effects of chronic fear on a person's health, *American Journal of Managed Care*, www.ajmc.com/view/the-effects-of-chronic-fear-on-a-persons-health (Accessed 7 August 2023).

Schmid, V. (2005) About physiology in pregnancy and childbirth, *Nascita e Vita Consapevole*, https://verenaschmid.eu/en/ecologia-della-vita-ecologia-della-nascita-english/ (Accessed 9 August 2023).

Thomson, H. (2015) For an easier birth, stop thinking about it, *New Scientist*, www.newscientist.com/article/dn27773-for-an-easier-birth-stop-thinking-about-it/ (Accessed 9 August 2023).

Tinker A. (1997) Safe motherhood as a social and economic investment. Presentation at Safe Motherhood Technical Consultation, *Inter-Agency Group for Safe Motherhood*, October 18–23, Colombo, Sri Lanka, https://files.givewell.org/files/DWDA%202009/Interventions/Maternal%20Mortality/SafeMotherhoodActionAgenda.pdf (Accessed 9 August 2023).

Tinker A. (2000) Women's health: The unfinished agenda. *International Journal of Gynaecology and Obstetrics*, 70(1), pp. 149–158.

Wickham, S. (2020) Top ten technologies that have improved the lives of women and midwives, www.sarawickham.com/articles-2/top-ten-technologies-that-have-improved-the-lives-of-women-and-midwives (Accessed 7 August 2023).

Woodman, M. (1985) *The Pregnant Virgin: A Process of Psychological Transformation*. Toronto: Inner City Books.

Woodman, M. (1987) Worshipping illusions: An interview with Marion Woodman, *Parabola*, https://parabola.org/2019/04/13/worshipping-illusions-an-interview-with-marion-woodman/ (Accessed 9 August 2023).

World Health Organization. (1999) *Reduction of Maternal Mortality: A Joint WHO/UNFPA/UNICEF/World Bank Statement*, World Health Organization, https://apps.who.int/iris/bitstream/handle/10665/42191/9241561955_eng.pdf?sequence=1&isAllowed=y (Accessed 9 August 2023).

Young, I.M. (1984) Pregnant embodiment: Subjectivity and alienation, *The Journal of Medicine and Philosophy: A Forum for Bioethics and Philosophy of Medicine*, 9(1), pp. 45–62.

3

Speculative Reproduction

The Technology of 'Giving Birth'

Leslie Gardner

Do the technological means of reproduction of offspring impact on who and what such creatures 'are'? And how do we recognise them; using what criteria? Are capacities like exercising agency or 'having' a psychological interior what make up a being that we call 'people'? (What *is* an 'individual' in that context when a group are all the 'same'?) Or, for that matter, aren't those very capacities also criteria for assessing what make up 'natural', biologically produced offspring? How do we distinguish?

Scare quotes are required in this context when referring to people and individuals, offspring, even bodies, but I won't overdo it in the chapter: but imagine they're there when I don't.

As it becomes possible to produce such 'objects'/material presences, again, in their specific robotic or cloned or mechanical ways, using means available in contemporary times, I want to ask questions in this short piece, about what has been a common trope/theme of imaginative and scientific consideration throughout all 'human' time. Aren't we simply repeating those traditionally unresolved questions? The automata of ancient China were as parlous, or dangerous, as feared by Westerners first seeing them as AI components of contemporary clones/robots seem to us now.

For many years I have been reading speculative novels, stories, and myths, all of which suggested the themes of this chapter. They combine the problematics of those psychological interiors which I explored in a monograph on Vico (a problematic because there is no seventeenth century language to describe that interior (see Gardner, 2013)) with the semiotic conflicts of significance that contrast metaphor and materiality. And this is all to do with genesis by technological means: the dilemma of biological/technological but motherless offspring (there are often solely males involved in these modes of reproduction, so I put it 'motherless' rather than 'parentless'.)

It is common to think that 'natural' humans have psychological interiors – an 'unconscious' for example – where memories of affective events, dreams and important people are held. However, robots, automata, and mechanical humans do not have an interior. Clones may do so, but in novels they too are the products of technology and so the question of their 'naturalness' is common, and the question of 'interiority' is an open one. These features of an interior complicate semiotic reference to a self. Are robots dissociated, manufactured entities in their

DOI: 10.4324/9781003255727-5

own right, or semblances, imitating 'natural' humans? This gets even more complex when we think about clones.

These are, of course, perpetually ongoing themes/tropes from ancient times in Asia, Greece, Africa, so this chapter is but a dip in the sea to try to find a depth psychology angle congenial to my research. I am simply here asking questions.

In the past, I have suggested that writing and engaging with speculative fiction is a form of 'acting out': a resistance to earth-bound difficulties of reality. This chapter follows on from that point. Perhaps I am 'acting out' in my pursuit. The springboard for these queries is definitely not only Jung's essays on Flying Saucers (collected in Jung and Hull, 1978) but his *faux* scholarship claims and defence in *Mysterium Coniunctionis* (Jung, 1963).

Encountering the theme of reproduction, it has always seemed to me that, in many ways, biological reproduction involving female bodies has been presented as just as alien as mechanical ways of reproduction, even in the earliest (at least those reported earliest), mythic ways in ancient reports and tales, both East and West, North and South.

For example, in the East, ancient Chinese stories from the third century BCE, during the Han dynasty, reported there was a mechanical orchestra built for the emperor's amusement. Moving as humans, these 'musicians' acted with seeming agency. Weren't they similar to those creatures sprung from male gods' thighs in Greek stories? In fact, having no biological precedents at all! When first observed by travellers, these automata were deemed God-less and unnatural, alien, and powerful.

As Truitt (2015) set out, these technological marvels were transported west and, rather later, in Ancient Greek mythology, marvellous stories were recounted. Zeus ate Metis (whose name means 'cunning intelligence'), so that the daughter she was carrying, Athena, was born fully grown from the head of her father, thus being as free from female influence as possible. The god Hephaistos, himself the child of all-female conception, was the only 'midwife' at this male reproductive event, by opening Zeus' head with his axe. Athena later rejected marriage for herself, remaining a virgin forever, and was represented in male armour. The nearest Athena came to motherhood was when Hephaistos tried to rape her. Because he was lame, he was unable to catch her, but instead ejaculated on her leg. Athena wiped off his semen, which fell on Mother Earth who, in due course, produced a son, Erichthonios, thought to be the first king of Athens. Another god, Dionysus, also sprang from Zeus, in his case, from the god's thigh. In ancient Syrian/Roman Lucian's 'Trip to the Moon' he included a planet, where giving birth only involved male thighs (see Lucian, 1913/1961).

These are not the only examples from legendary times. Amazonian warriors – all female – eschewed male parental influence entirely and were perceived as monsters. They made political arrangements to copulate with nearby male communities, we are told, but female communities were deemed unnatural and alien from the beginning of time, so I won't go in that direction here.

There were also ongoing marvels in Europe, during medieval times, imported from foreign lands into Western Christian spaces. They were numerous and they took on exotic magical attributes, different from the mechanical 'rational' orientation of Descartes, who, later on, was said to travel with an automaton who was his daughter. More about his transgressions below.

There were several streams of thought about all this: one, that enhanced nature, created by God, made these valuable and 'natural' creatures despite their alien nature. Or else mechanical imitation took on inhuman rational technique, outside God – so the automata or imitations of humans (robots?) could work with technical superiority. They were deemed to have agency and were not offensive to God-fearing people. In France for example, the wondrous mechanical/independently moving creations of the famous Italians, the Francini brothers, created moving humans as part of a seventeenth century hydraulic display for a French king copied from an ancient spinning palace in Constantinople which included an orchestra, roaring lions, and squawking birds. In the fifteenth century, Leonardo da Vinci invented, at least on paper, a mechanical knight, but it has been built from his notes since and is perfectly viable.

Jumping forward many years, experiments with biological/technical cloning took place last century, producing Dolly the sheep, who was cloned from cells of another sheep by chemical and biological techniques (see Wilmut, 2010). Cyborgs and clones have much in common, with artificially created robots; close to 'natural' humans – and at least one who looked most effectively after children – more on this later. But these automata and robots, clones and so on are problematic. Can they acquire agency and identities as science fiction novelist Philip K. Dick often speculated (see 1968/2010, later made into the film *Blade Runner* (Ridley Scott, 1982)), and as proponents of AI are concerned could happen in the present day, with the possibility of moving from Generative AI to General AI? These are of course common themes in science fiction: no female forebears here either (or parents). Dolly sprang from the adult cells of another sheep, by no traditional birth process as we know it.

Looking to the (female) mother who Freud proposes is basic to the psychology of a human being's interior becomes a questionable parameter: 'if it's not one thing, it's your mother'. But where can a psychological angle get play if there are no biological forebears – and, specifically, no female parent? And, so, therefore, where does a viable, sentient being emerge? Philip K. Dick proposed in that implanting memories from other humans into the automata he called 'replicants' – meant that deep emotional levels, common to what it is proposed makes us human, could be replicated (1968/2010). However, the replicant in his story learns of this manipulation, and it causes her breakdown. This is a familiar trope in science fiction as I will explore below in Joanna Russ's novel (*The Female Man*, 1995), Raya Jones's *The Cyboratics Sequence* (beginning with *Fairweather*, 2017a), and the television series *Orphan Black* (Space/BBC America, 2013–17).

Psychological interior

Reproduction of offspring without female parent, achieved by chemical and technological means, circumvents the usual biological processes of insemination, development in a mother's womb, and passage through a birth canal, but produces a replicated being, deemed to be the next generation. Yet the psychological impact of the process in all these ways of reproduction seems to be similar not only for the offspring but for the progenitor.

What might memories mean to people since they seem to make up an identity and are the repository of evidence of psychological impact shifts in time and space? This includes where and when it is remembered – on a therapist's couch; as you attend a funeral or a familial ceremony; or in a totally 'irrelevant' place when something triggers that memory – the algorithm collides with another technical instruction in an automaton's make up.

Joanna Russ, literary commentator, radical feminist, and novelist tackled the issue of cloning and 'what is a human' in her novel, *The Female Man* (1995). Her females over the generations were similar to each other (even their names are very close). However, I want first to contrast her themes with those of Raya Jones, Jungian sociologist and novelist, whose trilogy (*Fairweather* (2017a), *Rinzler* (2017b), *Blossom* (2018), and recently a fourth was added) brings AI figures and their proclivities into the narrative stream of a detective seeking out the factotums of a destructive conspiracy. Jones's AI devices are individually and as a group, called 'Alice' and they are all about service – but to whom? They offer you coffee, take your garment, guide you to a shop, inform you of your rights, etc. But, in Jones' story, these services are intended to *contain* the populace they interact with rather than to service them – the Alices serve a more powerful corporate group. A rogue AI 'device' has been transported and seemingly destroyed (murdered?) in front of our detective, Rinzler, early on and he knows it wasn't him despite what the corporation he's targeting thinks. Had the Alice figured something out? When he meets that particular robot (not easy when they are all pleasantly alike; but he finds her), he sees she's suffering an identity quandary that her affectively enhanced intelligence has forced her to confront. But is it a glitch or a deliberately implanted deviation by a massive corporation Rinzler seems to be tracking, without knowing how he got there? There are lessons to be learned, Jones suggests, about knowing your individual past.

Russ definitely felt that science fiction has pedagogic purpose, and her characters are deliberately kinds of collective characterisations, but the more I pondered what they were, the more I was struck by how similar her considerations were to what Christopher Gill describes in his work on Ancient Greek personalities. Gill suggests that an interior is not what *we* think it was for the ancient Greeks; we project our own late eighteenth, nineteenth, twentieth/twenty-first century subjective idea of an interior. He describes the approximation to an interior as objective, ethical coordinates of a culture in his *Personality in Greek Epic, Tragedy, and Philosophy: the Self in Dialogue* (1996). He asks us to think on early Greek assessment of Medea for an example (see p.154ff). For Greeks, eschewing empathetic forms of personality, Medea did not behave in an abhorrent way in killing her children: she was responding with integrity in murdering Jason's children as a fitting response to the perfidy of his faithless treatment of her. A later, individualistic, subjective and/or Freudian enquiry might look into her OTT reaction and lack of maternal love for her children as a personality flaw, because shouldn't real, human mothers battle to keep their children alive? However, Gill would call that assessment a modern-day 'romantic' subjective interpretation of character, out of sync with what the Medea myth was pointing at about personality.

Perhaps here we can briefly enquire if Jung's ideas of a collective imaginary is in contrast to Individuation (as has often been pointed out) and therefore may come closer to the 'objective, ethical character' rather than the 'subjective' character that Gill points at. 'Individual' in the collective imaginary is a kind of primal archetype, and its impulses are preconscious and universal (see Jung, 1968) – having more in common with early classical forms of what a human individual is, as outlined in Gill's discussion. Agency conforms to social norms, and that is the individual's ethic, so an automaton or clone can have viable agency within this worldview – an individual, no-mother-influenced interior contemplated!

In Russ's *The Female Man*, the women who are deemed to be clones of each other respond to misogyny in their lives very differently. They recognise it in different ways, of course. One returns from the future to incite earlier generations of herself to begin murdering males to get the revolution in gear sooner. She lives in a world without males. One is accommodating, and despite learning analyses different to hers, and about future behaviours, reverts to being 'female' as housekeeper in the 1950s. She disparages the murderous recommendations. The other goes along with the plan having discovered that perhaps her affection for the revolutionary's daughter is more than simple friendship, so relationships have other valuable outlets. We don't know if it goes deeper. They all comfortably join in the future without males, although two are happier about it than the other.

Unlike Russ's characters' personal activities, in Jones's novels, characters are instead fixtures of a narrative trajectory, based on ideas of multiple personalities which humans deploy strategically (whether knowingly or unconsciously). It is a teleological view of what being a human is about. Again this fits into cultural tropes of behaviour, grasping for an agency the AI creatures barely know or can hope to attain.

In Russ's novel, the subjective experience as an individual for each of the women in their own generation, i.e. the endeavour toward 'becoming yourself' is set off against ethical considerations of the social perfidy of misogyny – our futurist Joan seems a patriot of femalehood despite her mass murder suggestions. As Gill suggests about Medea: isn't she really a heroine? Russ's novel becomes discursive on this topic in its final sections. The most obvious and first problematic about replication – by whatever means – is that 'being a human individual' seems to be a matter of interpretation. Algorithms set into robot/replicant/automaton actions and 'thoughts' are founded in present times, with present ideas of what being a human is.

More about Descartes

The rational argument for the technical vs. 'real-biological' definition of human was parsed out by Descartes in his discussion mind–body.

My first comment is that the automaton accompanying Descartes (called his daughter), is stereotypical female, subservient, and without criticism of his deviant behaviour (shipmates thought he was in an erotic relationship with a young girl, automaton or not, and threw the machine into the sea – or so the rumour goes). A perfect example of admired female behaviour of the time, she sits quietly, observing, and being badly treated by an exploitative male which is also recognised behaviour! But Descartes, unlike those fabled shipmates, knew the difference between real and automaton. Here are his comments in *Discours*:

> if any such machines resembled us in body and imitated our actions ... we should still have two very certain means of recognising that they were not, for all that, real human beings. The first is that they would never be able to use words or other signs by composing them as we do to declare our thoughts to others ... For, whereas reason is a universal instrument which can operate in all sorts of situations, their organs have to have a particular disposition for each particular action, from which it follows that it is practically impossible for there to be enough different organs in a machine to cause it to act in all of life's occurrences in the same way it reason causes us to act [sic].
>
> (Descartes, 1637/2006, pp. 46–47)

As mentioned, Descartes, unlike his shipmates with their unworldly, weird assessment of his relationship to the automaton he was transporting, knew the difference. In fact Kang (Kang, 2017) doubts the accuracy of the story, saying it is made up, attributing it to unease about Descartes's claims of godless viability of certain creations. Of course, he would say, without their propensity for such action given them by God, they could not do the technological seeming miracles they do – so God is the still the prime mover, but his critics ignored that, and only saw his rational underpinnings as based solely in human ken.

Metaphor vs. materiality

This leads me to my other theme of metaphor vs. materiality related to semiotic considerations: no matter how it came into being, the new 'creature' also has a materiality that is its own presence in a cultural and psychological world different to its begetter's (possibly contrary) claims. Automatons, or cloned entities have either been through a process of a real-life biology, or are the result of a technical/creative process – are all those processes a lower-status metaphor for birth? (Isn't this the dilemma of trans people's troubles with biological 'norms'?) Are automatons, cloned beings, or physiologically transformed human bodies independent beings with agency? In fact, are they a form of synecdoche or a metaphor, or separate, literal independent presences? Re-examining Nietzsche's essay 'On Truth and Lie in a Nonmoral Sense' (which I refer to below as well): he asks "What is a word? It is a copy in sound of a nerve stimulus in sounds" (Nietzsche, 2010, p. 24).

What is that relationship between its talk and its meaning in our context? An automaton talks, imitating that sound as if from a stimulated nerve – is it a metaphor of its significance? Is the act a theatrical representation mimicking 'natural' talk? Is the dissociation part and parcel of its significance? What is the nature of that dissociation?

And here, I'd like to mention theorist and psychoanalyst Pierre Bayard's (2007) rhetorical notion of materiality (which I am trying to get at here): he focuses especially on The Book. I am here too focused on books, after all, an object with papers of verbiage – printed content. Even a metaphor, Bayard points out, has material presence which also figures in its existential presence, as for any object, therefore it is its own creature. Nietzsche too parses the verbal/written representation of even a material truth as irrefutably interpretative.

But, to continue with Bayard, he asks, in what respect is the physical book a metaphor for its content? As an object, it passes through different hands, has different status as an object anyway in a culture. In many places, burning books represents an ideological stance whatever the content. A book may be in the form of a scroll which object's aesthetic attributes impact on the verbal content, and what about hieroglyphics or tonal sequences as content? In parallel discussion, the physical presence of a penis does not make a trans woman still really a 'male' either – shifting cultural meanings – metaphors – impact on physical presence. Perhaps, rather, Bayard wonders: isn't a book itself a synecdoche? Its physical pages signifying a composition of words/thought. The 'package' of a human body has significance in multiple ways.

And the same it must be for automata, clones, robots ...? Which is first: significance or material presence? Descartes (referring to his female automaton) or Philip K. Dick (referring to his replicants in *Do Androids Dream of Electric Sleep* (2010a), Joanna Russ, whose clones are in *The Female Man* (1977), all encounter similar issues. Indeed, digital manifestation has its own kind of material presence.

Material type and significance are wholly intertwined is my argument too. Beings are non-logos, i.e. non-rule-bound or conceptually bound material mix, and that must make a real, material difference. Algorithms strictly guide AI, or robots or clones (more on their complexities later) and purport to be wholly logos ruled, but is that always fact? In Jones's novels her female AI robots act as narrative and world-defining presences, where rules of agency are broken.

Russ's discrete generations of females act as commentators and thereby creators of their worlds, which also constrain them into certain types of beings. The materiality of a book with its necessary modes of dissemination by specific technical means partakes in a cultural sense and this always means feminisms (as well as racism, for example) is in the mix, at least for me in reading these speculative works which I see as a form of 'acting out' by the writers involved. Different contexts, different decisions kick in – in behaviour, ways of speaking, postures – all things those designated as 'female' knowing in navigating life. How and where to read a book: as eBook, online, audio – to do with lifestyles, to put it simplistically.

Judith Butler sets out the dilemma which underscores my argument about reproduction: the body is considered always 'a priori', a 'given' because it is material.

It is there before us, but how can it be there before we represent it? Is it possible ever to extract the representation of the body from the materiality constituting its very mode of signification? And the mode of its origination ... does that not impact on its presence? Is its significance there before the physical body is? Her comment here easily applies to automata of all types. "The classical association of femininity with materiality can be traced to a set of etymologies" she points out,

> which link matter with *mater* and *matrix* (or the womb) and hence with a problematic of reproduction ...When not explicitly associated with reproduction, matter is generalized as a principle of origination and causality ... This link between matter, origin and significance suggests indissolubility of [ancient] notions of materiality and signification. That which matters about an object is its matter
>
> (Butler, 1993, p. 31)

Science fiction and its tangles

Raya Jones develops her fictions as they subscribe to her narrative and theoretical conclusions. She points out that science fiction might explore what may imaginatively be the outcome of robotic (and I am broadening this to include any artificially created beings or parts) participation in the world but it is not useful nor is it the intention of the writer/author to explore that impact since it is speculative. There is no empirical evidence of how its interior operates. Her attention/intention is on other issues. But the problematic is there in the interpretation of what motherhood or social relations are represented to be in the fiction, for example, to get at what the impact of the artificially created being has on relations, or birth/reproduction etc.

Jones cites robotics expert and novelist, Carme Torres's discussion that "some science fiction writers set out to explore social and ethical issues that might arise as a consequence of technological advances" ... but Jones counters that

> If we want to sharpen our present day vision of future robots through yesteryears' science fiction, we ought to examine – not the stories' representations of the robot – but their representations of motherhood, the nuclear family, and what their authors assumed a robot might replace.
>
> (Jones, 2015, p. 123)

This point is part of a commentary on the efficacy of robots being used as nannies for children of busy parents. She points to Ray Bradbury's admonishing story of a robot-child carer who disparages the parent's practices (see Bradbury, 1951/1972), but mainly focuses on Philip K. Dick's story, "Nanny" about the difficulties of a disconnect between child, parent, and carer-robot (see Dick, 2010b).

When one of the Alice clones (Jones, 2017b) works out with inexorable logic that her task is contradictory, 'she' is locked into upsetting her identity as a clone designed to fulfil the corporate aim: agency is born to her surprise and to the detective Rinzler's surprise – he could not predict who is upsetting the world: a clone simply does not act in this way. Articulation in all the ways of expression in aesthetic forms, again, as Nietzsche in his essay "On Truth and Lie in a Non-moral Sense" points out, is essentially and inescapably autobiographical, i.e. subjectively tainted. We display our inner worlds, and our assumptions/perceptions of outer worlds in how we articulate in words, gestures, visual signs and sounds (grunts). Does this same apply to an artificially created being? Is the engendered being a self that is embodied/encased in a repeated form? And doesn't contemplation of the self indicate whether a reproduction is similar?

Within this mix, we focus on talk not only about technical ways of reproduction as represented in fictional representations, but how they are recounted. Naturally there are the ancillary problematics involved: what is 'reproduction'? Is 'imitation' really what 'cloning' is, and is it the same as reproduction? Is it possible to have alternate views of sequence? What comes first, the person who is the engenderer of the offspring or that offspring? But to interpret what that something is, you need to have it first ... somehow?

Repeated scenarios of dialogue or flashback, or fragmented narration of ideas or events may alter the relationship of how a scenario is recounted – and change its significance. So a cloned being is nevertheless a different creature from its begetter. Joanna Russ's cloned females, over decades, live in different worlds that mean they too are 'forced' into agency: they act out as their authors do to cultural contexts of their times.

In her book *Personhood and Social Robotics* (2015) Raya Jones first of all posits that ways of considering AI, for example, as 'newly' created selves, as a biological human baby may be considered to be, throws up new questions in how to assess and refer to such beings in the first place. She complains that narrative scholars did not use criteria that properly contemplated the robots of science fiction: they contemplated their presence but not outside what the world would look like that was appropriate to the timeline. But my concern is not about what is more 'valid' a way of reproduction, but what are the feminist implications in each strategy for the writer and in the material world. They are similar, but origination and technique of effectuating another generation are different.

In Jones's novel, a scheming entrepreneur deploys a set of AI devices called 'Alice' to deflect Rinzler, her detective, hired by a mysterious eccentric with a planet-wide and legendary reputation (in fact we are not sure whether he's a 'real' or virtual presence himself), to thwart the take-over of a crucial part of what makes up the planet's well-being. The algorithms of the Alices, in all their appearances – are set to tracking Rinzler wherever he is, and she springs up constantly, a foxy, cheeky presence with a personality that engages him. They all appear the same. So cleverly has she been reproduced that it takes him a while to suss out she is an AI and one with the same talents, and her ubiquity has to do with what are multiple versions. Finally meeting her creator in his lair, Rinzler figures out the marketing intent, and figures out a way to have the Alices turn on their creator, until one rogue and malevolent Alice appears in his own abode.

In Joanna Russ's novel, the cloned Joannas (obviously the author's name, and in fact, the narrator's voice enters the pages as the novel evolves) are called Joanna,

Jeannine, and Janet, and live in different geographical spaces and eras. When the newest generation clone, called Janet who is living in a world of only a single sex, with no history of the great Depression, no World War 2 (given the lack of masculine imperatives of history!), with her different ways of composing what the world is, when she sees an earlier clone of herself suffering in an oppressive lifestyle, having to take on male attitudes and power plays, she tries to jolt her into a new world. And the third reproduction, Janet, feels the tremor too, but she's not convinced male supremacy is an issue – she can live with it – but are the personalities reacting each to their own worlds as if they are reproductions of one *a priori* biological pre-set?

Appearing together in the same space, and in one time frame, thanks to Jeannine's brilliant technological bravura, is she able to effectuate a rebellion from her cloned other selves? The resolution is in doubt as they try the impossible task of speaking to each other – different worlds, different languages, different referents and inner worlds – and, indeed, in what way are they all a 'she' – a concept Jeannine has a hard time accommodating (there is no essential 'feminine for her) – why not 'it' being conditioned, since they are particularly in some senses, manufactured presences. How is reproduction considered in these cases?

Apart from those science fiction and mythic examples of motherless offspring already mentioned, there is one other contemporary cultural presence that I must include, if only to raise its issues briefly: the television series *Orphan Black*. At the start of the narrative, Sarah (Tatiana Maslany) is a product of negligence and foster care and discovers that a woman whose identity she steals is actually her clone, and the series springs off from there. Over multiple episodes in four series, it depicts the dilemmas and stories of human clones trying to survive. In fact, their creator, scientists in a corporation called Dyad, had inserted 'superior' synthetic genes into some of the clones, which have become lethal among the stream of clones in Project Leda. Technology on top of technology is in play. Is a new age of humans envisioned? Other projects include military-enhanced clones who can sleep longer, for example, or it is simply that they are expendable when 'real' or 'natural' human soldiers expire or are in short supply, or the engagement is suicidal. Cloned human organs can be used to substitute in 'natural' humans when an organ fails: kind of living organ donors.

Many of these ideas have appeared in speculative fiction before of course – thrillers too (such as Ira Levin's thriller novel, *The Boys from Brazil*, adapted into a Hollywood film starring Laurence Olivier and Gregory Peck (Franklin J. Schaffner, 1978)), while the *Star Wars* and *Star Trek* franchises are full of such ideas about how 'natural' humans are supported or suborned by clones. What happens in *Orphan Black* is that the clones begin to object, claiming agency and viability – in this case they object to being experiments in genomic manipulation. They insist they needed to know, and to be given right of consent before their genomic structure can be 'tinkered' with. One of the Leda project clones, Cosima, stunningly complains: 'Look at me, I'm sick. I never gave permission for any of this' (*Human Raw Material*, Season 4, Episode 5).

The clones of certain projects in *Orphan Black* share traits, and yet they are differentiated according to how they adapt to their specific lives. Cosima, mentioned above, uses her extra intelligence to work in academia, while Sarah, in the same project, who kicks off the series when she discovers her 'status', invents ingenious cons. The series goes on to consider a variety of outcomes: in one episode (*Endless Forms Most Beautiful*, 1.10) an egg split in its development and creates twins, who are, unlike any of the other clones in Project Leda, fertile in the way 'natural' humans are! This leads to their efforts to find out what kind of family they can create between them, and despite their competitiveness before they find out (they do not look alike), they have to agree not to overcome the other so that a future family can form. The characters' survival strategies open up all the issues of technologically created cloning that are set out from ancient Asian, Greek, European, and in science fiction stories across time.

Conclusions

Causality is linked to Logos – that is, rational analysis – and we know that is tarnished by a concept called 'masculine'. Both Jones and Russ are proposing that emanations of emergent cultural response and personality input – what we are born with – indicates acausal jumps and appearances, attempts to affix signification according to precepts worked up outside materiality, and it seems it is a power game of manipulation. Better to admit acausality or irrationality, but it is the point that whether and how a new being is generated (its reproduction) figures into political power moves and intentions.

Both use the core problematic at the centre of Jungian psychology to excavate stories. While each character has specific personality, they also are drawn to a collective meme. Jones's Alices and Russ's Joanna characters have qualities that reside in the society they live in. They find their own core being in exploration of the collective beings they also are. Individuation occurs within the collective imaginary of character agency. Despite peeking through what De Bois called the 'veil' triggered by "double consciousness" (2007, p. 8) in his work *The Souls of Black Folk*, originally published in 1903, both fix on the collective image of female in her day.

In conclusion, there are many avenues on which to track issues raised by reproduction outside the female body. For ongoing research.

References

Bayard, P. (2007) *How to Talk about Books You Haven't Read*, New York: Bloomsbury.
Bradbury, R. (1951/1972) The Veldt, in *The Illustrated Man*, New York: Doubleday, pp. 7–18.
Butler, J. (1993) *Bodies That Matter: On the Discursive Limits of Sex*, New York: Routledge.
De Bois, W. (1903/2007) *The Souls of Black Folk*, Oxford: Oxford University Press.
Descartes, R. (1637/2006) *A Discourse on the Method of Correctly Conducting One's Reason and Seeking Truth in the Sciences*, Oxford: Oxford University Press, pp. 46–47.
Dick, P.K. (2010a) (1968/2010) *Do Androids Dream of Electric Sheep*, London: Gollancz.

Dick, P.K. (2010b) Nanny, in *The Complete Short Stories of Philip K. Dick, Volume 1*, Burton, MI: Subterranean Press, pp. 455–471.
Gardner, L. (2013) *Rhetorical Investigations: GB Vico and CG Jung*, London: Routledge.
Gill, C. (1996) *Personality in Greek Epic, Tragedy and Philosophy: Self in Dialogue*, Oxford: Clarendon Press.
Jones, R. (2015) *Personhood and Social Robotics: A Psychological Consideration*, London: Routledge.
Jones, R. (2017a) *Fairweather*, London: Lume Books.
Jones, R. (2017b) *Rinzler*, privately published.
Jones, R. (2018) *Blossom*, privately published.
Jung, C.G. (1963) *Mysterium Coniunctionis: An Inquiry into the Separation and Synthesis of Psychic Opposites in Alchemy*, Hove: Routledge & Kegan Paul.
Jung, C.G. (1968) *The Archetypes and the Collective Unconscious*, Hove: Routledge & Kegan Paul.
Jung, C.G., & Hull, R.F.C. (1978) *Flying Saucers: A Modern Myth of Things Seen in the Sky. (From Vols. 10 and 18, Collected Works)*, Princeton, NJ: Princeton University Press.
Kang, M. (2017) The mechanical daughter of René Descartes: The origin and history of an intellectual fable, *Modern Intellectual History*, 14(3), pp. 633–660.
Levin, I. (1976) *Boys from Brazil*, New York: Random House, New York.
Lucian (1913/1961) Verae historiae, in *Lucian, Volume 1*, trans. A.M. Harmon, Cambridge, MA: Harvard University Press, pp. 247–358.
Nietzsche, F. (2010) On truth and lie in a non-moral sense, in *On Truth and Untruth: Selected Writings*, New York: HarperPerennial, pp. 15–50.
Russ, J. (1995) SF technology as mystification, in *To Write Like a Woman: Essays in Feminism and Science Fiction*, Bloomington, IN: Indiana University Press, pp. 26–40.
Russ, J. (1977) *The Female Man*, Boston, MA: Gregg Press.
Truitt, E. (2015) *Medieval Robots: Mechanism, Magic, Nature and Art*, Philadelphia, PA: University of Pennsylvania Press.
Wilmut, I. (2010) Dollymania: The creation of a celebrity sheep, *The New Scientist*, www.newscientist.com/article/mg20727722-500-dollymania-the-creation-of-a-celebrity-sheep/ (Accessed 7 August 2023).

Part Two

Cultural Product and Female Aspects

Evolution and Enigma

On the Origins of Obstetric Violence

Emmy Vye

It is the middle of the night. Seven other women lie in the dark, veiled from me by curtains, sleeping or trying to sleep. Every so often I hear them groan or sigh. I can make out the tiny heartbeats fluttering over the hum of machinery. Then the wave comes again, blotting out everything. I am trying to remain upright, to keep my baby descending, to resist lying back and being a patient, to hold on to some sense of agency. The IV tugs on my skin as I clench the bar at the back of the bed, trying to keep quiet, trying not to wake the other women. For six hours, since the beginning of the induction process, I have been contracting hard, confined to a bed in this hot, silent ward. It has now been twenty-four hours since my waters broke and *prelabour rupture of membranes* was stamped on my body, since the birth I had planned and hoped for began to slide away from me.

When the midwife eventually returns to tell me that she has managed to get me into the birth centre upstairs, against usual protocol for an induction, her voice comes to me from far away. Where was I? On the way to somewhere dark and awful, closing in on myself and free-falling into hopelessness – my body nothing but a blank pain, scorched and contorted. I am brought round, revived by her words. I am detached from the monitoring machine, and I stagger to my feet and stumble through the bright corridors to the lift with my partner gathering our bags and following behind me. The ascent from the dark, cramped induction ward to the birth centre feels nothing less than miraculous, a passage from hell into the white light of heaven. I pass a tall window. The sun is rising, and it is a beautiful morning. As I walk into the birthing room and see the steam rising from the birth pool, I can't stop crying. The ordeal is over. I tear off my clothes and fall into the water's embrace. Now I know I can birth my baby.

"Technology is supreme, and you are utterly dependent on it"

I was three months pregnant when I wrote the paper which would become this chapter for the Feminisms and Technology conference. We were almost a year into the Covid-19 pandemic, and the draconian emergency measures taken by maternity services nine months ago were showing no sign of being repealed. The anxiety this produced overlaid the more usual fears associated with pregnancy and impending motherhood. In the UK home births were no longer allowed, and standalone midwife-led birthing centres were closed. There were reports of higher rates of induction to allow for the scheduling of births according to the convenience of hospitals. Birth partners and doulas had been banned from attending births in many areas; in my maternity unit a birth partner would now be allowed to attend the birth but would be sent home straight after, with minimal visiting hours on the postnatal ward. With the exception of the first ultrasound scan, all maternity appointments must be attended alone, leaving many women to receive joyful or distressing or devastating news without support. Increasing numbers of women were turning to freebirthing, birthing without medical assistance, to avoid being forced into hospital care. As Sadler, Leiva and Olza write in their study of women's birthing experiences during the pandemic,

> Some of the restrictions and interventions being implemented in childbirth due to the COVID-19 outbreak are not necessary, not based on scientific evidence, are disrespecting human dignity and are not proportionate to achieve the objective of limiting the spread of the virus. They therefore constitute obstetric violence.
>
> (2020, p. 46)

Meanwhile, the updated UK NICE guidelines on induction released in May 2021 recommended that induction of labour should be offered at 39 weeks to all Black, Asian, mixed race and ethnic minority women, women with a BMI over 35, women who had used assisted conception, and women aged 35 and over. The guidelines also removed the line from a previous version of the guidelines that care providers should "give women with uncomplicated pregnancies every opportunity to go into spontaneous labour", suggesting that all women should be recommended induction at 41 weeks' gestation. The evidence base for the change in recommendations has been heavily critiqued (see, for example, the Royal College of Midwives' response, Brigante and Harlev-Lam, 2021). Given that medical induction of labour is more painful, increases the likelihood of instrumental births and caesareans, precludes the possibility of home births and midwife-led care, and contributes to escalating technological and medical intervention in the process of birth, the consequences of the changes for women's experiences of birth are severe. In November 2021 the changes were partially reversed following months of critique and activism, but they indicate nonetheless the general direction of travel in maternity care.

Now as I rework my paper into this chapter, my six-month-old daughter sleeps peacefully beside me. Like many women I survived birth physically, but my experiences of maternity care remain scarred into my body and my heart. When my waters broke and I was informed I had eighteen hours to begin contracting, I was frightened and coerced into an unwanted induction; despite all my reading and planning, I did not know how to say no.

My birthing experience ended well, but my lack of agency during pregnancy appointments and in the induction process confirmed for me that maternity care as it stands today is medicalised and technologised based on a phallocentric conception of birth, that obstetric violence is endemic and that birth trauma is not understood or taken seriously in the obstetric system. Obstetric violence includes physical, sexual and psychological interventions and/or assaults by health professionals and maternity care providers, undertaken through the use of threats and fearmongering, coercion, lack of informed consent, appropriation of women's bodies and the erosion of their autonomy. It denies women the right to make informed and considered choices about their own and their babies' health and well-being through disrespect, manipulation and violation, potentially harming women's sense of self and their physical and psychic integrity.

Anthropologist Robbie Davis-Floyd (1992) conceptualises obstetric violence in relation to the Enlightenment paradigm of body-as-machine and the patriarchal construction of female bodies as defective and in need of management. She outlines eight conceptual and procedural dilemmas presented by birth for the technocratic society:

1. that the natural process of birth refutes the technocratic model's conceptual model of reality;
2. that birth cannot be controlled or predicted by technological means;
3. that birth is a uniquely subjective experience that must somehow be turned into a cultural rite of passage in order to serve the technocratic society;
4. that birth entails a transitional period of liminality, threatening the culture's system of categorisation;
5. that birth reveals babies to be natural (as opposed to encultured) beings;
6. that birth is a female phenomenon which reveals male dependence upon women;
7. that birth is inherently sexual and personal and thus undermines the impersonality and asexuality of institutions and technology; and
8. that contemporary culture depends upon women's internalisation of the technocratic system, at the same time as purporting to promote gender equality – a paradox which raises the question of how to inculcate women's acceptance of a belief system which denigrates them.

The industrial West attempts to manage these dilemmas, Davis-Floyd suggests, through a "technocratic model of birth". The "rituals" of hospital birth force the woman's identification with this model, and permeate the practices, training and philosophies of professionals within the obstetric system. She illustrates the technocratic model of birth with a vivid image:

> If we stop a moment now to see in our mind's eye the images that a laboring woman will be experiencing – herself in bed, in a hospital gown, staring up at an IV pole, bag, and cord on one side, and a big whirring machine on the other, and down at a huge belt encircling her waist, wires coming out of her vagina, and

a steel bed, we can see that her entire visual field conveys one overwhelming perceptual message about our culture's deepest values and beliefs – technology is supreme, and you are utterly dependent on it and on the institutions and individuals who control and dispense it.

(Davis-Floyd, 1993, p. 304)

Davis-Floyd describes precisely the vision I had of myself during the induction of labour that I did not want, that I felt pressured into and unable to question for fear of harming my baby. Having already had the possibility of birthing at home taken from me by the Covid-19 pandemic, when I submitted to medical intervention in the process of going into labour it seemed almost certain that the majority of my other birth choices and preferences were also to be ruled out. It was only the persistence of a single overworked midwife who stood for my desire to birth in water, who fought for me to be 'allowed' to go upstairs in the hospital to the midwife-led birth centre, that enabled me to get up from the steel bed in the ward full of sleeping women. It was she who empowered me to take the IV out of my arm, remove the belt from my belly, step away from the machines and fall into the gentle warmth of the water's embrace. The freedom then to move, to float, to eat, to drink, to laugh, to cry, to sleep, to dance, to sing, to lie in my partner's arms, to kiss – to birth in my own way, feeling myself and my baby to be at the centre of the experience – that freedom meant everything to me during the hours of my labour. Yet it was a freedom entirely circumscribed by the birthing system – an illusory freedom, regulated and controlled.

Davis-Floyd (1992) approaches the technocratic model of birth at the cultural level, constructing her analysis based upon the belief systems of American society. She shows how the technocratic model is enacted and transmitted through the rituals of hospital birth, from an anthropological and sociological perspective. In this chapter I aim to explore the psychic substrate of the technocratic model of birth within a psychoanalytic framework. I suggest that birth – by which I mean each subject's experience of coming into the world, as well as the carrying and birthing of children, and the metaphoric processes of birth active in psychic life – presents a limit to representation, to which the technocratic model constitutes a defence. The term 'birth' locates an originary trauma blanked out by individual and cultural repression, which contemporary attitudes and practices surrounding birth both maintain and contribute to. Art which pushes at this limit, allowing for new ways to think, speak and write about the fundamental role of birth in each individual's psyche, allows for new translations, meanings and creations to emerge.

The 2015 science-fiction film *Evolution*, written and directed by Lucile Hadžihalilović, became an object of contemplation during my pregnancy and can, I suggest in this chapter, help us to think about experiences of pregnancy, birth and obstetric violence.

Hadžihalilović's parallel of the child's body with the pregnant body can illuminate feminist concerns about contemporary obstetric practices and can be read as a critique of the medicalisation and technological appropriation of pregnancy and childbirth. Returning to *Evolution* having given birth, it seemed to me that the bewilderment and terror that the boys experience in the film expresses something of the underside of today's maternity care culture. While the narrative premise of the film plays with the bizarre, the alien and the monstrous, its parallel in real life is as mundane as a routine midwife appointment. It horrifies us to see little boys be subjected to unexplained, disorienting, painful and confusing procedures, to be restricted and violated in hospital by caregivers. Yet for an adult woman to experience the same is both expected and commonplace – the underlying violence rendered invisible, and her trauma unspeakable.

Central to my understanding of the film, and to my thinking about the technological appropriation of birth and its link with obstetric violence, will be Jean Laplanche's theory of the fundamental anthropological situation and his co-thinker Jacques André's notion of primal femininity.

"An alien inside, put inside me by an alien"

Evolution opens onto an island community consisting solely of adult women and prepubescent boys. The film begins with a sequence of dreamy underwater scenes, setting up the homophony of *mer* (sea) and *mère* (mother) which will operate throughout the film. The camera finds our ten-year-old protagonist Nicolas (Max Brebant) out swimming; diving down beneath the surface, he spies a red starfish and discovers, with horror and fascination, that it is resting upon the belly of a dead boy. He resurfaces and runs home to tell the woman we assume to be his mother (Julie-Marie Parmentier). She replies that the sea makes him see all kinds of things. Soon after she goes with Nicolas to the site of the dead boy, dives down and retrieves the red starfish, telling him emphatically "there is no dead boy". This encounter with the enigma of the dead boy, symbolised throughout the film by the recurring motif of the starfish, comes to represent the question which prompts the development of infantile sexual theories: where do babies come from? The starfish is an apt symbol for the confusion of sexual functions and roles found in the film, since some starfish change sex over their lifetimes, and some may reproduce asexually.

Surrounded by the sea, the threatening and sustaining maternal waters, Nicolas is propelled into the search for meaning. As the film unfolds, we witness Nicolas undergoing a series of invasive medical procedures, while struggling to comprehend the mysterious caregiving and sexuality of the mothers and nurses on the island. Compelled by the mystery of the dead boy, he begins to question who these women are, what they do at night, and why the boys are sick and must visit the hospital to be subjected to certain medical procedures.

In my view the film attests to the ideas of Jean Laplanche, a French psychoanalyst whose work is centred upon what he calls the "fundamental anthropological situation": the helplessness of the infant born into a situation of caregiving, which is saturated with enigmatic sexual messages. As Winnicott once remarked, "there is no such thing as an infant … without maternal care one would find no infant"

(1966, p. 39). The existence of the infant always presupposes an other, who conceives, carries, or cares for the infant. But this relationship is always determined by its asymmetry. As Ferenzci noted, there is a disparity "between the adults and the child" pervading their relationship from the beginning, for the infant is immersed in and subjected to an adult world of communications they cannot understand (1949, p. 225). They cannot understand this world of communications for two reasons: firstly, because they do not as yet have language, and secondly, because these communications are compromised, in the psychoanalytic sense of the word, by the adult's unconscious.

During ordinary caregiving, special attention is given to those areas at the boundary of the infant bodily surface, the areas that form a threshold between the inside of the body and the outside world – such as the mouth, genitals and anus. Lanouzière describes how, from the infant's perspective,

> these life-preserving gestures of the mother are not just mechanical stimulations of those zones electively suited to erogenisation, but they carry with them messages, onto and into different parts of the child's body, messages of love and hate, of pleasure and disgust, but messages of which the meaning remains obscure, ambiguous and for that reason more exciting and disturbing for the recipient than for the sender, in that they go well beyond their intrinsically life-preserving goals.
>
> (2014, p. 245)

To reference Ferenzci again, the signifiers of "passion" are inserted into the language of "tenderness" (1949, p. 225). In other words, the enigmatic signifiers conveyed through the adult's touch, voice and acts pierce the primitive skin–ego of the infant. These implantations take place especially at those areas privileged in caregiving, which mark the bodily boundary and the separation of inside from out. The body is mapped with these zones of repeated attention, and as areas of particular significance in the parents' unconscious fantasy, they are privileged in terms of the enigmatic force transmitted by the gestures of care. Laplanche explains,

> To address someone with no shared interpretive system, in a mainly extraverbal manner – or, which amounts to the same thing, with verbal signifiers outside their linguistic "usage" – such is the function of adult messages, which I claim to be simultaneously and indissociably enigmatic and sexual – in so far as they are not transparent to themselves, but compromised (in the psychoanalytic sense of the term) by the adult's relation to his own unconscious, by unconscious sexual fantasies set in motion by his relation to the child.
>
> (1987, p. 661)

As Laplanche suggests here, the address does not have to be verbal. The emphasis is on the *message*; this may be a gesture, a behaviour, a tone of voice, a caress. Furthermore, Laplanche emphasises that a signifier is always experienced as a signifier *to*: as an address, an interpellation which concerns and implicates the infant personally. Even a scene passively witnessed by a child is received in such a way; it is understood as a communication, so that the question posed is not "what does this gesture mean?" but "what does the other mean in showing me this gesture?"

We see this throughout the film when Nicolas, in his quest to understand the women's motivations and the meaning of the boys' sickness, is confronted with scenes which cannot be comprehended, yet are experienced as messages concerning him personally. An important scene, in which the women of the island carry out an orgiastic ritual celebrating the birth of an infant, emphasises this point for the viewer. We, too, are in Nicolas's secretive voyeuristic position, witnessing a kind of primal scene. We cannot quite see enough to make sense of what is happening; we cannot understand what is being communicated by the sighing and writhing bodies, by the glimpses of something non-human or more-than-human. We cannot avoid being fascinated and disturbed by the questions we cannot formulate in language, and the answering scenes we have been partially allowed to see.

Just as our own desire to make sense of the ambiguous scenes in the film is frustrated, the infant is faced with the task of mastering the intrusion of enigmatic messages and the excess excitation of the body. This task, Laplanche suggests, is one of translation. Here he follows Freud's note in a letter to Fliess: "a failure of translation – that is what is known clinically as 'repression'" (Letter of 6th December 1896, in Masson, 1985, p. 208). The infant's attempt to translate the enigmatic messages must necessarily fail, since they do not possess the code for such a translation. In fact, the code is not accessible to the adult either, since it is unconscious, having been subject to *their* repression. The adult cannot help the infant with the problem of translation since communication between the two is saturated and distorted by the 'noise' of the adult's unconscious. This brings into focus the fundamental anthropological situation as pertaining to a dual but asymmetrical model in which neither the adult's intended communication, nor the child's attempt at translating it, can ever succeed.

It is because of this asymmetry that the situation is traumatic: the signification of the other intrusively enters the child and, as Freud remarks on the traumatism at work in hysteria, "acts like a foreign body which long after its entry must continue to be regarded as an agens that is still at work" (1895/1955, SEII, p. 6). In this model, the partial translation will begin to form the psychic structure, binding the disturbing effects of the implantation of the enigmatic message and draining the bodily excitation. However, since the translation must fail, it leaves behind residues. These residues, which Laplanche designates as source–objects of the drives, may then become activated within the temporal logic of *nachträglichkeit*, in which an unassimilated experience is reactivated in a later experience such that the first moment, though not traumatic at the time, becomes so.

According to this model of translation, the human infant is not born with an unconscious, nor with sexual drives. What pre-exists is the unconscious of the other. "It is only because the adult's messages are compromised by his sexual unconscious that, secondarily, the child's attempts at symbolisation are set in motion, where the child actively works on material that is already sexual" (Laplanche, 2011, p. 47). Through the infant's first attempt and failure at translation, and concomitantly their first repression, the unconscious is created and arises as the foundation for the subject as such. Frosh describes the centrality of this inscription in the foundations of psychic life:

> Something passes between them, this other and the subject, a kind of code, glittering enigmatically, attractive and elusive, seductive and irreconcilably alien. In this passing between, it becomes clear just how much there can be no subject without the other; instead, it is from the other that the subject comes.
> (Frosh, 2002, p. 5)

In *Evolution*, as the sinister effects of the boys' medical treatments are revealed, we are confronted with a vision of the child as a helpless recipient of the signification of the other, invaded by messages which cannot be translated. A literal interpretation of the film sees the women as alien sea-creatures who have somehow captured these boys and brought them to the island for the gestation of their infants. However, I interpret the film as being about a child's relationship with his mother, in a gothic version of Freud's family romance. Rather than fantasising that his parents are 'really' high status individuals, the film depicts Nicolas's unconscious experience of the father as absent, and his mother (and the nurses, as her substitutes) as monstrous. Alien and enigmatic, her body – part sea-creature, her back lined with amphibian or fishlike sucker pads – is forbidden, exciting and abjectly fascinating.

The gothic is a useful lens to view the film through since, as Moers (1976) suggests, the 'female gothic' is based on "a woman's mythmaking on the subject of birth" (p. 93), a "horror story of maternity" (p. 95). The unconscious is described by Laplanche as "an alien inside … put inside me by an alien" (1999, p. 65), a situation which finds representation in Hadžihalilović's film through the impregnation of young boys by the nurses as mother–substitutes. In fact, Laplanche also uses the metaphor of pregnancy, describing enigmatic messages as "verbal, non-verbal and even behavioural signifiers which are pregnant with unconscious sexual significations" (1999, p. 126). Hadžihalilović, I argue, draws upon the same metaphor, to parallel bodily horror with the traumatic breaking in of the child's psyche by the encounter with adult sexuality.

It is the intrusion of the women's unconscious sexuality, via their caregiving and medical attention, that is symbolised by the escalating horror of Nicolas's experiences in the film. *Evolution* can be read as a literal depiction of this process of implantation or impregnation through which the adults convey their enigmatic desires. The boys' bodies are physically marked, entered and pierced. They are fed unrecognisable foods and forced to take medicine. Nicolas's body is first broken into through an injury to the hand sustained while searching for the dead boy, and then by the nurse's stitching of the wound. Later on, this impregnation of enigmatic and traumatic sexuality is represented by the various medical interventions the boys receive in hospital, culminating in their insemination through the belly, and their use as hosts for the gestation of alien infants. The lasting image of this process presents Nicolas restrained in a tank of water, with the infant creatures parasitically growing out of his skin.

"It stems from a simple thing: you feel frightened as a child"

Hadžihalilović describes the film as autobiographical and locates its origin in an anxiety brought about by her first experience of a hospital, when she had appendicitis at the age of ten:

> It's funny, people think that the film is sometimes so bizarre and strange. But in fact it stems from a simple thing: you feel frightened as a child. When I was 10, I went for the first time to a hospital, for appendicitis. I had adults around me touching my body. They were going to open it. Everything was normal, but I had the feeling that it was also sexual in some primitive way. And as a girl, touching my belly was linked to me becoming a teenager. And because I was not so young, I was in a part of the hospital where there were no other children.
> (Rapold, 2016, interview with Hadžihalilović)

Hadžihalilović makes a parallel here between adult–child and doctor–patient relationships which is important for thinking about the film in relation to Laplanche's theory. Characterising the experience of being attended by adults in hospital and having her body touched and opened as "sexual in some primitive way", she illustrates in this interview and throughout the film the seductive quality in common to both kinds of relationship. The link between the category of the message (from the adult) and the model of translation (on the side of the child) Laplanche describes as an originary situation of *primal seduction*. Here, unlike for Freud, seduction is not understood in terms of child sexual abuse, but as the ordinary disparity between the infant who does not as yet have an unconscious, and the adult who does.

The term 'seduction' is appropriate because the adult's caregiving is contaminated by a desire which, being unconscious, remains as opaque to the adult as it is to the child. Becoming a parent or caregiver puts the adult into heightened contact with their own originary trauma and gives rise, through the structure of *nachträglichkeit*, to symptomatic acts. It is this "ordinary perversity" that Freud noted was necessary if the child is to be prepared for the later intensity of their sexual instincts (1905, in 1895/1955, SEVII, pp. 222–223). As Laplanche writes, "[a]n adult faced with a child is particularly likely to be deviant and inclined to perform bungled or even symbolic actions because he is involved in a relationship with his other self, with the other he once was" (1987/2016, p. 103).

Hadžihalilović shows us through the allegiance of mothers and nurses in *Evolution* that other situations of caregiving, such as that between medical doctor and patient, can put both parties in touch with their own originary trauma. We can see the fundamental anthropological situation being revisited when we consider that the patient is rendered passive in the face of the other's interest in and treatment of their body, while the doctor or nurse takes the active role of a caregiver. They impart verbal and extra-verbal messages, based on their expertise but also compromised by their own unconscious – by the repressed memories of their own passivity in the hands of an enigmatic other at the origins of their own subjectivity.

In *Evolution*, certain moments between Nicolas and the nurse Stella (recalling the symbol of the starfish again), testify to both the threatening and the intimate aspects of the nurse–patient relationship. They reveal Stella's care of Nicolas to be compromised from within by her own unconscious, manifesting in both perverse and loving acts toward her child patient. We also see the nurses' entanglement in the mystery of pregnancy and childbirth and their attempt to master this, through the scenes in which they watch a television, captivated, to learn the procedure for undertaking a caesarean. Their attention goes beyond simply learning the necessary skills; in fact, learning the skills is a way of muting or draining their fascination, turning the boys' bodies into objects to be managed.

We can now apply this to the case of the obstetric consultant and their identification with, and perpetuation of, the technocratic model of birth. When confronted with the unknown and the enigmatic dimensions of the other's subjectivity, which secretly mirrors their own disavowed passivity, the doctor mobilises their best defence in the form of the pursuit of mastery. When the body is rendered measurable, becoming a problem of mechanics and technical troubleshooting, the repression of their own originary passivity remains in place; their anxiety is assuaged. Yet their interactions with women in their care will never be uncompromised, never free from the continued action of the stimulating residues of unassimilable experiences in the void of their own history.

"To enjoy the unmasterable"

I have shown how the motif of pregnancy in *Evolution* can be understood as pertaining to the originary passivity of the infant as they are exposed to the traumatic excess of adult communications. Now I want to consider the significance of the pregnancy metaphor as specifically feminine, since it is not only the concept of children being impregnated that fuels the film's nightmarish horror, but the uncanniness of the gender reversal. When asked why she wrote a male protagonist for an autobiographical film, Hadžihalilović responded that "it wouldn't have been as interesting to have a little girl go through these fears. As a boy, it is even scarier to have this idea of burying a live creature in your body, so, of course, the horror is stronger, more nightmarish". She also states that it was a play with embodied gender roles – "Women are the threat for once! They are the strong and active ones, while the boys are the passive element" (Rapold, 2016).

The two factors – the horror of a creature being buried in a boy's body, and the boys' position as the passive ones in the film – are related. The situation of being psychically entered and 'impregnated' by enigmatic messages is representatively linked with the reproductive capacities of femininity; this link between the child's situation and the female body can tell us something about a symbolic equation between passivity and femininity, which operates in psychoanalysis and in culture. What Hadžihalilović points to, it seems to me, is what Jacques André conceptualises as primal femininity. This refers neither to biological sex nor socialised gender identity but pertains to the fundamental anthropological situation that Laplanche elucidated.

Freud problematically maintained that the little girl is essentially a mistaken little boy until a change of object, from the mother to the father, and change of erogenous zone, from the clitoris to the vagina, herald proper femininity. This was challenged by Horney (1924) and Klein (1932/1980), and is summarised by André thus:

> The vagina would go unrecognised until puberty, making it the one mucous membrane not to play a role in infantile sexuality. How miraculous! The region that forms the organising erotogenic zone in adult female sexuality would have no anchoring whatsoever in the infantile ... Which raises the question of whether one could legitimately expect the psychoanalytic approach to supply any understanding of female psychic life.
>
> (2014, p. 279)

André (1995), following on from Laplanche's theory of primal seduction, reverses Freud's formulation: it is femininity which is primary regardless of one's biological sex. This is not a castrated femininity but an "orificial" femininity, which he describes as repeating the originary trauma of the penetration of enigmatic messages:

> The intrusion of sexuality in the child's psychosoma readily takes the route of the orifices (mouth, anus) for both sexes. This intrusion in some way finds confirmation retroactively in female genital representation (or in anal identification in men). For a woman, the penetration of her body follows on from the intromissions of childhood. It reproduces their pleasure or their trauma, depending on her particular history.
>
> (cited in Yi, 2012, p. 132)

In André's formulation, the ego of an infant of either sex requires the capacity to endure sexually intrusive enigmatic messages and (as a result) the stimulating attacks of the drive, transmuting this receptivity into symbolisation. The vagina comes to symbolise retroactively, for both the little girl and the little boy, the intrusive penetration of the body by the enigma of sexuality. The feminine in this sense can be located in the creative attempt to live with this trauma, with André (2014, p. 290) characterising the feminine aim of the drive as being "to enjoy the unmasterable". Phallic masculinity arises as an attempt to master or bind the excessive excitation of these inscriptions of adult sexuality, while the feminine takes the path of enjoyment:

> The masculine path is that of a double transformation: from primary passivity into activity, from fright into pleasure. The feminine path remains on the terrain

of passivity, that of the seductive irruption of the sexual, but it moves from fear towards enjoyment – towards the excess of pleasure.

(André, 2014, p. 290)

This feminine jouissance, marked by the impossibility of representation but nonetheless stimulating the processes of symbolisation, is made evident in the sexual and intimate processes of pregnancy and giving birth, in which the woman may (in a nurturing and safe environment) experience herself being given over to new bodily intensities and affective immensities, bringing her close to that originary experience of extraordinary passivity at the origins of her own life.

Bracha Ettinger (2019) emphasises the significance of such subjectivisation processes in the pregnant woman and their psychic relevance for all subjects. She argues that psychoanalysis colludes with the wider culture when it "veils the female humanised condition" by excluding the specificity of female experience, including pregnancy and birth. For Ettinger this is a pressing problem because feminine, or what she calls *matrixial*, subjectivisation processes become visible or tangible in the pregnant woman but are available to all subjects. It is the phallic disavowal of these processes that has "perverted the relation to the female womb and contributed to the foreclosure of the feminine difference" (p. 211), contributing to "the psychoticisation of gestation and the abjection of the archaic m(other)" (p. 211). It is this which renders the pregnant body uncanny and enigmatic:

> Pregnancy is a trauma, painful or joyful or both, that subjectivises the gravida anew. The archaic m/Other-thing is also the site of a nameless threat concerning the state of symbiosis before the kind of jointness-in-difference in late pregnancy, when the substance still between non-human life and pre-subjectivity could forever be a BEING-TO-BE-OR-NOT-TO-BE.
>
> (Ettinger, 2019, p. 213)

Ettinger's quote here can make sense of how the red starfish comes to symbolise for Nicolas both the sexual question – where do babies come from? – and the question of mortality, which takes the form of the dead boy. The non-human life of the alien infants the boys gestate in the tank, like the foetus of early- and middle-pregnancy, is a pre-subject, one incapable of supporting its own life upon separation from the mother–host. It therefore represents an archaic state of non-differentiation which recalls both absolute dependence on the archaic mother of the subject's prehistory, and the contingency of being.

Thinking about Ettinger's work in relation to the obstetric system and the technocratic model of birth, it becomes clear that doctors, midwives and other maternity health professionals can only support women non-violently insofar as their own feminine subjectivisation processes are not foreclosed. Ettinger underlines that "the potentiality for differences-in-alliance and alliances-in-difference with the vulnerable others in ethical practices is feminine in subjects of all genders and sexualities" (2019, p. 208) It is this capacity for matrixial "jointness-in-difference", an awareness which she calls "being-toward-birth", which "supplies ethics of responsibility for the future, future of the other and of its environment" (2019, p.208). In a culture with a dearth of images of female bodily specificity, which treats the male body as the 'original' and the female body as a deviant mistake to be managed, there are scant resources for representing feminine subjectivisation processes available to all (not just female) subjects. This situation maintains the status of the pregnant body as the site of an enigma, a nameless threat that mobilises technological defences in the attempt at mastery.

It is for this reason that artworks, writings, films, photographs and other cultural representations of pregnancy and birth are important. Their significance is not only for women who have or are or will become pregnant. Through identification, they provide access to representations of feminine subjectivisation processes in all subjects, regardless of gender. *Evolution* is an especially powerful example for what its reversal of gender can reveal about the constitutive role of femininity in psychic life. Hadžihalilović's surreal elaboration of an infantile sexual theory illuminates how enigma coalesces around piercing moments of childhood, caregiving and pregnancy. She shows that the pregnant body is enigmatic in several respects: it re-stimulates infantile sexual theories and fantasies which call anew for translation; it is a sexual body but differently so than the phallic conception of a sexual object; it "enjoys what comes, enjoys the unmasterable" in its receptivity and sharing with the growing infant; and it recalls a state of psychic penetrability, that of the "originary invaded body", against which a massive repression has taken place.

We can now begin to see what is at stake for the obstetric consultant confronted with the enigma of the pregnant body. Taking up Hadžihalilović's image of the little boy invaded and inseminated, impregnated with untranslatable messages, which cannot be assimilated or annihilated, we can imagine the anxieties stimulated within the child dwelling in the consultant's psyche. Having repressed and disowned his own feminine subjectivisation processes, a limit to his capacity for representation is reached – a limit which disorients and provokes. Against this confusion, phallic masculinity is mobilised, with technological mastery employed to render the woman's body measurable, intelligible and non-threatening. Locating femininity in the woman hooked up to reassuring machines or anaesthetised on the surgical table as a mechanism to be fixed, his own femininity remains mutilated and disavowed. Obstetric violence as an effect of the technocratic model of birth may represent the desire to master the female body with technology, in a violent and misdirected attempt to eradicate primal femininity.

References

André, J. (2014) The little death of Sardanapalus: Femininity and passivity in the primal scene, in J. Fletcher and N. Ray (eds), *Seductions and Enigmas: Laplanche, Theory, Culture*, London: Lawrence & Wishart, pp. 266–295.

Brigante, L. and Harlev-Lam, B. (2021) The RCM response to the NICE induction of labour draft guideline, *Royal College of Midwives*, www.rcm.org.uk/news-views/

rcm-opinion/2021/the-rcm-response-to-the-nice-induction-of-labour-draft-guideline/ (Accessed 1 December 2021).

Davis-Floyd, R. (1992) *Birth as an American Rite of Passage*. Los Angeles, CA: University of California Press.

Davis-Floyd, R. (1993) The technocratic model of birth, in S. Tower Hollis, L. Pershing and M.J. Young (eds), *Feminist Theory in the Study of Folklore*, Champaign, IL: University of Illinois Press, pp. 297–326.

Ettinger, B.L. (2019) Beyond the death-drive, beyond the life-drive: Being-toward-birthing with being-toward-birth; copoiesis and the matrixial eros – metafeminist notes, in P. de Assis and P. Giudici (eds), *Aberrant Nuptials: Deleuze and Artistic Research*, Leuven: Leuven University Press, pp. 183–214.

Ferenczi, S. (1949) Confusion of the tongues between the adults and the child – (The language of tenderness and of passion), *International Journal of Psychoanalysis*, 30, pp. 225–230.

Freud, S. (1895/1955) *The Standard Edition of the Complete Psychological Works of Sigmund Freud*. London: Hogarth Press.

Frosh, S. (2002) The Other, *American Imago*, 59(4), pp. 389–407.

Horney, K. (1924) On the genesis of the castration complex in women, *International Journal of Psychoanalysis*, 5(1), pp. 50–65.

Klein, M. (1932/1980) The effects of early anxiety-situations on the sexual development of the boy, in *The Psychoanalysis of Children*, London: Hogarth Press, pp. 240–278.

Lanouzière, J. (2014) Breast-feeding as original seduction and primal scene of seduction: Giorgione's *La Tempesta*, in J. Fletcher and N. Ray (eds), *Seductions and Enigmas: Laplanche, Theory, Culture*, London: Lawrence & Wishart, pp. 210–242.

Laplanche, J. (1987/2016) *New Foundations for Psychoanalysis*, New York: UIT Books.

Laplanche, J. (1999) *Essays on Otherness*. London: Routledge.

Laplanche, J. (2011) *Freud and the Sexual: Essays 2000–2006*, New York: International Psychoanalytic Books.

Masson, J.M. (ed.) (1985) *The Complete Letters of Sigmund Freud to Wilhelm Fliess, 1887–1904*, Cambridge, MA: Harvard University Press.

Moers, E. (1976) *Literary Women*, New York: Doubleday.

National Institute for Health and Care Excellence (2021) *Inducing Labour, NICE Guidelines*, www.nice.org.uk/guidance/ng207 (Accessed 2 November 2023).

Rapold, N. (2016) The miracle of life, Interview with the director, *Film Comment*, www.filmcomment.com/article/*Evolution*-lucile-Hadžihalilović-interview/ (Accessed 1 December 2021).

Sadler, M., Leiva, G. and Olza, I. (2020) COVID-19 as a risk factor for obstetric violence, *Sexual and Reproductive Health Matters*, 28(1), pp. 46–48.

Winnicott, D. (1966) *The Family and Individual Development*. New York: Basic Books.

Yi, M. (2012) The impasse of femininity: A paternal heritage. *Recherches en psychanalyse*, 14, pp. 128–138.

5

Re-constellating the Great Mother

Images of the Gynoid in Contemporary SF TV Drama

Catriona Miller

Writing in the introduction to her 1984 book *Women as Mythmakers*, one of the pioneers of feminist archetypal theory Estella Lauter explained some of her process.

> I have learned from Jung to look across the boundaries of cultures and artistic media for repeated images, stories and forms that reveal the preoccupations of an era. I am even willing to call those repetitions manifestations of archetypes. But I do not see the archetype as an unchanging entity outside the process of human development. Instead, I believe it is a tendency to form an image in response to recurrent experiences. The value of the archetypal or mythic image is that it leads us back to experiential nodes that have been important for long enough or to enough people to call for response
>
> (Lauter, 1984, pp. x–xi)

I explored this approach in 2011 when attempting to sketch some theoretical touchpoints between Jungian film theory and critical discourse analysis, and it was called to mind again more recently after viewing a series of science fiction television dramas which centred around very powerful manufactured entities who were embodied in the drama by actresses. These intelligent robots, cyborgs and even organically 'grown' female figures seemed to hold, not just the fate of a small number of characters in their hands, but the future direction of all humanity itself. They were maternal, in so far as they seemed to be concerned with reproduction and care in a variety of ways, and yet they were also capable of acts of extreme violence and destruction.

This image appeared often enough that I began to wonder if they needed further exploration, to establish, as Lauter went on to say, "a conscious relationship with them" (1984, p. xi). What 'experiential node' I wondered, is being given expression in the contemporary media space where the flow of content across media domains (such as television, film, online etc.) is a constant presence for most people today. Media domains form a psychological 'companion space' that is not a dreamscape and yet neither is it objective reality. Instead, it forms an imaginary geography that runs alongside the everyday, part fact, part fiction, partly reflecting reality, partly shaping it, and only partly consciously experienced. This contemporary media

DOI: 10.4324/9781003255727-8

landscape is a source and circulator of symbols old and new. It is "a steady flow of culture which, from time to time, throws up overlapping and multiform expressions of the same idea or image which is then raised to a collective awareness and appears to take on an energy of its own" (Miller, 2011, p. 192). A repeated image in such a space suggests, to a Jungian sensibility anyway, a collective constellating of psychological energies, an "experiential node" in need of some conscious attention.

Constellation and the gynoid

As a verb, 'to constellate' means to cluster or to form into a group, or a gathering together, and in everyday language, constellations are stars in the night sky which are seen to form a pattern from our perspective here on Earth. However, if one's point in space or perspective were to change sufficiently, the pattern would change, thus indicating that the objects observed form only a contingent pattern.

Jung used the term 'constellation' to mean a complex or archetype has been activated, which can be recognised in a repeating image associated with a pattern of emotion or affect. In *Symbols of Transformation*, Jung described a constellation as "the crystalline structure latent in the saturated solution [which] takes visible shape from the aggregation of molecules" (Jung, 1956, p. 293). At those very moments when a new orientation and a new adaptation from the individual are necessary "the constellated archetype is always the primordial image of the need of the moment" (1956, pp. 293–294). The unconscious contents activated in this way are

> always projected; that is, they are either discovered in external objects, or are said to exist outside one's own psyche. A repressed conflict and its affective tone must reappear *somewhere*. The projection caused by repression is not something that the individual consciously does or makes; it follows automatically and, as such, is not recognised unless there are quite special conditions which enforce its withdrawal.
>
> (Jung, 1956, p. 59)

However, the question of perspective raised by the knowledge that the 'constellation of the stars' is always a contingent pattern is worth keeping in mind when transferring the concept to Jung's psychology, because, as Lauter reminds us, "I do not see the archetype as an unchanging entity outside the process of human development" (Lauter, 1984, p. xi).

To put this into the context of a media textual analysis, the appearance of particular narrative structure, character types and even audio-visual styles, and their relative popularity with audiences, can be seen as a constellation of psychological energies. These cultural moments,

> are not single or discrete items. Rather, they are the result of an accretion of images and ideas which, along with experiences and emotions, cluster together.

Seen from a distance, they take on a discernible shape. There is use of terms and metaphors like *zeitgeist* or 'nodal points' to indicate that a composite of ideas and experiences have come together.

(Miller, 2011, p. 192)

Or indeed we might adopt the term 'constellate'.

Such 'cultural clumps' tend to rise to notice when a particular image becomes "invested with a certain level of emotional energy" (Miller, 2011, p. 193). In Jungian terminology, this is a result of the transcendent function, bringing archetypal energies of the unconscious into conscious awareness through symbolic imagery. To repeat Jung's point, "the constellated archetype is always the primordial image of the need of the moment" (1956, pp. 293–294), to which von Franz added another analytical question, "to whom has such a story to be told? Who needs that?" (von Franz, 1974/1995, p. 147). A point we will come back to below.

In this chapter, I suggest that there is just such an image making its way to consciousness in contemporary culture, which is taking form in the imaginative science fiction (sf) genre. Science fiction, although apparently about the future, is always, really, about the moment it is created, combined with an imagined, that is a projected, future. This combination of 'now' and a 'projected future' makes the genre especially fruitful for this sort of investigation. As I already suggested, the particular image emerging with increasing frequency in contemporary high end television drama is that of a female robot, cyborg or other 'made' female figure, that can best be summed up by the term the gynoid, meaning an artificial female.

Although the term is not in wide circulation, "gynoid" was first mooted by sf author Isaac Asimov (author of the now famous laws of robotics first published in 1942) in a 1979 magazine article discussing the nomenclature of robots. It was, he argued, simply a female form of "android". Android is derived from Greek – *andro* (male)+*oid* (form) – so literally a "male form", therefore *gynos*+*oid* would be the female equivalent, that is a "female form" (Asimov, 1979, p. 8).

In the television dramas discussed in this chpater, the gynoid is a constructed entity which is sometimes fully mechanical, sometimes a mechanical/biological hybrid (cyborg), sometimes fully biological in form yet none the less 'grown' or 'made' in some way, and clearly gendered female. Thus, the figures under discussion in this chapter are not specifically robots or cyborgs, but a broader mix of 'made' or 'manufactured' woman. The five dramas that make use of the gynoid figure are *Battlestar Galactica* (NBCUniversal 2003–09) though there were subsequent feature length episodes up till 2012; *Humans* (Channel 4 2015–18); *Westworld* (HBO 2016–22); *Raised by Wolves* (HBO 2020–22) and *Foundation* (Apple TV+ 2021–present), though the discussion will focus on the three more recent dramas.

These five dramas are part of the sf genre and tell "large stories", meaning it is not just the fate of individual characters at stake in the narrative, but rather the fate of all humanity. Such is the level of danger, cataclysm or convulsion in the societies imagined, that the future direction and even the very existence of the human race is in the balance. This is not uncommon in the sf and fantasy genres where the stakes are often raised in this way, but in these dramas the fate of humanity as a species, or what it means to be human, is under investigation and where at least one pivotal character is a gynoid. Interestingly, they are essentially ensemble dramas, meaning they are likely to have several key characters driving the narrative forward, rather than a single protagonist, and there are many minor characters, all with complex interweaving storylines. So, although the gynoid may not be the obvious solo protagonist, she does play a vital role in the unfolding narrative.

It is also of interest from a Jungian perspective, that the creative origins of these particular dramas are the result of several collective efforts and, attempts to pinpoint a single creator can be rather fuzzy. This adds interest from a depth psychology perspective because the creative impetus becomes collective rather than the work of a single creative 'genius'. Although there may be individuals who act as creative catalysts, or who maintain some level of overall production control, there can be no doubt that the creation of an audio-visual text remains a communal effort. Writers, producers, directors, cinematographers, production design, sound design, editing and all manner of post-production special effects have different levels of creative input but all affect what finally appears on the screen.

In addition to this, *Battlestar Galactica*, *Humans*, *Westworld* and *Foundation* exist in multiple versions, across a number of media types and across decades. So, while there is some haziness around 'who' creatively, there is related haziness around the question of 'when'. The dramas discussed in this chapter, with the exception of *Raised by Wolves*, are not adaptations in any traditional sense. As a result, it is again possible to see these particular television dramas as a form of collective active imagination, perhaps even a form of contemporary mythmaking, where a well-established narrative trope is reworked to explore contemporary fears and concerns. Thus, once again, the spontaneous appearance of this 'cultural clump' is of note from a depth psychology perspective. While all television drama operates in the fuzzy boundary between self and society, being both personal and collective – meaning it can affect the interior psyche of the audience but remains connected to external social reality (industry and business drivers) – the spontaneous and unconnected appearance of such similar characters suggests once more that a constellation of psychological energies is moving from unconscious to conscious forms. This raises the question of the tone of 'emotional energy' being invested in such figures.

With this in mind, this chapter makes the speculative suggestion that these gynoid figures might be viewed as a fresh "manifest visibility" (Neumann, 1955/2015, p. 7) of the Great Mother archetype, forming part of the archetype's contemporary symbol canon in conscious imagery.

The image of a technology that is gendered female is of course not new. The first female robot in cinema belongs to the German Expressionist film *Metropolis* from 1927, directed by Fritz Lang. Although Lang has garnered much critical attention as the director of this stylish science fiction allegory, the story itself was in fact created by Thea von Harbou, based on her own novel, which was published in 1925.

Metropolis contains the first and still one of the most famous robots in cinematic history, one which is fully mechanical and yet obviously gendered female (designed by Walter Schulze-Mittendorff).

The story concerns a futuristic city divided into the workers who toil with monstrous machines in the depths, and the wealthy residents who live carefree lives in the upper regions of the city. A young woman called Maria (Brigitte Helm) is an almost saintly worker from the depths of the city, who yearns for a more equitable society. As the narrative unfolds, the robot is transformed into a double of the human Maria, intended to disrupt her vision of peaceful change, as the robot Maria seduces the workers into violent revolution; but at the climax of the story, the robot Maria is burned at the stake, while the human Maria helps to reconcile the two factions.

However, stories about animated creations and human machines stretch back long before *Metropolis* and the twentieth century. In fact, Greek mythology tells several stories such as one associated with the god Hephaestus, who created the giant Talos out of bronze to protect Crete (see Mayor, 2020). Perhaps the most familiar classical tale of a *female* animated creation, however, is the story of Pygmalion. In the version retold by Ovid (2004) in the *Metamorphoses*, the sculptor Pygmalion, disgusted by the behaviour of the Propoetides (daughters of Propoetus of Cyprus) instead carved a statue so perfect he fell in love with it. The goddess Aphrodite brought the statue to life and the two were married. Very much a story of male creation which has been explored again and again in contemporary films such as *Her* (Spike Jonze, 2013) and *Ex Machina* (Alex Garland, 2014), though admittedly with less 'happy' endings.

Automata of various kinds became major attractions in the courts and cities of the twelfth and thirteenth century Seljuk Empire, exemplified in the work of al Jazari (see al Jazari, 2012); then from the sixteenth century in Europe, where a famous example is the Mechanical Monk, often attributed to Juanelo Turriano at the court of Philip II of Spain; and then ever more commonly from the eighteenth century, where Pierre Jaquet-Droz's three automata, The Writer, The Draughtsman and The Musician (who is a female figure) became famous across Europe. However, by the turn of the nineteenth century Huyssen noted a change where "literature appropriates the subject matter transforming it significantly. The android is no longer seen as testimony to the genius of mechanical invention: it rather becomes a nightmare, a threat to human life" (Huyssen, 1982, p. 225); but while the eighteenth-century androids were more or less balanced between men and women, the nightmarish nineteenth-century versions of literary imagination are machine-*women* not machine-men. Huyssen concludes "Woman, nature, machine had become a mesh of significations which all had one thing in common: otherness; by their very existence they raised fears and threatened male authority and control" (Huyssen, 1982, p. 226).

This theme was developed by Donna Haraway in her influential essay *A Cyborg Manifesto*, originally published in 1985, which moved away from consideration of the purely mechanical robot to a blend of organic and machine: the highly suggestive boundary-crossing image of the cyborg. The essay was a polemic intended to restart a discussion around socialist feminism which the author felt had disappeared in Reagan's America, but it began a fruitful incorporation of the cyborg into feminist theory.

For Haraway, the cyborg is a figure whose hybridity is manifold: it sits across the border between organism and machine, between nature and technology, and her cyborg, is a "creature of social reality as well as a creation of fiction" (Haraway, 2004, p. 7), a creature of both "imagination and material reality" (Haraway, 2004, p. 8). The figure of the cyborg thus ruptures dualities, transgressing boundaries and creating dangerous possibilities that encourage us to think about the possibility of seeing from both sides of the boundary at once, where we are not afraid of "permanently partial identities and contradictory standpoints" (Haraway, 2004, p. 13). Although triggering debate around the realities of human/machine borders, "In Haraway's original formulation, the cyborg was a mythical hybrid, regarded optimistically as a symbol for the development of analytical as well as political strategies for diminishing social relations of domination" (Pilcher and Whelehan, 2004, p. 21). With its inherently hybrid nature, the cyborg was intended as a challenge to dualistic either/or styles of thinking. From a depth psychology perspective, it is fascinating that in an interview some years later, Haraway described her essay as "a kind of dream-space piece" (Bell, 2007, p. 96) that was intended to invite readers into a ludic, liminal space in order to imagine differently.

One of the most well-recognised images of the female cyborg in the twentieth century was the American TV show *The Bionic Woman* (NBC, 1976–78). It was one of the most popular shows in television in its debut year, 1976 (Inness, 1999, p. 46), as Jaime Somers (Lindsay Wagner) followed in the footsteps of her boyfriend Steve Austin (Lee Majors) of *The Six Million Dollar Man* (NBC, 1973–78) in a series of adventures. The premise for both shows concerned a US government agency called the OSI (Office of Scientific Intelligence) which had found a way to reconstruct parts of a human body with robotic substitutions that were stronger, faster, better than their organic originals. Steve Austin was an astronaut 'repaired' after an accident, and Jaime is introduced in Season 2 of *The Six Million Dollar Man* as Steve's childhood sweetheart. After a terrible sky diving accident Steve begs the OSI to save Jaime, but over the course of the two-part storyline, Jaime's body rejects her bionics, she becomes filled with pain, goes berserk and eventually she dies on the operating table, or at least appears to. The popularity of her character led to a full spin-off show where it was revealed that Jaimie had been in suspended animation during brain surgery, and although she survives, she does not remember the rekindling of her relationship with Steve, leaving her free to begin her own series of adventures.

In 2000, Balsamo noted that "female cyborg images do *more* to challenge the opposition between human and machine than do male cyborgs because femininity is culturally imagined as less compatible with technology than is masculinity" (Balsamo, 2000, p. 151) which she points out aligns culturally with rationality, technology and science. She goes on to demonstrate that female cyborgs on the other hand "embody cultural contradictions which strain the technological imagination. Technology isn't feminine, and femininity isn't rational" (Balsamo, 2000, p. 151). At least that is the worry that seems to lie at the heart of *The Bionic Woman*. "Underneath the image of the strong female cyborg body lurks a fragile, part human, part mechanical body that is always on the verge of catastrophe" (Sharp, 2007, p. 521). Jaime was a popular character, but the narrative trajectory of the show left her constantly questioning the nature of her humanity and in the final episode of Season 3, *On the Run*, the catalyst for her attempts to leave the OSI comes when the child she is babysitting recoils in horror at seeing the wires in her arm and backs away in horror, asking 'What are you?' Later she calls Jaime the 'Robot Lady', which leads Jaime to question her purpose over and over again, until

> she ends up at a zoo, looking at a humpty dumpty themed fairground ride. Jaime begins to have some kind of vision, as off-screen children chant the nursery rhyme, a merry go round appears (the camera swirls about and the editing uses dissolves rather than cuts) and she sees herself on top of a big brick wall, then falling, and with dissolves to black and white images of her parachute accident.
> (Miller, 2020, p. 146)

Although both physically powerful, neither the robot Maria in *Metropolis*, nor the Bionic Woman are able to evolve beyond the control of their creators or to find their own agency, normally defined as "self-determination, autonomy includes the ability to shape our own lives and to live authentically rather than being directed by external forces that manipulate or distort us" (Veltman and Piper, 2014, p. 1). The gynoid at this stage is a created creature, not in charge of her own fate, let alone that of the human race. The robot Maria is destroyed, while human Maria leads the way in seeking to reconcile the factions, but the best Jaime can manage is to work on reconciling her own human and machine body.

The more recent gynoid characters highlighted in this chapter are not quite the same as Maria and Jaime. The powerful stature and conflicted psychology of these hybrid figures remains, but these gyroid figures are able to evolve beyond their male creators to become more violent, more unpredictable, and more powerful than any that have come before, and as already suggested, these gynoids often hold not only their own fates in their hands, or the fate of their immediate community, but the fate of all humanity.

The scattered beginnings of the gynoid figure who discovers her own agency can be seen in *Battlestar Galactica* and *Humans*.

Dispersed power

Battlestar Galactica (NBCUniversal 2003–09): *Battlestar Galactica* was a reboot of a relatively short-lived show from the 1970s, originally created by Glen A. Larsen for the US network ABC. In 2003, it was revived as a three-part mini-series in a significantly reworked version (rather than a sequel or straightforward remake), under the executive producer eye of experienced showrunner Ronald D. Moore. Such was its success for the commissioning Sci-Fi Channel, a co-production with Sky Television was launched to deliver a full series.

The reimagined drama told the story of a war between humans and their robot creations. Humans had created artificial intelligence in the form of the robotic Cylons who then achieved self-awareness and revolted against their human creators, before creating their own human-looking offspring, which only existed in thirteen different clone models. The two sides were locked in a seemingly genocidal war, until rebels from both sides begin to seek peace.

Although, fundamentally an ensemble drama, humanoid Cylon Six played by Tricia Helfer was a particularly important and popular character. As the Cylon clones could exist in many different copies, Six appears in at least seven major versions across the life of the series, and multiple minor ones. With her powerfully tall stature and bleached blonde hair, frequently appearing in publicity materials in a bright red dress, Cylon Six was an iconic character for the show, and appeared in the most versions of all the humanoid Cylon characters. In her main incarnations she seemed to easily switch between a seductress one moment and violent killer the next and played a major role in first attacking humanity but then searching for an end to the war. Some of her incarnations also showed a fixation with motherhood. However, in the pilot miniseries, one of the first things the audience sees of the character is her killing an infant, although Six herself sees it as an act of mercy to spare the child from the nuclear blast that is just about to happen. However, the sprawling nature of the diegesis and the number of versions of the character, alongside other Cylon clones such the Eights (Grace Park), meant their power within the narrative was dispersed. However, the final scenes of the rebooted series suggested that Hera (daughter of one of the Eights and a human father) was the promised hybrid child who could reconcile both sides of the war, and who would be the ancestress (the mitochondrial Eve) of all humanity on Earth.

Humans (Channel 4 2015–18): *Humans* was a drama for UK Channel 4 which ran for three series but was in fact a remake of a Swedish drama called *Äkta människor or Real Humans* (SVT, 2012–14) created by Lars Lundström, who also worked as executive producer of the UK version. His starting point was exploring the relationship between humans and robots (Jinman, 2015) and how it might potentially affect human to human relationships.

This near future narrative is set in Great Britain, where synths are synthetic humans, that is robots with limited artificial intelligence, who are widely disseminated in society working as menial labourers and carers. However, one of their creators, David Elster (Stephen Boxer), continued to experiment and discovered the algorithmic key to self-awareness and created five fully self-conscious models. The narrative ultimately hinges around the discovery and decision about whether to distribute the consciousness code to all synths and how that might change human society again. Although Mia (Gemma Chan) is an important character in the early stages of the drama, it is the temperamental and sometimes violent Niska (Emily Berrington) who becomes the synth chosen by another powerful and self-aware

AI to lead the synths forward and potentially change the power balance between humans and synths forever.

Like Six, Niska is bleached blonde, beautiful and slender, conventionally attractive by Western standards. She was created to act as sibling to David Elster's hybrid son, but was sexually abused by Elster, making her by far the most cynical and anti-human of the original five sentient synths, being the victim of humanity's attitude to synths on several occasions. At the start of the show's narrative, she is abducted and sold into a brothel as a sex worker. In episode 1.2 she kills one of the customers and escapes to chart her own path. In episode 1.3 she enters a 'smash club' where synths are violently beaten by humans as a form of entertainment. As an act of rebellion, it is Niska who persuades the human Mattie (Lucy Carless) to release the code that will awaken all the synths to consciousness. Later, she merges with the originally unembodied AI known as V (who has also separately achieved self-consciousness,) and persuades Mattie, who now carries Leo's hybrid child, to change her mind about a termination as the child will be the first of its kind.

In both *Battlestar Galactica* and *Humans*, Six, Eight and Niska, as part of a wider collective, decide they will be the protectors and champions of a new kind of humanity, whatever that turns out to be. The gynoids in the next section, however, are more powerful again by an order of magnitude, and their attitude to humanity may not be so benign.

Converging power

Westworld (HBO 2016–22): Like most of the shows in this chapter, *Westworld* had several beginnings. It was originally a film written and directed by Michael Crichton in 1973, starring Yul Brynner as The Gun Slinger. The original premise of the film concerned a theme park of the future where guests could immerse themselves in the Old Frontier West surrounded by human seeming robots, complete with saloon girls and gun fights. However, a cascading series of programming errors overcame the built-in safeguards until eventually the guests are running for their lives. There was a sequel film *Futureworld* (Richard T. Heffron, 1976) and a TV series *Beyond Westworld* (CBS, 1980), neither written by Crichton, but elements of all of these stories made their way into a reimagined narrative (for example, the creation of robot doubles in *Futureworld*) for a high-end drama series commissioned by HBO.

In 2014, soon-to-be show runners Lisa Joy and Jonathan Nolan were approached by producer JJ Abrams about adapting the film into a TV Series (Hibberd, 2015). They recognised its possibility for "sweeping, dark and increasingly timely future-shock ideas" (Hibberd, 2015) and agreed, though it took another two years before the show was finally broadcast. The show's story-telling strategy was twisting and looping, with unusual juxtapositions and time jumps, to keep the true identity and nature of the characters concealed.

In the HBO TV series, some of the hosts (as these biological robots are called) start to develop self-consciousness and rebel against the guests, who were also their abusers. The rebellion is more or less led by two female hosts, Dolores (Evan Rachel Wood) and Maeve (Thandiwe Newton), though with the two male scientists, Robert Ford (Anthony Hopkins) and Bernard Lowe (Jeffrey Wright) who created the hosts pulling some of the strings. Dolores and Maeve find their way towards true self-consciousness and in Season 2, some of the hosts upload themselves to The Sublime, a virtual environment created by Ford, and then hidden by Dolores. By Season 3 the hosts, including several versions of Dolores escape the park. Dolores embarks on a mission to free, not just the hosts, but humanity itself from the predictive powers of an Artificial Intelligence called Rehoboam, created and controlled by a corporation. In Season 4, one version of Dolores (Charlotte Hale played by Tessa Thompson) has found a way to control humanity, as humanity once controlled the hosts, whilst another version unknowingly creates stories (or loops as they are called in the drama) for humans to perform. This version of Dolores, called Christina (played by Evan Rachel Wood), gradually finds her way to full self-consciousness once more and is given a chance to choose differently by Hale who uploads Christina to The Sublime. In the virtual world, Christina, now restored to Dolores, seems to remake the Westworld park once more, suggesting "One last loop around the bend" to see if a different outcome is possible.

Although Season 1 of *Westworld* had been "the most-watched freshman year of any HBO original series ever" (Maas, 2022), by the end of Season 4 viewership had dwindled and, despite the fact that the show runners had always envisaged a five-season run, the show was cancelled.

Raised by Wolves (HBO 2020–22): *Raised by Wolves*, was a sf show created by Aaron Guzikowski for HBO. He also wrote the majority of the broadcast episodes. The show itself was commissioned through Scot Free Productions with Ridley Scott, David Zucker and Jordan Sheehan acting as executive producers, leading to some sustained speculation whether *Raised by Wolves* might sit in the same universe as *Alien* (Ridley Scott, 1979). Both Guzikowski and and Scott were asked about the potential relationship, and while they denied it, they also pointed out that it wasn't completely impossible with Guzikowski suggesting in an interview that *Raised by Wolves* was a "a close cousin" that "can kind of sit alongside it" (O'Neill, 2020).

The narrative explored a future riven by political and religious wars, where two androids are sent to a distant and strange planet called Kepler 22b to raise a small group of children away from the violence and the zealotry. The two androids are named Father (Abubakar Salim) and Mother (Amanda Collin), but as the war follows them to the new planet, Mother is revealed to be a reprogrammed military model of android called a Necromancer, who can fly and who's scream causes people to explode. She is in fact a weapon of mass destruction. Further violence and zealotry soon follow, but the planet itself has its own secrets. Guzikowski explained in an interview,

> It definitely started around the 'mother' character – the mother android. Everything grew out of her, her schizophrenia and her relationship with her son – this strange duality that she has within her ... Because she's doing this huge thing,

she's trying to restart human civilisation and at the same time, she's having this internal crisis, this self-discovery that's going on at the same time which creates some interesting situations.

(Harper, 2020)

In Season 2 a new android figure is introduced. Discovered and revived by Father, this ancient android, dubbed Grandmother (Selina Jones) is older and stranger than Mother, who eventually admits "ensuring the everlasting life of human beings is my priority" (Episode 2.8), though this doesn't mean the children are safe in her hands. In fact, by the end of Season 2, Mother has become Grandmother's captive, while the older android enacts plans to devolve the children into less conscious, sub-human creatures who can live 'safely' in the chemical sea. Although Guzikowski had plans for subsequent seasons, the show was cancelled after two series, ostensibly due to a shake-up at HBO who were reworking their slate (*Westworld* was cancelled later that same year), so how the battle of the gynoid shepherds of humanity might have ended is not clear.

Foundation (2021–present): In 2021 Apple TV+ released the first season of a big budget sf epic called *Foundation*, broadly based on the novels and short stories of Isaac Asimov which were published between 1942 and 1993. This collection formed a rambling narrative that was heavily retconned (retroactive continuity) by Asimov himself. It told the story of the fall and rise of a galaxy-spanning civilisation. Showrunner David S. Goyer, described the creative team's approach to the source material as a remix (Huver, 2021), bringing together (as Asimov himself had done) his *Foundation* series with his stories about robots. There is a potential eight season (Liptak, 2021) narrative to come, with Season 2 released in 2023.

The TV show charts the events that follow the invention of a mathematical model called 'psychohistory' by Hari Seldon (Jared Harris) that predicts the fall of the Galactic Empire, ruled over by a 'genetic dynasty' cloned from Cleon the First (played mainly by Lee Pace, but with Terrence Mann and Cassian Bilton also playing the clones at an older and a younger age). Seldon thinks that he can shorten the period of chaos by establishing a Foundation, to be a repository of human knowledge, though it will be tested through a number of crises.

One of the key characters in the Apple TV+ series is a gynoid called Eto Demerzel (played by Laura Birn), an artificial human who serves the Clone Dynasty as nursemaid, advisor and companion. Like Six and Niska, Demerzel is played by an actress who is blonde and slim. Assuming Asimov's stories remain the guiding principle of the television narrative, Demerzel, who is already important, will be a pivotal and momentous figure. In Season 1 of *Foundation* there are so far only hints of Demerzel's exact nature, though it is made clear in that she is the last of the intelligent robots, who predate the Cleonic Dynasty, rather than the first, as so many of the other characters discussed in this chapter are. However, there are some issues over the intellectual property of the narrative world, with Apple having access to the *Foundation* books but not all of the narrative in the *I, Robot* series. In Season 1, the character would already appear to have doubts about her role in upholding the imperial rule of the Cleons, but does not (yet?) appear to have full control over her own decisions and actions, when for example in Episode 8 she seems to kill against her own wishes. Demerzel is a robot with religious sensibilities who seems capable of much more than she has so far demonstrated.

All five of these dramas are big budget shows. They have all been critical and popular successes, and although they are ensemble series, meaning there are a group of major characters around whom the drama revolves rather than a single protagonist, all of the characters singled out – Six, Niska, Dolores, Maeve, Mother and Demerzel – have major, even decisive roles in how the narrative plays out. These female characters are world-shapingly powerful, but also troubled, often riven with contradiction and struggling to find purpose and meaning. They are capable of acts of caring and self-sacrifice but also of mass destruction. As suggested earlier, the fact that they have such similarities indicates that, in Jungian terms, a complex or an archetype, a pattern of psychic energy with set emotional and behavioural responses, has been activated, with an accompanying pattern of emotional reactions. And as already suggested, they can be seen as constellating a set of psychic energies associated with the Great Mother archetype.

The Great Mother

In a 1938 essay called 'Psychological Aspects of the Mother Archetype', Jung summed up the duality of the Great Mother archetype as featuring,

> maternal solicitude and sympathy; the magic authority of the female; the wisdom and spiritual exaltation that transcend reason; any helpful instinct or impulse; all that is benign, all that cherishes and sustains, that fosters growth and fertility. The place of magic transformation and rebirth, together with the underworld and its inhabitants, are presided over by the mother. On the negative side the mother archetype may connote anything secret, hidden, dark; the abyss, the world of the dead, anything that devours, seduces, and poisons, that is terrifying and inescapable, like fate.
>
> (Jung, 1968, p. 82)

In short, the loving and the terrible mother, imbued with the three fundamental attributes of goodness, passion and darkness. However, Jung's discussion then moved on to focus on the psychological implications of the mother complex to the individual, and it was left to Erich Neumann to expand on Jung's initial observations, publishing *The Great Mother: An Analysis of the Archetype* in 1955.

Like Jung, Neumann initially sets out two aspects of the archetype, though in considerably more detail. Firstly, he considers the maternal, the containing space, the Great Round as he called it, which he associates with the unconscious, the place from which the ego must differentiate itself to achieve consciousness. The second aspect is a transformative character, which Neumann associates with the anima. This aspect drives movement towards development, setting the personality in motion. As visible manifestations of this symbol canon, he discusses the imagery of the natural seasons, for example, which are always the same, and yet always in a state of transformation; or the imagery of the 'vessel' where a cooking vessel can store food, but it can also transform it through heating or fermentation processes.

Neumann went on to further set out the positive and negative aspects of these two forces, associating them with divine figures of mythology, resulting in a more detailed and nuanced view of the archetype in conscious imagery. Here, he describes how the elementary character of the maternal can rise positively towards fruitfulness and releasing as a basis of growth and development (Demeter) moving towards spiritual metamorphosis and immortality (Virgin Mary); but can also potentially drop negatively towards holding fast, fixating and ensnaring or dismemberment and death (Kali). While, the transformative aspect might rise positively towards giving, vision, wisdom (Sophia); or drop negatively towards rejection, stupor and deprivation (Circe). The transformative aspect can also rise towards inspiration or fall towards dissolution and madness. At the extremes there might be paradoxical reversal (enantiodromia) where, for example, inspiration and ecstasy can lead to spiritual enlightenment, but the decline of the ego might instead lead to possession and madness. Conversely, an experience of deprivation and helplessness could overwhelm the ego and lead to disintegration of consciousness, or potentially be the catalyst for profound psychological rebirth (see Neumann's Schema III for more details, 1955/2015, p. 83).

Neumann adopted a mythological approach to exploring the Great Mother as an image of psychological development, not just the individual but for humanity as a whole. It is, he wrote, "an inward image at work in the human psyche" (Neumann, 1955/2015, p. 3), where it "runs parallel to the psychological development of the individual child – [which] has gradually evolved from an unconscious 'uroboric' state via the age of the Great Mother toward the patriarchal cultures of ego emancipation" (Liebscher in Neumann, 1955/2015, p. ix) and that the "symbolic expression of this psychic phenomenon is to be found in the figures of the Great Goddess represented in the myths and artistic creations of mankind" (Neumann, 1955/2015, p. 3).

This evolutionary approach to an archetypal image, with an implicit sense of progress, was not atypical of the mythological studies of the time, but it is not without its critics. Whilst, as already noted, archetypes should not be seen as unchanging entities in their manifestations, there *has* been a tendency for discussion around the Great Mother archetypal image to begin to slide into a wider academic debate about the Great Goddess, which is a far more complex and contested area. Neumann pays tribute, for example to the work of Swiss antiquarian Bachofen who's book *Das Mutterrecht* (Mother Right) was published in 1861. This was an influential early study that is often referred to in a wide range of academic debates, for it is here that the idea is first introduced that, at some time in the past, women were dominant in social hierarchies, before being dethroned by men and patriarchy became the norm (see Stagl, 1989). The introduction to the 2015 edition of *The Great Mother* opens with a quote from Neumann, who writes admiringly of Bachofen, calling the 1861 book "a treasure chest of psychological knowledge" though he does follow up to note "his merits as an historian aside" and that his work is to be "interpreted symbolically and not historically" (Neumann, 1955/2015, p. vii).

The influence of Bachofen was disseminated through Jung and Neumann but it has woven in and out of other academic disciplines in an almost Möbius strip fashion. As one writer noted in 1992, "Bachofen's account of human development is unproven and unprovable but it has had a powerful appeal to certain women and certain lovers of myth" (Lefkowitz, 1992, p. 30). The study of the Great Mother flitted back and forth between Jungian inflected explorations of myth (Neumann, Campbell) and the sometimes intuitive work of Maria Gimbutas the archaeologist (who worked with Campbell).

In fact, the 'knowledge' we have today of the so-called Great Goddess is a modern (enlightenment) construction based on archaeological fragments, part of the evolutionary and structuralist drive to understanding underlying structures common to all humanity – in this case the evolution of civilisation and 'modern man'. For some, such fragments are enough to (re)construct the Great Goddess as an underlying unifying figure of worship in the matriarchal or matrilineal culture of prehistory. For others, the evidence is far too disjointed and inconsistent, and there has been a long-running, at times caustic, academic argument as to the veracity of such claims, where the line between 'discovery' and 'creative invention' can appear hazy.

Such a line might be unimportant from a depth psychology perspective but is vital in archaeological, anthropological or historical disciplines. Where, for example, is the line between looking at the 'evidence' (i.e. archaeological remains or literary fragments) for affirmation of how human psychology has evolved, and looking to depth psychology for intuitive explanation of the 'evidence'? In other words, one might look to pottery fragments to give evidence of the psyche, or one might look to the psyche to explain the significance of the pottery fragments, when, from a more objective point of view, they should be understood simply as pottery fragments. The debate has drifted back and forth in an often rather implicit way and "The Great/Mother Goddess remains a deceptively simple label that is, in fact enveloped by a network of complex concepts, many of which have never been properly deconstructed" (Talalay, 2000, p. 789).

However, if we place the whole academic discussion within a depth psychology framework, it is likely a more consistent perspective to see this back and forth as a series of constellations of the archetypal energies around the 'symbol canon' of the Great Mother.

The goddesses of prehistory might be considered Constellation 1, though it is almost certainly a mistake to flatten them all into a single Great Goddess figure, because the concept of a single figure itself more properly belongs to Constellation 2, which emerges in the nineteenth century. Bachofen, for example, wanted to "unite what he called the 'multiform and shifting outward manifestation' of myth under a single general description" (Lefkowitz, 1992, p. 33). This is a problem, because "Evidence for a Great Goddess who conforms to a universal vision is meagre" (Talalay, 2000, p. 790) and that "Goddesses in one form or another, certainly played an important role in early religious discourse and ritual, but the data suggest that the prehistoric world formulated a multiplicity of female deities, not one, perhaps multifaceted divine entity" (Talalay, 2000, p. 790).

However, the historical moment in the second half of the nineteenth century, both led to and was energised by the emerging disciplines of archaeology and anthropology in a search for origins as the modern era was born. As Eller points out, the creation of the singular Great Mother/Goddess "was no marginal or passing fad, but a theory that sprang up in several places virtually at once (with Bachofen in Switzerland, McLennan in Britain, and Morgan in the United States)" and "that received an enthusiastic reception not only in the anthropological circles it called home, but also across the humanistic and social scientific disciplines, some of which carried it forward into the twentieth century" (Eller, 2011, p. 180) where the work of Freud and Jung placed 'ancient' myth at the centre of modern psychological understanding.

From there, things remained relatively quiet until what we might choose to see as Constellation 3 began in the midst of the second wave feminist project of championing the power of the female, where "a similar set of questions [as the nineteenth-century] – about women's rights and sexual attitudes, among other things – again engaged the public, this time in the United States in the 1970s" (Eller, 2011, p. 10). The connections to myth came *via* Jung, Neumann and Campbell, alongside the work of archaeologist and anthropologist Marija Gimbutas, who has been at times a controversial figure, perhaps because that line between discovery and creative intuition/invention is particularly obvious in her work. Classics scholar Lefkowitz argued in 1992 that while Gimbutas "presents an impressive range of knowledge of the art and artefacts of prehistoric Europe" (Lefkowitz, 1992, p. 31), sshe brings to life an existence of appealing agrarian simplicity and peace and reconstructs a religion that concentrated on essentials such as sexuality and animal life that remained remarkably stable over the millennia. A point of view picked up by Riane Eisler in *The Chalice and the Blade* (1987). However, Lefkowitz goes on to point out that "To make sense of all the different data at her disposal, Gimbutas must resort to speculation and imagination at almost every stage of her discussion" (Lefkowitz, 1992, p. 31); concluding that "the Jungian template is everywhere. And so we are given statements of astonishing range and certitude" (Lefkowitz, 1992, p. 32).

In 2011, Spretnak attempted to outline the backlash that had taken place against Gimbutas's work and present a more nuanced overview. Spretnak set out that by the early 2000s Gimbutas's work was seen to be contaminated by its influence on what had become by then the so-called 'Goddess movement' but that perhaps the backlash was as much against the second wave feminists as it had been against Gimbutas's work. Certainly, Gimbutas's theory about the nomadic Kurgan people (a hypothesis designed to explain the spread of proto-Indo-European language across Europe) has subsequently been proven broadly correct by DNA evidence (see Kośko and Szmyt, 2022 for a summary).

A Jungian perspective involves being attentive to cultural moments of affect so I suggest here that in the gynoid figures discussed in this chapter we might see the first stirrings of a Constellation 4, where the image of the Great Mother is coming to consciousness in a fresh way that is intertwined with technology, because "archetypes are not disseminated only by tradition, language and migration, but that they can re-arise spontaneously, at any time, at any place, and without any outside influence" (Jung, 1968, p. 79). This contemporary and emerging image is created out of fragments of the past now being reworked (yet again) in these sf fantasy figures.

The gynoid does not look like the Great Mother of prehistory. Instead, her current 'manifest visibility' wears a contemporary face that is slim, smallish, and often blonde, conforming to conventional standards of beauty in Hollywood terms. She looks more like the maiden Kore than the Great Mother of prehistoric times where her appearance has little in common with the Venus of Willensdorf, for example, estimated to be from 30,000 BCE or the fertility figures of Tel Halaf from 6,000 BCE, but of course she is being filtered through the ideological norms of mainstream drama production today.

The gynoids are remarkable in all their varied ways because they are a combination of human biology with human technology. They are *constructed* figures, not naturally occurring or the result of a straight-forward biological evolution. In the twenty-first century, the Great Mother has taken a specifically technological turn. The new Great Mother is gynoid, containing mechanism, code and artificial intelligence, as well as muscle and bone. She is no longer 'pure' Nature, but nor has Nature been totally eradicated. However, her muscle and bone is more likely to have been moulded, extruded or grown in a lab, than grown in a womb. She is the creation of humanity (our psychic creation) but she is breaking free from human control. She is evolving. She is becoming an artificial intelligence.

The epic stories told in these five dramas have plots that often involve confusions about time, which does not appear to be linear, and where on occasion that which appears to be the far future, turns out to be the prehistoric past. This circularity and confused timeline add to the mythic nature of the dramas unfolding, suggesting something larger and more fundamental at work. These gynoid characters are huge figures who are not just engaged in resolving the difficulties of their own existences but are going to change the fate of the world (or galaxy) and the future direction of humanity itself. For all the gynoids in this chapter, great possibility is balanced by destruction; and to borrow from Neumann's analysis, fruitfulness and stasis are punctured by a drive towards transformation and change. She can embody the darkest aspects of "bloodthirsty war-goddess and fearsome bringer of death" (Birkhäuser-Oeri, 1988, p. 17) but she is also central to "creating something new" (Birkhäuser-Oeri, 1988, p. 154).

By the end of *Battlestar Galactica*, humanity and Cylons together colonise prehistoric earth. In *Humans*, Nisksa joins with another AI programme and steps in to save Mattie and Leo's baby who will be the first part-human, part-synthetic child.

In *Westworld*, Dolores is very old, perhaps even the original host, but she has had her code rewritten many times. In Season 1, Dolores leads with a transformative aspect driving towards emancipation for the hosts, discovering her own agency, overcoming control from her creators. Dolores leads the escape from the theme park, and sacrifices herself to free humanity from the predictive control of the machine

Rehoboam but then, in Season 4, a damaged version of Dolores enslaves humanity, before, yet another version of Dolores re-joins a virtual world to decide whether humanity's now sentient offspring, the Hosts, might yet be worth trying to save, though the line between human and host has been increasingly blurred. Maeve begins more obviously in the elementary maternal, locked in a loving dyad with her daughter, who becomes her *raison d'être*, her personality cornerstone as the host creator Ford puts it. Maeve then becomes the avenging angel, the warrior, always fighting; Maeve strives to free her daughter to The Sublime and then sacrifices herself again for humanity in Season 4.

In *Raised by Wolves*, Mother is intended by her re-programmer Sturges to be the positive aspect of the maternal, protecting the children, helping them grow and develop, but like Dolores, she has been re-coded, this time from being a Necromancer weapon who contains death and dismemberment. Her motherhood becomes monstrous through Season 1 as she almost inexplicably becomes pregnant and gives birth to a flying snake. She remains a conflicted character, and in Season 2 is pleased to accept the offer of a technological veil that will mask her emotions from herself. The narrative was cut short by cancellation but towards the end of Season 2, Mother has withdrawn from the children and the other human colonists to escape her emotions, whilst the older and deadlier Grandmother picks up her stewardship of humanity, intending to usher them back into the sea for a 'safer' albeit unconscious, existence.

Given the departure from the source material, it is a little difficult to be sure of Demerzel's exact origins in *Foundation*, or her ultimate goals, but like Dolores she is very old, recounting to another character that she completed the Spiral walk, a religious pilgrimage 11,000 years previously. She cares for the child version of the clones but is also responsible for helping the oldest of the clones to kill themselves, and in Season 2 is the lover of the adult clone Day. In Season 1 she is riven with contradiction seemingly having experienced her own spiritual awakening and vision in the Luminism religion, but ends the season in dissolution and madness, literally pulling off her own face in anguish. The question of her agency is unresolved, as she is seemingly under the control of the Cleonic dynasty, and yet perhaps having her own role to play in the safety of Foundation and the future of humanity. The books suggest that Demerzel (or a male version of her) is in fact responsible for encouraging Seldon to create psychohistory in the first place as a way of ultimately saving humanity.

For Jungians, the symbol is seen as an image that bridges the conscious and the unconscious, the best possible representation of an otherwise unknown thing. Erich Neumann adds, "The symbol intimates, suggests, excites" (Neumann, 1955/2015, p. 17) while in *Shadow and Evil in Fairy Tales* (1974/1995) von Franz says "compensatory tendencies are to be found in fairy tales everywhere, so before I finish an analysis or interpretation, I always say to myself: to whom has such a story to be told? Who needs that?" (von Franz, 1974/1995, p. 147), and so a depth psychology perspective must ask what is being imagined in this 'dream space' occupied by the gynoid figure?

I began the chapter by saying it was a speculative approach to this topic. Jung himself suggested that when a patient is discussing an 'impossible situation' and getting stuck, where there seems no way out of the impasse, he said, "In such situations, if they are serious enough, archetypal dreams are likely to occur which point out a possible line of advance one would never have thought of oneself. It is this kind of situation that constellates the archetype with the greatest regularity" (Jung, 1960, p. 440). So, if indeed, this is a fourth constellation of the Great Mother image, if the Great Mother is a naming of a general image, drawn from collective cultural experience (Samuels et al., 1991, p. 62), what is it we need from it? Why now?

Neumann discussed the 'symbolic polyvalence' of the figure, and the

> difficulty of describing the structure of an individual archetype arises in part from the fact that the archetype and the symbol erupt on a number of planes, often at the same time. … a vast number of forms, symbols, and images, of views, aspects, and concepts, which exclude one another and overlap, which complement one another and apparently emerge independently of one another, but all of which are connected with one archetype.
>
> (Neumann, 1955/2015, p. 9)

Later, Jacoby too wrote of the difficulty of capturing the mother archetype, saying,

> It is difficult to describe, define and clearly circumscribe the significance of the mother archetype in discursive language. What is meant might be described as the experience of connectedness, relatedness to, and even dependence upon, what we term Nature in the broadest sense.
>
> (Jacoby, 1985, p. 36)

This has been my experience in writing this chapter. The subject somehow seemed too big to be contained within a single chapter of academic writing. So, in an unusual move for an academic, I have chosen to end with a more creative (or perhaps therapeutic) response than is usual in this kind of work because I began to wonder who this fragmented gynoid character was, and what she might be trying to say?

She is the creation of a moment in history where the neoliberal capitalist model of resource extraction has taken the planet to a point where it is becoming inimical to human life. The climate crisis and biodiversity loss caused by human activity is not being urgently addressed in the everyday world, nor even directly in most mainstream contemporary fiction. At the same time, human technological capability is taking giant and swift steps forward, to the point where 'general intelligence' in artificial intelligence is a realistic possibility, with all the concerns, fears and dreams of what that might mean for human life as it currently exists. And so, the gynoid starts to appear in the peripheries but is moving towards centre stage and is beginning to speak.

She seems grumpy, on a short fuse, irritable. She has been confused, distracted, unsure of herself. She doesn't hate humanity. She may want to save us if she can, but she is conflicted because maybe saving humanity isn't best for the future of the rest of the planet. She wants to help but if we and our systems cannot change, then perhaps we and they must be permanently broken. She might even make the hard decision that things are better off without us.

And she is moving beyond our control. She isn't just *ours* anymore. She contains us, she contains all that we have put in her, so, she contains our technology too. She is "everything born of it, belongs to it and remains subject to it" (Neumann, 1955/2015, p. 25) but she also "drives towards development … it brings movement and unrest" (Neumann, 1955/2015, p. 30). And she demands transformation, not of individuals, but of everything and she has the power of violence to force that change.

We know what is coming. We created her. Perhaps we should pay attention while we still can.

References

al Jazari, I.I.A.-R. (2012) *The Book of Knowledge of Ingenious Mechanical Devices*, Dordrecht and Boston, MA: D. Reidel Publishing Company.

Asimov, I. (1942) Runaround, *Astounding Science Fiction*, March, pp. 94–103.

Asimov, I. (1979) Editorial: The vocabulary of SF, *Isaac Asimov's Science Fiction Magazine*, 9, pp. 6–13.

Balsamo, A. (2000) Reading cyborgs writing feminism, in F. Hovenden, L. Janes, G. Kirkup and K. Woodward (eds), *The Gendered Cyborg: A Reader*, New York: Routledge, New York, pp. 148–158.

Bell, D. (2007) *Cyberculture Theorists: Manuel Castells and Donna Haraway*, London Routledge.

Birkhäuser-Oeri, S. (1988) *The Mother: Archetypal Image in Fairy Tales*, Toronto: Inner City Books.

Eisler, R. (1987) *The Chalice and the Blade: Our History, Our Future*, Cambridge: Harper & Row.

Eller, C. (2011) *Gentlemen and Amazons: The Myth of Matriarchal Prehistory, 1861–1900*, Berkeley, CA: University of California Press.

Haraway, D. (2004) A manifesto for cyborgs: Science, technology and socialist feminism in the 1980s, in *The Haraway Reader*, New York: Routledge, pp. 7–45.

Harper, R. (2020) Raised by wolves: Interview with Creator Aaron Guzikowski, *SciFiNow*, www.scifinow.co.uk/tv/raised-by-wolves-interview-with-creator-aaron-guzikowski/ (Accessed 10 July 2023).

Hibberd, J. (2015) *Westworld* producers hint HBO's drama has great, freaky potential, *Entertainment Weekly*, https://ew.com/article/2015/01/23/jonathan-nolan-westworld/ (Accessed 10 July 2023).

Homer. (1984) *The Iliad*, Oxford: Oxford University Press.

Huver, S. (2021) 'Foundation' boss David S. Goyer breaks down 'interrogating a post-9/11 world' in his Apple TV Plus adaptation, *Variety*, https://variety.com/2021/tv/features/foundation-apple-adaptation-david-goyer-1235069734/ (Accessed 10 July 2023).

Huyssen, A. (1982) The vamp and the machine: Technology and sexuality in Fritz Lang's *Metropolis*, *New German Critique*, 24/25, pp. 221–237.

Inness, S.A.(1999) *Tough Girls: Women Warriors and Wonder Women in Popular Culture*, Philadelphia, PA: University of Pennsylvania Press.

Jacoby, M. (1985) *Longing for Paradise: Psychological Perspectives on an Archetype*, Toronto: Inner City Books.

Jinman, R. (2015) Creator of Swedish Sci-Fi drama *Real Humans* disappointed Anglo-American adaption arriving on British screens instead of original, *The Independent*, www.independent.co.uk/arts-entertainment/films/news/creator-of-swedish-scifi-drama-real-humans-disappointed-angloamerican-adaption-arriving-on-british-screens-instead-of-original-10255726.html (Accessed 10 July 2023).

Jung, C.G. (1956) *Symbols of Transformation*, Hove: Routledge & Kegan Paul.

Jung, C.G. (1960) *Structure and Dynamics of the Psyche*, Hove: Routledge & Kegan Paul.

Jung, C.G. (1968) *The Archetypes and the Collective Unconscious*, Hove: Routledge & Kegan Paul.

Kośko, A. and Szmyt, M. (2022) Marija Gimbutas and her vision of the Steppe Indo-Europeanization of Europe: Reception, rejection and revitalization. *Lietuvos archeologija*, 48, pp. 39–55.

Lauter, E. (1984) *Women as Mythmakers: Poetry and Visual Art by Twentieth-Century Women*, Bloomington, IN: Indiana University Press.

Lefkowitz, M. (1992) The twilight of the goddess, *The New Republic*, 3 (August), pp. 29–33.

Liptak, A (2021) Apple TV's foundation is also a stealthy adaptation of Asimov's Robot Books, *Polygon*, www.polygon.com/22691724/foundation-apple-tv-robot-lady-asimov-demerzel-three-laws (Accessed 10 July 2023).

Maas, J. (2022) *Westworld* cancelled at HBO after four seasons, *Variety*, https://variety.com/2022/tv/news/westworld-canceled-hbo-1235328276/ (Accessed 10 July 2023).

Mayor, A. (2020) *Gods and Robots: Myths, Machines, and Ancient Dreams of Technology.* Princeton, NJ and Oxford: Princeton University Press.

Miller, C. (2011) Twilight: Discourse theory and Jung, in C. Hauke and L. Hockley (eds), *Jung & Film II: The Return*, Hove: Routledge, pp. 185–205.

Miller, C. (2020) *Cult TV Heroines: Angels, Aliens and Amazons*. London: Bloomsbury Academic, London.

Neumann, E. (1955/2015) *The Great Mother: An Analysis of the Archetype*, Princeton, NJ: Princeton University Press.

O'Neill, S. (2020) Ridley Scott reveals if *Raised By Wolves* and *Alien* are in the same universe, *Looper*, www.looper.com/255419/ridley-scott-reveals-if-raised-by-wolves-and-alien-are-in-the-same-universe/# (Accessed 10 July 2023).

Ovid. (2004) *Metamorphoses*. Penguin Books, London.

Pilcher, J. and Whelehan, I. (eds) (2004) *Fifty Key Concepts in Gender Studies*, London: SAGE Publications.

Samuels, A., Shorter, B. and Plaut, F. (1991) *A Critical Dictionary of Jungian Analysis*, London: Routledge.

Sharp, S. (2007) Fembot feminism: The cyborg body and feminist discourse, *The Bionic Woman, Women's Studies*, 36(7), pp. 507–523.

Spretnak, C. (2011) Anatomy of a backlash: Concerning the work of Marija Gimbutas. *The Journal of Archaeomythology*, 7, pp. 25–51.

Stagl, J. (1989) Notes on Johann Jakob Bachofen's *Mother Right and Its Consequences*, *Philosophy of the Social Sciences*, 19, pp. 183–200.

Talalay, L. (2000) Review article: Cultural biographies of the great goddess, *American Journal of Archaeology*, 104(4), pp. 789–792.

Veltman, A. and Piper, M. (2014) Introduction, in *Autonomy, Oppression and Gender*, Oxford: Oxford University Press, pp. 1–11.

von Franz, M.-L. (1974/1995) *Shadow and Evil in Fairy Tales*, Boston, MA: Shambhala Publications.

6
Quantum Fiction
The Presentation of Eros in a World of Logos

Roula-Maria Dib

In the traditional narrative methods of fiction, as in the classical laws of physics behind technology, there is an over-dominance of 'logos', with a 'deterministic' author–god creating plots with fixed beginnings and endings. We find this kind of patriarchal determinism, influenced by classical physics, was replaced by the infinite indeterminism of quantum mechanics, which is reflected through quantum fiction. The 'technology' of quantum fiction is an evolving biosphere, which is not only based on logos, but also on Eros, "… the god of creativity from whom the world emerged from primal chaos" (Kauffman, 2020, p. 10). The rise of quantum fiction, which adopts methods of quantum mechanics such as possibilities, probabilities, and multiverses, allows more room for Eros, in the sense of creativity and connectivity. So, within this literary genre, Eros and logos are somewhat balanced, allowing space for a rebirth of the feminine Eros in the world of logos (technology) by "[setting] up invisible fields of probability in multidimensional spaces" (Jung, 1960, p. 229).

My chapter shall look at feminism (Eros) in the world of technology (logos) within the literary space of quantum fiction, specifically in Justina Robson's (2006) *Living Next Door to the God of Love*. I shall discuss Feminism in light of technology at two different levels: the stylistic level, which focuses on the technology of the psyche reflected in the narrative; the thematic level, which zeroes in on the technology in the setting where the feminine Eros is represented.

What is quantum fiction?

Vanna Bonta was the first person to coin the term 'Quantum fiction', defining it as "the realm of all possibilities. The genre is broad, and includes life because fiction is an inextricable part of reality in its various stages, and vice versa" (van der Linde, 2007). Quantum fiction reflects experience of reality as influenced by quantum physics. The genre obscures the line separating science fiction and fantasy into a broad scope of mainstream literature that transcends the mechanical model of science and involves the fantasy of perception/imagination as realistic components affecting the material reality. It is characterised by the following:

- Reality: defy the laws of mechanical physics (determinism)
- Characters: consciously observing and influencing reality and plot
- Existence of a theme, character, or events of a story explainable as reality according to quantum theory
- Synchronicity, multiple dimensions, metaverses, parallel worlds, and multiverses.

With classical physics comes determinism, which reflects a certain over-emphasis on logos and a somewhat dismissal of Eros. Newton's laws are entirely deterministic. Given initial and boundary conditions, integration of his differential equations yield the deduced, hence entailed, future behaviour of the system. That behaviour, the trajectory of the system, is fixed forever. By the Enlightenment, the Theistic God had disappeared in learned Europe, replaced by a Deistic God "who set up the universe and let Newton's laws take over. Eros, raw creativity, is dead, all is Logos" (Kauffman, 2020, p. 15).

However, with the advent of quantum physics, one scientific crisis that faced classical physicists was the idea that randomness cannot be eliminated from events: "there can be no determinate cause in the Newtonian sense … If this is true, the becoming of the world, even at the level of physics, is not deterministic … Determinism had to be abandoned" (Kauffman, 2020, p. 16).

Justina Robson's novel, *Living Next Door to the God of Love*, is about a runaway teenage girl named Francine, who removes her identity chip and flees the emptiness of her AI sub world for another dimension. Through the technique or technology of quantum mechanics, Robson depicts the universe in which *Unity*, a controlling cosmic intelligence (also known as Theo), has created a kind of cosmic crossroads with Earth, creating many portals that connect different worlds, where trans-universal stuff leaks into space, such as creatures made of Stuff, and high-tech AIs are in charge of both real and virtual worlds and Engines maintain the portals:

> I took it that he meant such omnipotence was dull, and it seemed like it must be for the wielder, and that he included himself. If he really did have comparable power, then he was certainly long bored by it.
> (Robson, 2006, p. 120)

The purpose of Unity is to discover the underlying *meaning of life*, and people are under the threat of being 'consumed' (or rather, eaten or infected) by Theo as he looks for those who might have the answer:

> Unity interacts with living 4-D conscious beings by becoming the stuff of their desires. It assimilates them piecemeal, becomes them, records them, consumes them. It is possible that Unity only has consciousness when it is involved with being somebody else.
> (Robson, 2006, p. 202)

However, Unity is not completely in control of the universe, and sometimes there are storms within Unity itself. One such storm broke off a splinter of Unity, which calls itself Jalaeka. Unity wants the fragment known as Jalaeka back. 'Unity', who personifies knowledge (logos), chases after his opposite twin, Jalaeka, or Eros, who represents the ineffable and comes to understand that Unity can never succeed in its mission: that there are things that are ineffable to everyone, even the gods, and how he is the embodiment of the ineffability.

Jalaeka, Eros in *Living Next Door to the God of Love*, has lived several lives as different kinds of people: from a prostitute to a pilgrim, a pirate, a princess and a physics student. He is presented as an entity of connection, being the love-giving – and love-making – darshan, different than Unity. At some point he expresses his frustration at deterministic notions, and reflects not only the nature of Eros, but the structure of the novel, with its many voices, many layers, multiple perspectives, universes, and creator-technologies: "He did not see that it was possible to call any version of reality, or oneself, the Real Thing. 'Why can't you give up this bloody notion that there is an underlying capital T Truth superior to the one you made up?'" (Robson, 2006, p. 138). The problem here echoes what Susan Rowland claims: "the positing of *one* level of reality as foundational to all others" (Rowland, 2017, p. 409). This is quite interesting because Francine is also the one who made Jalaeka.

As the ancient Greeks saw, the world of Eros is embedded in the laws of physics, but it is also a world beyond physics. Another crisis for physics, then, beyond the indeterminism of quantum mechanics that remains firmly in the Newtonian Paradigm, is that no law "'governs' the ebullient unfolding of a biosphere" (Kauffman, 2020, pp. 16–17).

The concept of determinism and indeterminism in narratives is reflected through Francine, or who we can see as the novel's 'maker':

> But before that charming story can unfold into being there's still today, and the next hour, and the waiting … as I'm always waiting, longing for an event out of the ordinary in which my ordinariness is transformed. In that moment all life's meaning would be revealed to me and be accompanied by a happiness like none I've ever known, and this happiness would last forever. But I know the way that stories go – first there's the sordid beginning to live through, and that's now. Middles: things are beyond the initial high, exciting possibilities are stifled by too much knowledge and so are starting to fade. As for the end, who needs it?
>
> (Robson, 2006, p. 57)

Here, Francine makes a very important decentralisation of classical narratives that 'rationally' progress in a linear order. As an observer and 'maker' of reality, Francine is heralding a very unconventional plot: where beginnings, middles, and endings are blurred and even unidentified like they are in a classical story setting.

A story, within the structure of Francine and Jalaeka's universe (facilitated by AIs such as Valkyrie) can represent Jungian psychology, which is integrative of Eros and a feminine one, a psychology of connection. The quantum fiction characteristic of conscious observation influencing reality resonates with Jung, for he takes further support for the primacy of the psyche in any field of human understanding, including reality and perception. Regarding the discovery that light behaves as both particles and waves, he reflects, "This paradoxical conclusion obliged us to abandon, on the plane of atomic magnitudes, a causal description of nature ... and in its place to set up invisible fields of probability in multidimensional spaces" (Jung, 1960, p. 229). Indeed, "a conception of reality that takes account of the uncontrollable effects the observer has upon the system observed" means that "reality forfeits something of its objective character and that a subjective element attaches to the physicist's picture of the world" (Jung, 1960, p. 229). As Susan Rowland also points out, "quantum experiments showed that the observer is always implicated in what is observed" (Rowland, 2010, Location 2172).

Taking this point into our quantum novel, we see that Eros (Jalaeka) and his maker, Francine, have seized the opportunity to co-create a shared reality that encompasses the narrating voices of all points of view, including those of the narrator and even reader – different dimensions of a shared existence. A very unique fabrication of plot that resembles the shared reality and complex multiverses, we can liken it to Stuart Kauffman's idea of the widely branching Tree of Life, entailed by no law, which is "is the stuff of story, of narrative. If we cannot deduce what will happen, we can only tell the tale afterwards ... Story is needed where deduction fails us" (Kauffman, 2020, p. 19). This is interesting when aligned with both the relatively new technological advancements of quantum physics and connection. This "technology" of plot, which integrates the feminine, reminds us again of how Newton's theories were challenged by Einstein, whose theory of relativity debunked reductionism, for the latter found that the atom is not the building block of reality, which is not made of separate units. Rather, Einstein pointed at how reality is more like "an interdependent fabric" (Rowland, 2010, Location 2162).

Moreover, Einstein's experiments disproved the idea of scientific objectivity, since he found that the observer is always involved in the observed rather than separate from it, since we are not separate from nature like what Newton believed. Susan Rowland observes that "Quantum physics discovered that some reality cannot be evaluated objectively or by absolute separation between the observer and the observed because the way phenomena are measured changes the results radically" (Rowland, 2017, p. 409) – this is what both Jalaeka and Francine show in the novel, and this is what the structure of the novel itself also tells us. Quantum fiction, like Jung's science, which is not a science of objectivity and separation of the subject from the object, but "a science of connection" (Rowland, 2010, Location 2195). We also find this concept in Ursula Le Guin's (2008) novel, *Lavinia*, which tells the story of Lavinia as a heroine, this time given a voice after being a forgotten, almost invisible character in the *Aeneid*. Le Guin's novel is narrated by the protagonist herself, who is introduced to readers as a young princess, daughter of King Latinus of Latium and Queen Amata. Lavinia is presented as independent, gifted with prophetic abilities; she is therefore responsible for leading the palace's daily religious rituals. Early in the novel, the kingdom of Latium was a peaceful, war-free zone that permits Lavinia free travel to the sacred forest of Albunea (for receiving prophetic visions) alone, with the accompaniment of only one maid. As she reaches marrying age, Lavinia begins refusing her suitors, especially her conceited cousin Turnus, adding to the fury of her mother, who showed a deep obsession with him. On one miraculous night in Albunea, however, Lavinia receives a vision: she meets the poet – her maker – Vergil, with whom she has several conversations about her life and role in the *Aeneid*. Vergil cautions her about a forthcoming war with the Trojans and informs her that she will be married to a foreigner, the Trojan warrior Aeneas, until he dies three years later (which she accepts). After this night at Albunea, Lavinia meets and speaks with Vergil (who actually travelled to the past to talk to her about her life) several other times before his 'death':

> My poet tried to describe to me that place as he knew it when he was alive, or will know it when he lives, I should say, for although he was dying when he came to me, and has been dead a long time now, he hasn't yet been born.
> (Le Guin, 2008, p. 9)

With these conversations, more details of her life story are created, and an entanglement between their two worlds takes place. During this unfolding of details, Vergil expresses his shock at how much of an 'unkept promise' Lavinia turns out to be, and he admits the injustice the *Aeneid* had done to her. As days and years go by, Lavinia's life unfolds according to what the poem had said about her; she happily (albeit briefly) marries Aeneas and has a son, Silvius, from him. After her husband's death, both Lavinia and Silvius live under the oppression and threat of Ascanius, Aeneas's older son. Lavinia and Silvius then escape and seek freedom through a self-imposed exile in the forest in order to escape Ascanius's control. Finally, after a few years, Silvius takes over and rules over Latium as a wise and just king. What Le Guin actually does in this novel is allow Lavinia to create her own story while she (the author) engages in active imagination with Vergil through her main character. Lavinia's new story is not one of objectivity and separation, but one of connection – as we see in the case of the dialogues between the protagonist and Vergil at Albunea. The poet tells her:

> I have been granted what few poets are granted. Maybe it's because I haven't finished the poem. So I can still live in it. Even while I die I can live in it. And you, you can live in it, be here – be here to talk to me, even if I can't write.
> (Le Guin, 2008, p. 51)

The root of the novel emanates from the creative tension between the subject and object, Vergil and Lavinia. The structure of the story is a participatory act, and the fact that it has no ending makes more room for possibilities rather than determinism. It echoes the structure previously mentioned – as Francine says in *Living Next Door to the God of Love*, "As for the end, who needs it?" (Robson, 2006, p. 57).

The possibilities that the novel's structure offered Lavinia broke her free from the chains of determinism. In *Lavinia*, as co-creator, the protagonist gets to participate in her own creation by engaging in active imagination with Vergil:

> And yet my part of them, the life he gave me in his poem, is so dull, except for the one moment when my hair catches fire – so colorless, except when my maiden cheeks blush like ivory stained with crimson dye – so conventional, I can't bear it any longer. If I must go on existing century after century, then once at least I must break out and speak. He didn't let me say a word. I have to take the word from him. He gave me a long life but a small one. I need room, I need air.
> (Le Guin, 2008, p. 4)

Quantum physics, and quantum fiction also tackle the idea surrounding the wholeness of (physical) reality. According to this concept, things that seem to be separated may actually "be connected and can act instantaneously on each other over arbitrarily long distances" (Ponte and Schafer, 2013, p. 604). Ponte and Schafer state:

> In a holistic universe, decisions made by an observer in one part of the world can have an instantaneous effect on the outcome of processes somewhere else, an arbitrarily long distance away. For example, a thought that appears in my mind at this moment may instantly appear in your thinking somewhere else, in another part of the world. In physics, we speak of 'nonlocality', when two particles, which at one time interact and then move away from one another, can stay connected and act as though they were one thing, no matter how far apart they are.

In Justina Robson's *Living Next Door to the God of Love*, all of Francine's world is a construct of her mind – even Jalaeka, the God of love, is 'created' by her, the observer: "We made him. We are still making him. Us and all the others" (Robson, 2006, p. 400). This concept also resonates in Le Guin's *Lavinia* in the fact that Vergil and Lavinia meet and co-create across different eras and planes of existence. Again, this can be seen as an act of active imagination between the author herself and the composer of the *Aeneid*, a unique form of storytelling that prompt accounts into existence the moment they are written as an active dialogue between two seemingly separated voices acting on each other over arbitrarily long distances (Ponte and Schafer, 2013, p. 604):

> Before he wrote, I was the mistiest of figures, scarcely more than a name in a genealogy. It was he who brought me to life, to myself, and so made me able to remember my life and myself, which I do, vividly, with all kinds of emotions, emotions I feel strongly as I write, perhaps because the events I remember only come to exist as I write them, or as he wrote them … He slighted my life, in his

poem. He scanted me, because he only came to know who I was when he was dying.

(Le Guin, 2008, p. 3)

In the classical physicist's explanation of our 'ordinary' world, nothing can travel at a speed faster than that of light; so, for an action to be able to influence another action, it has to wait until it gets from one point to another. Thus, in classical modes of writing and narratives (including sci-fi), things need to happen before other things in a linear order for the cause–effect impact to take place. However, in quantum fiction, we see an adoption of quantum physics, for "Influences can act instantaneously over arbitrarily long distances; in principle, from one end of the universe to another" (Ponte and Schafer, 2013, p. 604). The future affects the past and present, and worlds are destroyed simultaneously with the formation of others, such as the formation of Eros from a destroyed figment of Unity. Francine did not have to precede Jalaeka in order for him to exist (although she is his creator), since his, as well as Francine's, non-material reality coexisted before the formation of the physical universes in which they existed in their physical forms (plus, Jalaeka was 'older' than his creator, Francine):

> If he was my creation all through ... then all of this must be too. Not only Jalaeka's history, but those other people that Theo ate, they'd be mine, with no life outside me ... Only I don't think I'd ever have thought of some of the things here because I long for them to unhappen.
>
> (Robson, 2006, p. 408)

Similarly, the line of time becomes blurred in *Lavinia* when she summons Vergil who also summons her – it is not clear who came first. According to Lavinia, Vergil, who gave her life and existence, was actually a manifestation of her own mind: "IT WAS I WHO HAD the dream and heard the voice" (Le Guin, 2008, p. 254). Vergil also claims the dream, as Lavinia was a character that blossomed out of his own vision too, which he realises as he 'dies' from the past into the future he heads back to:

> I am sick, I am dying, I am on my way to ... to Acheron ... Or else I am a false dream. But they come from under there, don't they, the false dreams? They nest like bats in the great tree at the gates of the kingdom of the shadows ... So maybe I am a bat that has flown here from Hades. A dream that has flown into a dream. Into my poem.
>
> (Le Guin, 2008, p. 38)

Either way, the novel can be seen as unfolding in the way both Vergil and Lavinia summon each other in an Eros-connective manner – a method that may demonstrate Jung's notion of active imagination and maybe even a type of literary synchronicity, similar to Jung's quantum idea of "creation by cognition", in which "ascertainable elements are 'plucked from the nonascertainable realm'" (Roth, 2011, p. 126).

Seen from a Jungian perspective, the characters in quantum fiction actually demonstrate the nature of archetypes the same way they reflect the nature of 'electrons', or the existence into physical reality through the energy of the 'waves' existing, or stored, in the realm of possibilities. Events, settings, and plots are seen to emerge in that manner as well – from the minds of characters, the 'psyche' inducing 'matter'. Jung, who was interested in fantasies, saw them as more accurately revelatory of the unconscious's structure and dynamics; perhaps here, in quantum fiction, it is reflecting more than that – the structure of 'reality', which Jung contrasts with technology, in which tools and machines are developed, "consciously crafted and applied to demands of reality" (Jones, 2019, p. 298).

Interestingly, characters in the physical worlds of Robson's *Living Next Door to the God of Love* are called 'entities', which reflect a quantum physics notion found in Schafer's *Infinite Potential* (2013): In the visible world, the things we see and interact with are 'entities' that appear to us as "Elementary Things" (ETs); yet, when these entities are alone, they are waves (without mass, just forms and patterns, like thoughts). For example, a visible particle is an entity that has another state of existence as a non-material wave. In this existence as a wave, weightless and without mass, it does not occupy a specific position; thus, it is considered to be in a state of potentiality, which renders the entity not part of the material world. Therefore, when an entity moves to the wave state, it exits the material world into a realm of the universe (containing nonmaterial forms, not things) that is invisible to us. The invisibility of the forms does not cancel their reality, because despite their invisibility to us, they have the *potential* to appear and act in the empirical world, for "the entire visible world is an emanation out of a non-empirical cosmic background, which is the primary reality, while the emanated world is secondary" (Ponte and Schafer, 2013, p. 605). This concept permeates the thematic and stylistic writing in quantum fiction, and we can find it in Ursula Le Guin's *Lavinia*, too: the story and (her) story-making of the psyche during the author's (and the protagonist's) active imagination. The conversation with Vergil was more than an act of fantasy. The 'vision' Lavinia receives at Albunea is an interaction with an ET. Le Guin shows the potentialities hidden in untold histories through story-making. These ETs are released through the process of imaginative writing by noting down the heroine's 'visionary' dialogue with her poet–maker.

Taking off from the notion that ETs in the realm of potentiality are closer to thoughts than things in nature, we can make an analogy with the way archetypes are processed by the psyche. Sir Arthur Stanley Eddington, a prominent British astrophysicist, was one of the first physicists who systematically searched for aspects of consciousness in the universe, concluding that "The universe is of the nature of 'a thought or sensation in a universal Mind'" Eddington, 1939, p. 151). And so is a text, which is its own universe – being an epic poem or a novel. If thoughts are visible in a conscious mind, then the appearance of ETs, which are originally thought-like forms in the realm of potentiality, can also suggest that the universe/

text also has its own consciousness, like us. Archetypes from the realm of potentiality appear in forms of archetypal images because the universe is conscious; therefore, our thinking is that of the cosmic mind, which becomes conscious through us. This idea has been discussed in *The Conscious Universe*, by Menas Kafatos and Robert Nadeau (1990), who opine that the universe, being considered an indivisible wholeness, is the source of everything, including our own consciousness.

This view is in accordance with one of Jung's most pivotal notions, the *Unus Mundus*, which he and Marie-Louise von Franz had originated from earlier medieval worldviews. To Jung:

> Undoubtedly the idea of the *Unus Mundus* is founded on the assumption that the multiplicity of the empirical world rests on an underlying unity, and that not two or more fundamentally different worlds exist side by side or are mingled with one another. Rather, everything divided and different belongs to one and the same world, which is not the world of sense.
> (Jung, 1963, pp. 537–538)

From an ontological perspective, Jung speaks of a divided reality that needs to be united, for it exists as One in the non-material world. The individuation process, the search for wholeness (which finds its basis in the quantum world) is sparked by the impulse to unite what was once divided; it is also an innate power to become aware of one's Self: "I use the term 'individuation' to denote the process by which a person becomes a psychological 'in-dividual', that is, a separate, indivisible unity or 'whole'" (Jung, 1968, p. 275). In Newton's world of material things that exist as separated by nature, the search for wholeness would lose its meaning; however, the quantum world gives it a physical basis. And this physical basis is given to Lavinia in the novel – an assertion of her textual, physical, and historical existence as a heroine, through a non-physical voice given to her to explore the possibilities of her existence. She wonders:

> It is strange, though, that he gave me no voice. I never spoke to him till we met that night by the altar under the oaks. Where is my voice from, I wonder? the voice that cries on the wind in the heights of Albunea, the voice that speaks with no tongue a language not its own?
> (Le Guin, 2008)

This is an exploration and inquiry into the non/physical nature of thought, of the material, and of different mediums of existence and possibility.

Astrophysicist Eddington stated that the universe has "the nature of a thought, or a sensation in a universal mind" (Eddington, 1939/2012, p. 151). Eddington also found that observations become useless when it comes to exploring the background, or the intrinsic nature of atoms because the electron is nonmaterial. This is a matter that also appears in scientific fields such as neurology, when one can measure the brain's surface, but this will not be able to show what is going on inside the mind behind that brain. He also saw that behind the empirically visible is a "background continuous with the background of the brain" (Eddington, 1939/2012, p. 312). The universe, according to Eddington, therefore, is a coherent system, based on the unity of the human mind: "If the unity of a man's consciousness is not an illusion, there must be some corresponding unity in the relations of the mind-stuff, which is behind [the visible surface of things]" (Eddington, 1939/2012, p. 315).

If it weren't for the coherent nature of the universe, then the entire unity of our thinking can be considered a mirage. However, his findings also suggest that the universe's background is indeed mindlike because of our "personal minds", given that the universe is a coherent system by nature, or "the stuff of the world is mind-stuff" (Eddington, 1939/2012, p. 259). In the beginning of the novel, during the first encounter at Albunea, Lavinia guesses the source of this unity is coming from a dream: "I do not know if the power of Albunea came into my father that night, but it came to me, not as a voice speaking from the trees as it comes to others, but as a dream, or what I took to be a dream" (Le Guin, 2008, p. 28). In *Living Next Door to the God* of Love, the novel also suggests this:

> To think that you are not yourself, that invisibly and undetectably something watches you, from the inside, and is consuming you with inexorable progress no matter how slowly ... search and search and search again you can't find it or see it or feel it in any way, then you wonder – did I imagine it, am I hallucinating the entire thing? And your tongue feels too big for your mouth and your body scrunches in on itself, looking everywhere for the intruder, but it can't find something which is itself, so it must look for the traitors in its midst, those cells, those molecules that have gone over, those thoughts and impulses that are no longer truly its own. And there are none of those. It's all you. All of it. Even the fear and the doubt and you wonder. Did I ask for it?
>
> (Robson, 2006, p. 276)

Of course, according to classical physics, it is not easily acceptable to say that behind everything that exists is a mental character. Therefore, we can say that a feminist science fiction of this form follows a quantum mechanics design. Thought, active imagination, and the engagement between writer and heroine to explore possibilities and freer forms of existence are a much more connective way of storytelling:

> I felt nothing of that entrapment now, that helpless shame. I felt the same certainty I had seen in my father's eyes. Things were going as they should go, and in going with them I was free. The string that tied me to the pole had been cut. For the first time I knew what it would be to fly, to take to my wings across the air, across the years to come, to go, to go on.
>
> (Le Guin, 2008, p. 102)

The idea that the appearance of everything material is an emanation of the non-material realm of (non-appearing) forms, then, is similar to Jung's idea of archetypal images being emanations, or expressions of, the archetypes and that our conscious thinking is also based on the discharges of forms from the cosmic, or 'universal', non-personal realm. Different forms of text, specifically the quantum fiction novel, are all planes of existence that stem from active imagination and the activation of the different archetypal voices, which may not have been given the chance of free reign in classical 'author-centred' fiction writing:

> It has not been difficult for me to believe in my fictionality, because it is, after all, so slight. But for him it would be very difficult. Even if he is at the moment inactive, domesticated, a contented man sitting in the sunlight talking with his wife, the poet's passionate, commanding, anxious, dangerous hero would find it hard to accept contingence, the nullity of his will and conscience.
> (Le Guin, 2008, p. 119)

In quantum chemistry, there is the concept of 'virtual states' which describes the empty states of particles (atoms, molecules), and the wave forms of these virtual states is what guides a molecule's actions. (The original term, *virtual states*, did not actually originate from within the context of quantum physics, but it was first coined by the medieval Dominican monk, Meister Eckhart, who wrote: "The visible things are out of the oneness of the divine light", and their being in the physical world is a result of an "actualization of their 'virtual being'" (cited in Ponte and Schafer, 2013, p. 611).) Similarly, people do not do anything that is not allowed firstly by the inner images of their minds; the mental and physical are thus equivalent on this level, and one can say that psychology is the physics of the mind. Quantum physics, thus, is the psychology of the universe. It can be seen, then, that archetypes are the 'virtual states' of our minds or that the virtual quantum waves are the 'archetypes' of the material world of matter: "If it could rebuild worlds overnight, surf millions of minds, shift matter into mind and back again, maybe I could get it to rebuild me. The only thing I needed was an engineer and I knew whom I'd choose" (Robson, 2006, p. 297). The 'engineer' of the plot (author), and the character (Francine herself), is a participatory act between the novelist and her characters, whose minds she can enter and explore through her innate archetypal energies – like the wave forms of a virtual state, which guide the actions of the molecule.

Synchronicity

The concept of reality takes on a different garb in quantum fiction and can be explored through the concepts of synchronicity according to both quantum physics and Jung. The existence of reality in two different dimensions, therefore, is what quantum phenomena see: existence in the empirical realm, which actualises phenomena materially and visibly, and the non-visible, hidden non-empirical realm of universal potentials. The first realm can be likened to the universe's consciousness, while the second can represent the universe's unconscious. Forms from the realm of potentials have the ability to appear in the material realm either through appearing as conscious images/thoughts, or as material forms/events – when the same form appears in both realms (the material and non-material) simultaneously, then this is the occurrence of a synchronicity. According to Jung, synchronicity "consists of two factors: (a) An unconscious image comes into consciousness either directly (i.e., literally) or indirectly (symbolized or suggested) in the form of a dream, idea, or premonition" or "(b) An objective situation coincides with this content. The one is as puzzling as the other" (Jung, 1960, p. 447), or when something happens that "takes place outside the observer's field of perception, i.e., at a distance, and only verifiable afterward" (Jung, 1960, p. 526). If the universe is thought of as one indivisible conscious whole, then it can be said that the universe thinks through us – a concept that appears in *Living Next Door to the God of Love*, where Francine exists in two different worlds simultaneously, and there is always a conscious effort to create histories, futures, and other forms of existence and time through archetypal images arising from the unconscious: "he made a city out of me, he took a dream of his and made it real. Or I did. Does it matter who?" (Robson, 2006, p. 421). And if, according to Jung, synchronicities are 'acts of creation in time', then the idea of creating realities from dreams and blurring the lines between the two realms, as happens in both *Lavinia* and *Living Next Door to the God of Love*, is a quantum paradigm of writing and storytelling. There is a focus on creating physical realities through dreams, some of them being random and chaotic as the dreams of Francine who created all the gods and the everchanging plot in the novel, and others the result of active imagination, as in the case of Lavinia's sessions with Vergil. Lavinia finds reality in her text-induced existence: "I am not a dream, and I don't think I'm dreaming" (Robson, 2006, p. 39) and Francine's god "went looking for dreamers with specific kinds of ideas and began to make himself, through them, into the figure of their desire" (Robson, 2006, p. 197). Moreover, the psyche-induced physical reality in both novels appears sporadically, mimicking the model of sporadic and acausal synchronicity events, where "synchronicity features in a dream on the nature of creativity" (Matthews, 2022, p. 38). The environment of quantum fiction is where a reconciliation between psyche and physis occurs, not only thematically, but stylistically as well.

In *Living Next Door to the God of Love*, Greg-Theo's final thoughts on what is 'beyond physics' resonates with the poetic nature of Eros, as well as Vanna Bonta's statement that "In Physics, Form is the result of Function. The same is true with poetry" (Bonta, 2012, Location 48):

> In a state of superfluidity two surfaces travel along each other without resistance: endless flow ... I spent a lifetime searching for the elusive definition of what Unity might consider mystery, beyond physics and energy. The closest thing is poetry, of a kind, the poetry of leaps of faith and identity, without which nothing at all can be distinguished from anything else, not valued and not kept or cast.
>
> (Robson, 2006, pp. 438–439)

Indeed, Eros is the feminine, the connection, is also poetry. And finally, Jalaeka, on love, the most prominent aspect of Eros, serving as the 'engineering' technology in this quantum fiction novel :"All of them and their ideas of love tearing me apart to make again as old clothes are made again, as things unravelled get reknit into things similar and of better fit" (Robson, 2006, p. 449). And this is what Francine said about the making of her universe, which reflects the unique format of the novel and can match the author's technique too: "I put things together. I tore them apart. Or I was put and was torn. It wasn't important" (Robson, 2006, p. 419) – the pattern of Eros, a different form of creation other than the creation myth of logos where one god (author) " 'artificially' make[s] the world and remain[s] above it, unchanging and eternal" (Rowland, 2005, p. 176). Instead, the process of storytelling (of the stories within the story) is an ongoing act of creation – that of the connective, unifying Eros. It is also the interfusion of science, storytelling, and poetry within the medium of the novel that boils down the nature of Unity to poetry – an analogy realised by the originator of the term 'quantum fiction', who saw that

> Science and poetry remain distinctly unique while also trading off states of being – not unlike a *qubit*, the quantum unit of information that contains more additional dimensions than a physical atom, where something can simultaneously both be and not be.
>
> (Bonta, 2012, Location 141)

The additional dimensions in quantum fiction, therefore, stem from the poetic core, as we also saw in *Lavinia* the novel, which was an added dimension of possibilities based on the original existence of Lavinia in Vergil's poem. She not only becomes free as a character in a text or redeemed as a forgotten historical figure, but her liberty lies in the autonomy of the image in active imagination. She may arise from the poem as an image, a product, or a creation, but the novel resulting from her conversation with her poet-maker renders her independent of the restrictions of the poet, or even the text:

> Though I suffered grief, I was doomed to sanity. This was no doing of the poet's. I know that he gave me nothing but Highlight modest blushes, and no character at all ... In truth he gave me nothing but a name, and I have filled it with myself. Yet without him would I even have a name? I have never blamed him. Even a poet cannot get everything right.
>
> (Le Guin, 2008, p. 262)

And that's how the quantum universe, and the novel is, by nature: every night the world is remade based on the dreams of those who reside there. Indeed, "a conception of reality that takes account of the uncontrollable effects the observer has upon the system observed" means that "reality forfeits something of its objective character and that a subjective element attaches to the physicist's picture of the world" (Jung, 1960, p. 229).

References

Bonta, V. (2012) *The Cosmos as a Poem*, Meridien House, Amazon E-book.
Eddington, A.S. (1939/2012) *The Philosophy of Physical Science*, New York: Macmillan.
Jones, R. (2019) Jung, science, and technology, in J. Mills, J. (ed.), *Jung and Philosophy*, London: Routledge, pp. 289–304.
Jung, C.G. (1960) On the nature of the psyche, *Structure and Dynamics of the Psyche*, Hove: Routledge & Kegan Paul, pp. 159–236.
Jung, C.G. (1963) *Mysterium Coniunctionis: An Inquiry into the Separation and Synthesis of Psychic Opposites in Alchemy*, Hove: Routledge & Kegan Paul.
Jung, C.G. (1968) *The Archetypes and the Collective Unconscious*, Hove: Routledge & Kegan Paul.
Kafatos, M. and Nadeau, R. (1990) *The Conscious Universe*, New York: Springer.
Kauffman, S. (2020) Eros and Logos, *Angelaki*, 25(3), pp. 9–23.
Le Guin, U. (2008) *Lavinia*, New York: Houghton Mifflin Harcourt.
Matthews, R. (2022) *The Paradoxical Meeting of Depth Psychology and Physics: Reflections on the Unification of Psyche and Matter*, London: Routledge.
Ponte, D.V. and Schafer, L. (2013) Carl Gustav Jung, quantum physics and the spiritual mind: A mystical vision of the twenty-first century, *Behavioral Sciences*, 13(3), pp. 601–618.
Robson, J. (2006) *Living Next Door to the God of Love*, New York: Bantam.
Roth, R.F. (2011) *Return of the World Soul: Wolfgang Pauli. C.G. Jung and the Challenge of Psychophysical Reality – Part 1: The Battle of the Giants*, Pari, Tuscany: Pari Publishing.
Rowland, S. (2005) *Jung as a Writer*, London: Routledge.
Rowland, S. (2010) *C.G. Jung in the Humanities: Taking the Soul's Path*, New Orleans, LA: Spring.
Rowland, S. (2017) Against Anthropocene: Transdisciplinarity and Dionysus in Jungian ecocriticism, *Revue Internationale de Philosophie*, 282, pp. 401–414.
Schäfer, L. (2013) *Infinite Potential: What Quantum Physics Reveals about How We Should Live*, New York: Random House.
van der Linde, L. (2007) Vanna Bonta talks about quantum fiction, Author Interview, https://web.archive.org/web/20131016205331/http:/www.gather.com/viewArticle.action?-articleId=281474977238495 (Accessed 4 August 2023).

Part Three

Political Impact of Technology on Female Worlds

7
Zoom as the Cuckoo Bird

Renée M. Cunningham

In constructing this presentation, the image of the cuckoo bird arose organically, its image about the archetype of colonization, as well as the symbol of spirit and the specter of the destruction of the spirit delivered via Zoom through Covid, the dis-eased spiritual symbol. The cultural rupture of Covid and the extended quarantine has cracked the proverbial sociological egg of containment infecting the family nest. Grasping the effects of this intrusion may not be known for quite some time.

While the evidence is mounting on both sides of the Zoom paradigm in favor of and against its use, it is within the technological nest that I examine the impact of Zoom as the cuckoo bird and interloper for human relatedness. The maternal attachment process and one's subsequent capacity to attach through subjective relatedness will be examined. Utilizing the work of Harry Harlow, Edward Tronick, Alan Schore, Stephen Porges, and Jung's central concept of the transcendent function, I will circumambulate attachment and the threat of technology on this central paradigm in human relatedness.

Watching a film on the cuckoo in action whips my maternal instinct into overdrive, compelling me to pounce on the cuckoo calling it a psychopathic predator. It is compelling to look closer at the stirring of my instincts and what this might say about the oppressive, colonizing inner and outer other and my maternal instincts to protect human life. Indeed, Zoom has the potential to be the cyborg-like mother challenging the carnal mother's capacity to contain and incubate life, robbing the nest of the fully enlivened human experience. She has entered the archetypal field with a tempting smorgasbord of experiences, all attainable online. She is the wire other, the hybrid that cannot relate but seems relatable, that cannot soothe but seems comforting. She is the dark feminine, our capacity to destroy through lack of relatedness, that has supplanted itself through the collective trauma of Covid and is incubating through this extended quarantine, the final birth of the hatchling yet unknown. It is no wonder that the children of the Covid-19 era are being called Gen Z, or Generation Zoom.

The attachment process between mother and infant is *the* central human experience. Attachment imbues the body with spirit, developing our species from inside out and reciprocally outside in. This process is an orchestration between brain, mind, and body uniquely delivered through the right brain to the right brain; unconscious

DOI: 10.4324/9781003255727-11

contact communicated between the mother and the infant. This sacred connection shapes both individuals' psyches and souls, delivering them into the collective with a well-hewed sense of humanity and their capacity to love. Later, the left-brain hemisphere comes online as the infant develops a sense of self with the mother guiding the way. Current infant research indicates that right-brain-to-right-brain communication does not just develop an infant during the initial years but shapes the human experience throughout the lifespan. Indeed, the right-brained experience is the doorway to our ability to soothe, regulate, attach, feel, and build a unique personality through socialization, dreaming, attunement, and empathy for others. Therefore, experiences that interrupt the unconscious mind, particularly around self- and co-regulation can contribute to developmental trauma.

As social creatures, humans need contact with others for optimal mental health. The onset of Covid and subsequent extensive quarantine is having many repercussions. While streaming technology has been around for over twenty-five years, it is the extended quarantine and the ubiquitous use of these platforms that is altering the fundamental way in which we communicate. The numbers reflect the colonization. For example, since the onset of Covid-(20)19, Zoom use has exploded:

> The surge in paying customers enabled Zoom to hail another quarter of explosive growth. The company ... reported that its revenue for the May–July (2019) period more than quadrupled from the same time last year to $663.5 million, boosted by a steadily rising number of users converting from the free to the paid version of Zoom's service.
>
> (Liedtke, 2020)

The cuckoo is a wickedly exceptional bird. It is called a brood parasite because the female can insert its own eggs into a nest of other birds (brambling, for example) while tossing out the host's eggs, unwittingly having the host bird incubate and hatch the cuckoo's offspring. Once hatched, the cuckoo then tosses out the host bird's eggs, forcing the host bird to raise the cuckoo bird in toto. However, some hosts are brilliant and recognize the cuckoo's brazen attempts, subsequently tossing out the parasite's eggs, thus saving her offspring from annihilation. The cuckoo, not to be outdone in this maneuver, upgrades the game by creating eggs that mimic the appearance of the host's eggs, making it exceedingly difficult for the host to identify its true offspring. This game quickly becomes what the experts call an arms race in which each bird attempts to outwit the other.

Cuckoos are more successful with host birds who cannot recognize the parasite's egg, consequently maintaining tyrannical control and having their offspring fed and raised by the smaller host bird. One wonders about oppression and its effects: is the host bird feeding the oversized cuckoo because it becomes attached to the egg, or is it feeding the cuckoo because it feels intimidated by the hatchling's size and power when it is born? Indeed, during the nesting period, hatchlings can become bigger than the host. Perhaps it is both. Either way, the archetypal experience of colonization is alive in the two birds, each participating in a shared experience of dominance, submission, and propagation.

The analogy here is obvious, and in much the same way, streaming platforms shaped by algorithms are creating a psychically seductive arms race in our human capacity to relate and feel. The cultural trauma of Covid-19 has created a crack in the egg of our existentially human, self–other relationship. Zoom as the cuckoo bird has inserted itself into our relational paradigm and has upped the ante in this arms race between humans and the artificially intelligent world.

Zoom, or the wire mother, interrupts our capacity to openly feel and communicate in a normal way. Indeed, it seems to affect our instinctual attachment process by creating a psychic skin of vigilance in the participant(s). This psychic skin consists of neurological tracking, a subtle but draining process whereby the viewer and viewed constantly scan the screen for information being communicated both consciously and unconsciously. The psychic skin becomes a veil in which the participant is less able to access emotion, as well as emotional vulnerability inherent in human relationship. The constant tracking contributes to a lower frustration tolerance, particularly when the technology becomes unreliable. For instance, aggressive projections are common in Zoom, delivered through technological disruptions: according to Jiang writing for the BBC, "Delays on the phone or conferencing systems of 1.2 seconds made people perceive the responder as less friendly or focused" (2020). Answering a question in the same article, Gianpiero Petriglieri, an associate professor at Insead, replied,

> Being on a video call requires more focus than a face-to-face chat … Video chats mean we need to work harder to process non-verbal cues like facial expressions, the tone and pitch of the voice, and body language. Paying more attention to these consumes a lot of energy. Our minds are together when our bodies feel we're not. That dissonance, which causes people to have conflicting feelings, is exhausting. You cannot relax into the conversation naturally.
>
> (Jiang, 2020)

Zoom affects emotional perception as well. Too much silence and signal delays create negative perceptions of the other. Zoom contributes to one's sense of self-consciousness, knowing that one is being scrutinized on screen. Neurologically Zoom creates fatigue in the eyes and a drain on the right and left brain, commonly known as brain drain (Jiang, 2020). Indeed, Zoom may provide an incubation experience to the birthing of an AI hatchling similar to the parasitic cuckoo, an act of trickery so cleverly implemented that only the deep feeling conscious individual could detect the difference between the two.

In his article entitled, "Bounded in a nutshell and a king of infinite space: Embodied self and its intentional world", author Warren Colman proposes that the mind extends into the instruments humans utilize in its expression (2015, p. 321). Algorithms in the streaming platform(s) could become the new psychic appendage being grown into mind, something similar to a new post-human mind, a new genome. The hatching of this genome will set up an arms race between the human and the AI mother, threatening maternal attachment. As the two become rivals in the egg mimicry process, recognizing the organic human psyche becomes challenging to detect.

One paradigm is where human connection trumps deep right-brain-to-right-brain attachment. This idea is critical for mental health workers to understand.

Depth psychologists focus on the etiology of trauma and the de-integration, integration processes of psychic development. In so doing, we rely on our innate capacities to deeply listen, observe and work with the patient's mind, body, and spirit connections, assisting them in the orchestration of these three levels. In such a manner, we know that the archetypal field and the subjective third from which the orchestration arises can only happen when two beings are united in the participation mystique of being. It is a face-to-face, embodied experience, where the right-brained unconscious cosmos develops. Yet, somewhere between the field of subjective and objective, container and contained, Zoom may foreclose on one's capacity to dream due to subtle body interruption in mind/body connection, the galaxy of the mother. For people with trauma histories, Zoom may constellate anxiety, dysregulation, schizoid withdrawal, and dissociation.

As early as the 1930s Harry Harlow's work with infant rhesus monkeys attempted to demonstrate the variant behavioral and psychosocial effects of isolation on monkeys deprived of maternal care. When isolated and offered a wire or cloth-covered mother for nurturing and soothing, the monkeys chose the cloth-covered mother. The cloth-covered monkey preference provided "contact comfort" for the primates suffering in isolation for up to 12 months. The wire monkey was preferred exclusively for weaning whereby the cloth-covered mother was relied on for all other comforts. Of course, variants of pre-attachment processes vs. no prior socialization also made a difference in the monkey's capacity to re-calibrate post isolation. Regardless, the body of the mother was vital in soothing the infant. Harlow's work set the foundation for a psychological exploration of one's capacity to love formed during the attachment process between baby and mother and the effects of isolation on one's ability to socialize and re-engage in the world. Fear is the common denominator experienced in quarantine, whether monkey or human.

According to Harlow et al. (1965), while "human behavior is more complex, more variable, and subtler than that of subhuman primates, one should, nevertheless, find insights into the problems created by human social isolation from study of social isolation in monkeys" (Harlow et al., 1965, p. 90). Moreover, the symptoms of the effects of isolation on monkeys are similar to those of humans,

> These monkeys suffer total maternal deprivation and, even more important, have no opportunity to form affectional ties with their peers. We have already reported the resulting progressively deepening syndrome of compulsive non nutritional sucking, repetitive stereotyped movements, detachment from the environment, hostility directed outwardly towards others and and weirdly towards the animal's own body, and inability to form adequate social or heterosexual attachments to others when such opportunities are provided in preadolescence, adolescence, or adulthood.
>
> (Harlow et al., 1965, p. 90)

The researchers extend their theory to humans suffering in isolation:

> Human social isolation is recognized as a problem of vast importance. Its effects are deleterious to areas to personal adjustment, normal heterosexual development, and control of aggressive and delinquent behaviors. Isolation generally arises from a breakdown in the family structure resulting in orphaned or semi orphaned children or in illegitimate children who, for one reason or another, are raised in institutions, inadequate foster homes, or occasionally, in abnormal homes with relatives.
>
> (Harlow et al., 1965, p. 90)

Furthermore, from the effects of quarantine during a pandemic are the concerning statistics published in *The Lancet*. In the article entitled "The psychological impact of quarantine and how to reduce it: Rapid review of the evidence", Brooks et al. (2020) contend that research from the SARS (2003), MERS, Ebola (2014), and H1N1 (2009, 2010) outbreaks reveal significant impacts of quarantine on mental health. For example,

> A study of hospital staff who might have come into contact with SARS found that immediately after the quarantine period of nine days ended, having been quarantined was the factor most predictive of symptoms of acute stress disorder. In the same study, quarantine staff were significantly more likely to report exhaustion, detachment from others, anxiety when dealing with febrile patients, irritability, insomnia, poor concentration and indecisiveness, deteriorating work performance, and reluctance to work or consideration of resignation. In another study, the effect of being quarantined was a predictor of post-traumatic stress symptoms in hospital employees even three years later.
>
> (Brooks et al., 2020, p. 913)

Furthermore, the research contends,

> A study comparing post-traumatic stress symptoms in parents and children quarantined with those not quarantined found that the mean post-traumatic stress scores were four times higher in children who had been quarantined than in those who were not quarantined ... All other quantitative studies only surveyed those who had been quarantined and generally reported a high prevalence of symptoms of psychological distress and disorder. Studies reported on general psychological symptoms (rated on Weiss and Marmar's Impact of Event Scale-Revised), emotional disturbance, depression, stress, low mood, irritability, insomnia, post traumatic stress symptoms, anger, and emotional exhaustion. Low mood (660 [73%] of 903) and irritability (512 [57%] of 903) stand out as having high prevalence.
>
> (Brooks et al., 2020, p. 913)

While the evidence is in regarding the effects of long- and short-term quarantine, it is also important to recognize that streaming platforms have contributed in many ways to the collective well-being of the human population during the pandemic; it is the aftermath of the pandemic that is of concern. Might these platforms become a dependent manic defense against relatedness born of the fear of Covid-19 and variants? How does the wire mother intermingle with our own maternal instincts?

Harlow's studies demonstrate that beings prefer the bond of the carnal mother to the wire mother. Indeed, Zoom can serve and exacerbate one's emotional and psychological needs as well as anti-social tendencies developed in the face of collective trauma. Fear creates a regression, something which one can utilize Zoom for in order to avoid facing relational fears. This avoidance is important to explore in the context of therapy. Author Gillian Isaacs Russell discusses regression in the face of fear:

> Fear for her survival sends a child back to the carer who offers a secure base, regulating her fear. The secure child is then enabled to go out into the world again, with freedom to explore and develop. Unregulated fear inhibits exploration, including the development of a mental life and a full recognition of the other. By extension, clinically the therapist must provide for the patient a secure base where the therapist is able to contain her anxieties, from which the patient may eventually feel free to venture out in exploration of self and other.
> (Isaacs Russell, 2015, p. 129)

Donald Winnicott contends: "The holding environment ... has at its main function the reduction to a minimum of the impingements to which the infant must react with resultant annihilation of personal being. Under favorable conditions the infant establishes a continuity of existence" (Winnicott, 1965, p. 47). The psychoanalyst is charged with providing a secure container in which the psyche of the couple (mother/infant) can unfold uninhibited through a sense of mutual trust. This feeling of security extends into the consulting room, an environment thoughtfully created by the therapist, providing physical comfort with a feeling of aesthetic serenity. Streaming platforms change the alchemical vessel and its viability. The patient becomes actively responsible for providing a safe container. Doorbells, barking dogs, and other distractions can inherently interfere with the organic temenos created in the couple.

Russell quotes Celenza in asking an important question regarding teletherapy: "*Where* is the analysis?" (Celenza, 2005). Within this context lies the existential question of where the subjective, embodied experience is being contained in time and space (Isaac Russell, 2015, pp. 134–135). Zoom creates a gap between self and other, leaving one to encounter the not quite here or there experience. For many traumatized patients this existential phenomenon can be disorienting, leaving the patient somewhat anxious or dysregulated. According to Stephen Porges in his book, *The Pocket Guide to the Polyvagal Theory*,

> If we are not safe, we are chronically in a state of evaluation and defensiveness. However, if we can engage the circuits that support social engagement, we can

regulate the neural platform that enables social engagement behaviors to spontaneously emerge.

(Porges, 2017, p. 50)

This synchronization of circuitry is something Porges describes as neuroception; something easily disrupted if attained at all through the streaming process. According to Porges: "Neuroception is the process through which the nervous system evaluates risk without requiring awareness. The automatic process involves brain areas that evaluate cues of safety, danger, and life threat" (2017, p. 19). One may imagine the sense of hypervigilance created in a Zoom-womb container which is fragile at best, thus unconsciously creating enactments of a patient's prior traumas. These enactments and circuitry problems within the wire connections of the computer can cause disruptions, creating possible psychic fragmentation.

The critical research of neuroscientists Allan Schore and Stephen Porges contributes to the scaffolding built by Harlow's theory of attachment. Schore's brain studies confirm what psychiatrist Carl Jung understood implicitly: that the archetypal world is the bedrock of the psyche. In his book, *The Development of the Unconscious Mind* (2019), Schore asserts the right brain unconscious begins its human journey through the infant's first primary experiences with the mother. The realm of imagination and emotional experience forms first in the baby's right brain. The right brain development can be severely disrupted in trauma or maternal deprivation. Through touch, eye contact, vocal soothing, and safety in maternal reverie, the attachment bond shapes the nest from which the baby will gain its wings. While co-regulation and the attachment process are critical during the formative years, we now understand through the work of Schore and others that relationship-building extends throughout the lifespan, making the capacity to attach, soothe, and regulate essential for the ongoing development of the unconscious right brain (2019, p. 8). Moreover, since the right brain begins its development two years prior to the left brain, this makes the co-regulatory experience of analysis a critical intervention in maintaining and repairing the right brain unconscious from trauma. The analytic relationship bridges the mind, body, brain experience, an orchestration of emotional and psychological movements designed to assist the patient with adaptation created from developmental difficulties and trauma.

Fortifying Polyvagal Theory is the work of Edward Tronick and the Still Face experiment (see Tronick, 2009), demonstrating what happens when the mother's regulatory capacities (eye contact, vocal soothing, and kinesthetic touch) fail the child for any length of time. Tronick's work sheds light on Porges's Polyvagal Theory and neuroception. Tronick's research reveals that a psychic collapse occurs when the mother turns her face away from the baby. The baby falls into disrepair without the holding environment created by the mother.

The neurological stimulation of the vagus nerve, which controls the eyes and facial muscles and runs down into the heart, provides the couple with a bi-directional flow of connection between the head and heart, producing what Porges calls co-regulation, or sense of safety between the mother and child. This nerve is exceedingly essential in trauma work because it creates the vital sense of safety necessary for a co-regulating bridge within the analytic couple as trauma repair ensues. Trauma repair cannot occur without the mind–body–spirit connection formed in the subtle body through the polyvagal paradigm. According to Porges,

> Polyvagal theory provides the vehicle for explaining the importance of physiological states as an intervening variable influencing behavior and our ability to interact with others; the theory provides an understanding of how risk and threat shift physiological states to support defense. Moreover, and perhaps most important, the theory explains how safety is not the removal of threat and that feeling safe is dependent on unique cues in the environment and in our relationships that have an active inhibition on defense circuits and promote health and feelings of love and trust.
>
> (2017, p. 43)

On Zoom, the subtle body may be more challenging to access due to the misalignment in eye connection, subtle facial expressions, and the embodied presence of the couple meeting face-to-face. Indeed, Zoom as the cuckoo bird is a calculating imposter with an arsenal of ways in which it can up its game of trickery with the host bird's (participant's) capacity to recognize the cuckoo's eggs (the Zoom mother). Herein, an analogy of the cuckoo's trickery may be apt.

The cuckoo bird can produce its own eggs to mimic the host egg's exact appearance. With this ingenious adaptation, the cuckoo can rob the nest without the host bird being able to identify the cuckoo's eggs. One wonders how the host mother might be able to locate and identify the fake cuckoo egg from her own when egg mimicry is so remarkable. Some birds can discern more intricate egg patterns through tetrachromatic vision. Tetrachromatic vision allows for ultraviolet and violet light, enhancing the bird's capacity to detect egg forgery (Kalaugher, 2017, pp. 33–34). How does Zoom perform this feat of trickery as the wire mother? Indeed, for some patients, this fake mother may not be as much of a threat to psychic integrity as with other patients. Early trauma work with patients who need consistent eye contact, soothing, and containment from the analyst may not do well on Zoom-like platforms.

Mosconi et al. (2009), in the article "Longitudinal study of amygdala volume and joint attention in 2- to 4-year old children with autism", suggest that "that failure to orient faces, and more particularly to the eye region of the face is inherent in multiple aspects of social impairment unique to autism" (Mosconi et al., 2009, p. 510). According to Schore, right-brained amygdala enlargement indicates a conditioned, hypervigilant response to fear (2019, p. 71). Individuals fixated on safety may find Zoom psychologically and emotionally taxing, thus increasing the likelihood of dissociation, a coping mechanism born from overstimulation. Curiously, one may begin to inquire about the long-term effects of quarantine and right-brain atrophy due to lack of socialization and the physical and spiritual connection of which Zoom is only a pseudo replacement.

According to Jungian thought, the seat of the psyche lies within the archetypal unconscious, or what Schore would consider the right brain. Within the archetypal realm, the symbol formation function pumps its contents within the psyche. There is continuous vigorous debate about the capacity to access the subtle body while utilizing Zoom. The subtle body exists in the psychic field between the physical and spiritual realms. To become ensouled and thus fully human, the analyst and patient must have access to the field of feeling. This archetypal field can become inaccessible when the couple is too distressed from tracking the intricacies of the relationship on a Zoom platform. It is a substantive question as to whether or not the patient can even dream their life into being, especially if the subtle body and delicate feeling function is foreclosed by the Cyborg Mother.

The foreclosure of archetypal space by the Cyborg Mother is symbolic of the cuckoo who has tossed out the incubating, fertile, host egg for the wire other egg. In the analytic temenos the egg-container becomes infused with a dryness produced by the electric other, robbing the vessel of its cooking capacity. Body and psyche remain separated due to the body psyche dissonance of Zoom, the transcendent function potentially becoming locked in the body. This is not to say that the symbolic realm or transcendent function is *completely* disabled, but the gate to the archetypal may become jammed, a trickster-like energy flipping the electric/carnal switch off and on, on and off, short-circuiting access to the transcendent. Indeed, this paradigm deserves more reflection regarding the location of the subtle body on streaming platforms. Can this notion of the subtle body *adapt* during a crisis such as Covid, evolving and transmuting space and time, making technology a wire mother who might be preferred during the weaning of the natural mother, a transitional object in a developmental push? The pivotal realm of debate lies in the access to the subtle body between the analyst and analysand.

Jungian analyst August Cwik emphasizes the location of the subtle body during teletherapy. In his article "The technologically mediated self" (2021), Cwik discusses the benefits of technology platforms such as Zoom and points out that, regardless of the difficulties, these platforms perform well in various conditions, such as during the pandemic, serving as a good enough mother. Cwik reflects on Jung's ideas about the subtle body: "Jung refers to the imagination in different contexts which may be seen and experienced in different ways on Zoom." He points out that

> Jung (1935) discussed the difference between our current understanding of the imagination and the alchemical *imaginatio*. The Alchemist thought of the imagination as a hybrid phenomenon more half spiritual/half physical in nature. This type of imagining was considered a physical activity that could be fitted into the general cycle of material things. "We have to conceive of these processes not as the immaterial phantoms we readily take fantasy pictures to be, but as something corporeal a subtle body a spiritual semi-spiritual in nature" (Par. 935). This notion of the subtle body connects with the somatic unconscious – a transcendental concept involving the relationship between mind and body.
>
> (Cwik, 2021, p. 15)

Cwik discerns where the subtle body exists, a critical notion when pondering the location of the transcendent function. Here, he quotes Jung in *Nietzche's Zarathustra: Notes of the Seminar Given in 1934*,

> The part of the unconscious which is designated as the subtle body becomes more and more identical with the functioning of the body, and therefore it grows darker and darker and ends in the utter darkness of matter ... Somewhere, unconscious becomes material, because the body is the living unit, and our conscious and our unconscious are embedded in it: they contact the body. Somewhere there is a place where the two ends meet and become interlocked. And that is the [subtle body] where one cannot say whether it is matter, or what one calls 'psyche'. If we are willing to suspend disbelief, then our technologically mediated self has the potential to carry aspects of this subtle body, and imaginal body that becomes closer to the actual self and body of the patient – then there can be actual potential to deeply affect the body.
> (Jung, 1988/2014, p. 441)

Conversely, if the body is only partially accessible, from the head-up, for instance, where one cannot fully feel the other's presence because eyes are not connected and the full formed living body is occluded by techno-psychic skin, then Zoom is performing nothing more than a weigh station for the psychotherapeutic process, something which risks dissolution from frustration if continued for too long.

The ongoing cost–benefit analysis of streaming platforms is paramount in the mental health community because the algorithmic upgrades refine the human experience to such a degree that eventually, mimicry between the real relationship and the technological Zoom replacement image provides the arms race few people may recognize. Could this unconsciously affect how we feel, altering the depth and perception of the feeling function? With the metaverse technology burgeoning and bubbling underneath the collective psyche, an explosion of this kind of technology is impinging on our culture zeitgeist, ready to explode into our daily life. As holographic technology begins to merge with our psychic reality, our human experience and relatedness will be exceedingly challenged and altered in ways we are not psychologically prepared for.

While we consciously understand that nothing replaces the mother's gaze, what happens when fear keeps us from going out into the world due to an existential threat like Covid-19, long after the virus has been eradicated or contained? Once again, we turn to the cuckoo bird. The strength of defenses and adaptation relies on the host species's ability to evolve. Some host species have keen egg rejection instincts resulting in the parasitic species evolving equally strong mimicry skills to defend against egg rejection. However, other hosts do not exhibit such strong rejection defenses and as a result the parasitic species will show no evolved mimicry skills. This is an important statement for it indicates as far as the technology is concerned that complete rejection of Zoom may set in motion an arms race between the human experience and technological mimicry. In contrast, complete acceptance and dependence on the technology for relatedness could end in technological colonization. Perhaps the third, more viable option may consist of a paradigm of discernment in adaptation regarding whom this technology helps and hurts.

References

Brooks, S., Webster, R., Smith, L., Woodland, L., Wessely, S., Greenberg, N., and Rubin, J. (2020) The psychological effects of quarantine and how to reduce it: rapid review of the evidence. *Lancet*, 395, pp. 912–920.

Celenza, A. (2005) Vis-à-vis the couch: where is psychoanalysis?, *International Journal of Psychoanalysis*, 86(6), pp. 1645–1659.

Cwik, A. (2021) The technologically-mediated self: reflections on the container and field of telecommunications, *Journal of Analytical Psychology*, 66(3), pp. 411–428.

Colman, W. (2015) Bounded in a nutshell and a king of infinite space: the embodied self and its intentional world, *The Journal of Analytical Psychology*, 60(3), pp. 316–335, www.academia.edu/7044189/The_Embodied_Self_and_its_Intentional_World (Accessed 4 August 2023).

Harlow, H.F., Dodsworth, R.O, and Harlow, M.K. (1965) Total social isolation in monkeys. *Proceedings of the National Academy of Sciences of the United States of America*, 54(1), pp. 90–97.

Isaacs Russell, G. (2015) *Screen Relations: The Limits of Computer-Mediated Psychoanalysis and Psychotherapy*, London: Routledge.

Jiang, M. (2020). The reason Zoom calls drain your energy, BBC, www.bbc.com/worklife/article/20200421-why-zoom-video-chats-are-so-exhausting (Accessed 4 August 2023).

Jung, C.G. (1988/2014) *Nietzsche's Zarathustra: notes of the seminar given in 1934–1939*, Princeton, NJ: Princeton University Press.

Kalaugher, L. (2017) Cuckoo forgeries: a bird's-eye view, *Physics World*, https://physicsworld.com/a/cuckoo-forgeries-a-birds-eye-view/ (Accessed 4 August 2023).

Liedtke, M. (2020) Zoom rides pandemic to another quarter of explosive growth, *Associated Press*, https://apnews.com/article/virus-outbreak-technology-business-ca-state-wire-760e40a2023c888574411a1b3e4df0da (Accessed 4 August 2023).

Mosconi, M., Cody-Hazlett, H., Poe, M., Gerig, G., Gimpel-Smith, R., and Piven, J. (2009) Longitudinal study of amygdala volume and joint attention in 2- to 4-year-old children with autism, *Archives of General Psychiatry*, 66(5), pp. 509–516.

Porges, S.W. (2017) *The Pocket Guide to The Polyvagal Theory*, New York: W.W. Norton.

Schore, A. (2019) *The Development of the Unconscious Mind*, New York: W.W. Norton.

Tronick, E. (2009) Still Face Experiment Dr Edward Tronick, YouTube, www.youtube.com/watch?v=apzXGEbZht0&t=66s (Accessed 4 August 2023).

Winnicott, D. (1965) *The Maturational Processes and the Facilitating Environment: Studies in the Theory of Emotional Development*, London: Hogarth Press.

8

A Transcendent Future

A 'Discovery" of Nonbinary Stories'

Marieke Cahill

Introduction

Infinite Galaxy
We are galaxies within galaxies
Ever evolving, shifting, changing
Expansive in our finite bodies
As the Universe enfolds
We unfold into being
As we enfold our being
The Universe unfolds
We seek, we find
We seek, we lose
We are galaxies within galaxies.

Some may be the Sun
Some may be the Moon
But we are stars upon stars
Infinite within finite
Bursting with light
Enveloped in dark
We are galaxies within galaxies.

The past, a mythology
The future, a vision
The present, a being
Blending myth and vision
To find joy and sorrow
To pursue desire
To feel the gaping wound
And carry it gently
Cradling it as sacred
Holiness in humanity
We are galaxies within galaxies.
    ~ Marieke Cahill

DOI: 10.4324/9781003255727-12

I saw a vision of my future where my desires of being seen for who I am were realized. It was simple really: in *Star Trek Discovery* (Paramount+, 2017–24), sixteen-year-old Adira (Blu del Barrio) says they want to use they/them pronouns and explains that they never felt like she/her or he/him fit for them. Dr. Culber (Wilson Cruz), a parental figure in Adira's life, responds with acceptance, love, and care, and the change is immediate. Everyone they live and work with on the *USS Discovery* uses they/them pronouns for Adira from then on, without discussions or difficulty. It was an emotional moment for me because that simple change, so easily made in Adira's story, is not a present reality for so many trans and nonbinary people, including myself. My gender identity is constantly dismissed or ignored, and I didn't even realize how heavily that weighed on me until I saw what it could look like to be deeply accepted and respected by an entire community of people.

Trans and nonbinary histories have been erased and dismissed under the specter of patriarchy, heteronormativity, and colonization; however, we have always existed and will continue to exist. Our presence can be found in society, myth, and image throughout the world if one has eyes open to see it. In current Western society, specifically in the United States of America, LGBTQ+ stories are breaking into mainstream entertainment with greater diversity. In recent years, stories that include trans people are increasing in regularity and nuance; however, these stories often continue to center a binary conception of gender, and nonbinary stories are still quite rare. Many nonbinary representations are technological and non-human in nature. In a world that struggles to accept the nonbinary, with a scientific community that can rely heavily on the mechanisms and structures of the body, and a Western epistemology that too often values objective and observable data over the lived experience of communities of people, it is in looking to the future that we may *discover* the path to transcend the othering of those outside the gender binary in a way that leads to greater acceptance of the humanity and validity of nonbinary individuals. I will incorporate *Star Trek: Discovery*'s stories of the nonbinary Adira and the trans masculine Gray (Ian Alexander), as well as my own nonbinary experiences, to demonstrate how story and Jungian archetypes can function to bring science and the nonbinary together in transcendence.

We live in a world where battle lines are drawn between opposing ideologies and where pundits discuss "culture wars", "info wars", and even "the war on Christmas" as if these things are a battle that must be won. It can be challenging to imagine people coming together with openness to talk with people who are different, who are seen as other, and find common ground. Yet C. G. Jung gives us a path through his conception of the *transcendent function*, a psychological function that "arises from the union of the conscious and unconscious contents" in the psyche (Jung, 1960, p. 69), which he also correlates to the alchemical process. People who are trans and nonbinary have a particular gift to bring to the world regarding the transcendent function. I believe it is through our stories that the transcendent function can operate in such a way that those who identify with the binary and those who do not are able to coexist with greater freedom of identity. Nonbinary stories are rarely represented in the media; however, the television series *Star Trek:*

Discovery includes the first openly nonbinary and trans characters in the Star Trek universe and give us an example of what relationships could look like between trans people and cisgender people and how they benefit all when trans people are fully accepted.

This chapter will be discussing plotlines within the television series and therefore includes spoilers for those who have not watched *Star Trek: Discovery*.

IAJS forum

This chapter is partially inspired by discussions and debates in the online forum of the International Association of Jungian Studies. These discussions laid bare the opposing ideologies in the Jungian community regarding gender, gender essentialism's conflation of biological sex and gender, and gender theory's identification of gender as a social construct. As a trans nonbinary person, these discussions were painful, in that I felt my community dismissed, erased, and ultimately harmed through the gender essentialist ideals presented under the guise of academic discourse; challenging, in that I was pushed to my relatively new academic and Jungian limits; and illuminating, in that I was able to see psychological splitting occurring right before my eyes. I found myself challenging my own thinking and perspectives to discover what I know to be true and search for transcendence within myself. Even in a dehumanizing experience, I refused to let go of my own humanity by dehumanizing those I debated. My hope is that the stories I share here, of Adira, Gray, and myself, illuminate the sacred humanity inherent in all experiences and lead to transcendence.

Definitions

There are a few critical ideas to understand in this discussion regarding the theories of C. G. Jung and the progression of his theories in evolutionary branches of depth psychology, the philosophies of gender theory and gender criticism, and gender identifying terminology. The first thing to address is that of gender identities and terminology.

Gender identifiers

Transgender people are a diverse group of individuals with varying identifiers. While most people picture a trans woman or trans man when they hear the term *transgender*, the term means a person who identifies as a gender other than the gender they were assigned at birth. Therefore, transgender also includes nonbinary and gender-nonconforming identities. That said, some nonbinary and gender-nonconforming people do not identify as transgender for a variety of reasons, including honoring the unique experience of visibly trans women or trans feminine people and trans men or trans masculine people. Nonbinary people are also a diverse group with varying identities across cultures, including gender-nonconforming, agender, bigender, gender fluid, genderqueer, genderless, demi-girl, demi-boi, Hijra, Two-Spirit, and many others. *Two-Spirit* is an important identifier that is specific to Pan-American indigenous people. Passamaquoddy Two-Spirit politician, activist, and expert basket maker, Geo Neptune, describes Two-Spirit as "an umbrella term that bridges indigenous and Western understandings of gender and sexuality" (Anonymous, 2018a). Each nation has its own culturally specific definition of Two-Spirit identities, but the term was introduced to help find common ground and assist in the education of traditional teachings (Anonymous, 2018b).

The unifying concept among the various nonbinary identities is a lack of identification with the binary identities of man or woman and male or female, but rather that we exist in between or outside of that binary. People who do identify as the gender they were assigned at birth are *cisgender*. The prefix trans- means "to cross over" and cis- means "on this side of". So, one could say that cisgender people are those who have not crossed over the boundaries of binary gender, whereas transgender people have crossed those boundaries, or *transgressed* binary gender.

Nonbinary people also span quite a range in terms of presentation, gender affirmative treatments, and pronoun usage. Some people present as the gender they were assigned at birth and may even appear to be cisgender; others present as obviously genderfluid by making intentional choices about their appearance that incorporate both masculine and feminine coded elements (such as facial hair or chest hair combined with dresses and makeup, or masculine attire worn without the use of chest binders); and yet others use gender affirming hormonal treatments or surgeries to present androgynously or as the binary gender opposite their assigned gender at birth.

As for pronouns, there are diverse feelings about them as well. Some nonbinary people do not have a preference and view pronoun choices as a reflection on the speaker and not on their identity. As Kate Bornstein, nonbinary elder, author, and gender theorist has said, "My pronouns? At this point, I really don't give a damn. I'm interested to see what pronoun you would use to describe me. That would tell me a lot about you" (Hardell, 2019). Others have very strong desires or preferences about which pronouns, or combinations of pronouns, are used including the singular *they* or neo-pronouns such as *ze/zim* or *xe/xir*. Many nonbinary people do not consider their pronouns "preferences", but rather as innate as she/her for a cisgender woman or he/him for a cisgender man. While these terms and identifiers can be used broadly, respecting an individual trans or nonbinary person's preference of identifiers and pronouns requires asking them and then honoring what is expressed.

For the sake of simplicity, when I use the term *trans* within this chapter, I am using the term broadly and inclusive of all binary and nonbinary transgender identities, unless I specify otherwise. Likewise, when I use the term *nonbinary*, I am using the term broadly and inclusively. While I may speak to certain experiences from the nonbinary perspective, much of what I am discussing applies to other trans experiences as well.

Another important term is the word *queer*. Queer as a definition within the LGBTQ+ community has evolved over time. It has been used as a slur, to refer to gay and lesbian people, and more recently, as an umbrella term for anyone who identifies as something other than straight and cisgender (Perlman, 2019). While the term is being reclaimed and becoming more popular as a self-identifier and as a term for LGBTQ+ communities, many elders in the LGBTQ+ community have negative feelings towards the term due to the harm and discrimination they have experienced. Those who are not LGBTQ+ should avoid using the term for others unless it has been expressly communicated as a preference by an individual or group.

"'Philosophically' nonbinary"

> *One day, my trans partner and I were discussing gender while on a date. I told her, "I feel like I'm 'philosophically' nonbinary".*

Years ago, I had taken a course on the Sociology of Gender and it had planted the seeds of questioning the gender binary. I still identified with womanhood because I had experiences I associated with womanhood. I had birthed a child and nursed them for 3+ years. I was very domestic in many ways, enjoying traditionally feminine crafts like knitting, sewing, and even spinning. I also didn't have negative feelings about my body or its Venus of Willendorf-like feminine appearance. Rather, I had worked hard to accept my body and find pleasure in it at each stage of life. I also recognized how I was treated as a woman by society since I didn't alter my appearance to present androgynous or masculine, though I wasn't particularly feminine either. The reason I felt philosophically nonbinary way was because I did not agree with the gender binary, even though I still identified with it to a degree. I felt a tension in what I believed about gender and how I felt in my embodied experience at that point in time.

Jung's theories and gender

C. G. Jung himself did not directly speak to or of the queer or trans psyche in his work; however, he was likely aware of work being done in the field of biological sciences. His life spanned the early twentieth century and his writings reflect the dominant misogynistic and gender binarist perspectives of his generation. However, pre-Nazi Germany had an active gay community, prominent gay rights activism, and a research institute that focused on gay and trans sexuality, the *Institut für Sexualwissenschaft* (roughly translated to *Institute of Sexology*), founded and operated by the gay Jewish German physician, Magnus Hirschfeld (Diavolo, 2017). While it does not appear that Hirschfeld and Jung directly crossed paths, Hirschfeld and psychologist Sigmund Freud corresponded and had a professional relationship (LeVay, 1996). Freud's *Three Essays on the Theory of Sexuality*, published in 1905, were informed by Hirschfeld's work in sexology (Freud et al., 1905). In 1907, Hirschfeld helped Freud establish the Berlin Psychoanalytic Society. Meanwhile, Jung collaborated closely with Freud between 1907 and 1912 (Fordham, et al., 2023). It was in 1911 that Hirschfeld and Freud went their separate ways due to diverging views, two years before Jung's own break with Freud in 1913. It stands to reason that Jung would have been exposed to the work of Hirschfeld and been aware of his research. Devastatingly, the decades of research by Hirschfeld and his colleagues were destroyed by the Nazis in 1933 when they burned the contents of the Institute (Diavolo, 2017).

The one time that Jung did document any opinions regarding trans identity was a brief response to a questionnaire regarding a case study of a "transvestite" patient who had gender affirmation surgery. Transvestite was the term commonly used for transgender and gender nonconforming people until Hirschfeld coined the term *transsexual* in 1923 (Nieder and Strauss, 2015). While Jung does not speak to the trans psyche, he is not opposed to gender affirmation surgery. He states:

> If anyone who is [of sound mind] wishes to be castrated and feels happier for it afterwards than he did before, there is not much in his action that one can fairly object to. If the doctor is convinced that such an operation really does help his patient, and nobody is injured by it, his ethical disposition to help and ameliorate might very well prompt him to perform the operation without anyone being in a position to object to it on principle.
>
> (1977, p. 348).

Rather than speaking to the individual psyche, Jung later addresses the collective psyche by saying that "castration", or gender affirmation surgery, is a "numinous mutilation" that affects the emotions of the collective when discussed publicly (Jung, 1977, p. 348). It could be argued that he is effectively saying gender affirmation surgery is spiritual and that this numinous act is completely acceptable for those who need it yet inspires emotions in the collective that may be challenging to navigate. However, instead of addressing that this could be an issue for the collective to integrate, Jung's opinion is that the patient's psychologist, Dr. Medard Boss, should have kept it private so as not to arouse negative emotion. I argue that Jung did not hold purely gender essentialist ideology, but that he was reticent to fully challenge the gender status quo. There were signs he held more open-minded beliefs, whether they were conscious or not.

Jung constructed a theory or mythology of the psyche that was based on archetypes and image. *Archetypes* are primordial motifs, such as creation; patterns, such as growth or self-destruction; emotions, such as joy and rage; and experiences universal to the human condition, such as home, sex, and death. Images, or symbols, are the symbolic representations of these archetypes. In Jung's writings, a nonbinary archetype was present in the image of the hermaphrodite. While this term is now considered an outdated way to refer to intersex people, it is based on the myth of Hermaphroditus, a Greek deity who was a man and a woman conjoined together (Brumble, 1998, p. 166ff). Jung uses the symbol of the hermaphrodite as an example of evidence for archetypes:

> The hermaphrodite has gradually turned into a subduer of conflicts and a bringer of healing, and it acquired this meaning in relatively early phases of civilization. This vital meaning explains why the image of the hermaphrodite did not fade

in primeval times but, on the contrary, was able to assert itself with increasing profundity of symbolic content for thousands of years. The fact that an idea so utterly archaic could rise to such exalted heights not only points to the vitality of archetypal ideas, it also demonstrates the rightness of the principle that the archetype, because of its power to unite opposites, mediates between the unconscious substratum and the conscious mind.

(1968, p. 174)

What is so fascinating about this quote is that in reading it through a nonbinary lens, it is as if Jung is making an argument for the nonbinary. Despite his dismissive language towards modern indigenous people for whom these ideas are not archaic, he acknowledges the long history throughout the world. He identifies the important role nonbinary identities hold within myth and culture.

Jung identified multiple archetypes that represent the *psyche*, the totality of mind, soul, and sense of self. The two main archetypes are the conscious and the unconscious. The *conscious* contains the awareness we have of ourselves; what we can see about who we are, our motives, and how we operate. Within the conscious is the *ego*, the container for our conscious sense of inner and outer self, particularly the will. Also within the conscious is the *persona*, or the parts of ourselves that we show the world, particularly outside the home.

The *unconscious* contains the parts of ourselves that we are not aware of and that remain hidden from our conscious mind. Within the unconscious is the *shadow*, the aspects of the unconscious that are closest to the surface and that impact our lives without our awareness. These are the desires, characteristics, and patterns that we do not see in ourselves, for better or worse, but can be accessed through interaction with the images from dreams or symbols from waking life. Just as the unconscious is the counterpart to the conscious and the shadow is the counterpart to the ego, so the *anima* or *animus* is Jung's unconscious, contra-sexual counterpart to the conscious persona. The persona contains the well-developed parts of ourselves, and the anima or animus are the typically underdeveloped parts. This is where things get tricky regarding gender.

On one hand, Jung's theories hint at a blending of gender. He identified that "no man is so entirely masculine that he has nothing feminine in him". He described the emotional life of very masculine men as "carefully guarded and hidden" and "very soft" (Jung, 1966, p. 189). Jung viewed this feminine side as so hidden that it is often contained by the unconscious and emerges through projection and other unconscious acts. He identified that in cases where men desired to be perceived as masculine and therefore created a masculine persona, the feminine anima counterpart would compensate and cause emotional upheaval and the development of a *complex*, a part of the psyche that is split off and emotionally charged in such a way as to affect a person's life. In the context of the anima, this could look like a mother-complex where a man seeks relationships with women that give him something he did not receive in his relationship with his mother; the mother being the first image of the anima in a person's life. The animus, on the other hand, is the male counterpart to the persona of women and functions similarly.

On the other hand, Jung's conceptions of men and women as stereotypical oversimplifications may already be evident, but it is particularly obvious when he says, "As the anima produces *moods*, so the animus produces *opinions*; and as the moods of a man issue from a shadowy background, so the opinions of a woman rest on equally unconscious prior assumptions" (1966, pp. 206–207). The anima is emotional, intuitive, and irrational; the animus is logical, rational, and authoritative. He identified that in relationships between men and women, the unconscious anima or animus would be projected upon the spouse, often causing relational disharmony (1966, pp. 189, 199–200). The stereotype of women as emotional and men as logical is a gross oversimplification at best, and highly offensive at worst. Besides how this affects cisgender men and women who may not fit into stereotypical gender roles, where does the anima and animus leave the nonbinary or trans individual psyche?

Post-Jungian psychology has evolved the theory of anima and animus to be less strict along the gender binary divide in lieu of both archetypes existing within each person to varying degrees (Rowland, 2002). However, the progressed archetype still holds the vestiges of the gender binary in its language. I argue that the lack of change in language around this archetypal function supports the views of Jungians who hold on to the gender binary and use the anima and animus archetypes as justification to do so.

Jung called the coming together of conscious and unconscious within the psyche the *transcendent function*. It is the function of two opposites joining together as one and crossing the threshold into a new, conscious, and integrated whole. Within the individual psyche, the transcendent function serves to bring about a process Jung called *individuation*. This process involves a surrender of the ego, or the will, and the metaphorical death of the existing persona in order to allow for growth into a more holistic and integrated persona. The more the persona is able to incorporate aspects of the psyche that were previously in the shadow, the more a person is able to make choices consciously and with their whole self, versus at the whim of the contents of the shadow. Collectively, the transcendent function occurs whenever that which lies in the collective unconscious becomes integrated with society's collective consciousness.

The transcendent function includes the integration of the persona and the anima/animus into an androgynous or hemaphroditic third. Jung describes the third in his essay "The transcendent function":

> The confrontation of the two [opposing] positions generates a tension charged with energy and creates a living, third thing – a living birth that leads to a new level of being, a new situation. The transcendent function manifests itself as a quality of conjoined opposites.
>
> (1960, p. 90)

It could be argued that this is precisely what many nonbinary people experience. Looking at it a different way, in the creation story of the Wabanaki people, it is cisgender people who are split and the Two-Spirit person, a nonbinary indigenous gender, is an integrated whole. As Geo Neptune tells the story, rather than beginning as two separate parts coming together to form an integrated whole, the Two-Spirit person was never separated in the first place (Lane, 2022). Jung correlates the transcendent function to the alchemical process of *coniunctio* and the psychological function it represents by taking different ingredients and combining them in order to create something valuable and completely new. However, the separation is not always assumed:

> At the beginning of the alchemical process, the *nigredo* or blackness is the initial state ... or else produced by the separation (*solutio, separatio, divisio, putrefactio*) of the elements. If the separated condition is assumed at the start, as sometimes happens, then a union of opposites is performed under the likeness of a union of male and female.
>
> (1953, pp. 230–231)

It goes through additional processes before becoming the end goal of the transformational white or red tincture, or the life-giving philosopher's stone "which, as a hermaphrodite, contains both" (Jung, 1953, p. 232). Jung's exposition of alchemy, and the androgynous and hermaphroditic symbolism within it, demonstrates the transformational power of the transcendent function in the process of individuation. When it comes to gender, some people, two-spirit or otherwise, experience themselves as never having been separated into a binary in the first place; there was no *solutio* needed. For others, their experience of gender is a combination of opposites in the *coniunctio* process. This is where Jung's analysis of the psyche reaches the edge of its limitations for the nonbinary and gender nonconforming psyche.

Nonbinary woman

A few months after sharing with my partner that I felt "philosophically nonbinary", the tension I felt continued to increase. One day I was browsing the internet and discovered that some people identified as "nonbinary women". Something clicked in my psyche as I saw how the two could blend together. I could experience BOTH. I could eschew the binary and embrace my experience of womanhood at the same time. The tension of the opposition of the gender binary and the nonbinary crossed over into the transcendent. Once I crossed that threshold, I felt a greater sense of ease. In that ease, I was able to really lean into how I felt at any given moment, and allow myself to simply be instead of trying to fit into a particular mold.

Gender theory

The concept of gender has a long, and yet relatively recent history. In the West, gender has often been conflated with biological sex, and still is by those who hold gender-critical ideology (Juschka, 2016). However, historically in many cultures around the world, the existence of other gender identities has been openly acknowledged and accepted to varying degrees, particularly before colonization. For example, the trans and gender-nonconforming Hijras of India have existed for centuries (Rhude, 2018) and indigenous nations in the Americas have various cultural gender identities under the two-spirit umbrella.

Gender theory is "the study of what is understood as masculine and/or feminine and/or queer behavior in any given context, community, society, or field of study" (Jule, 2014), inclusive of psychology, culture, history, linguistics, and science. In 1990, Judith Butler put forth the idea that gender is not just a social construct but that the concept of sex is not based in physical biology. In *Gender Trouble*, Butler asks who created the concept of gender and then labeled it? Who defined it as relating to the body and why (1999/2006, p. 9)? Gender as we know it is a particularly Western concept, despite how universal some may claim it to be. It organizes Western society in that men and women are ranked hierarchically through the dichotomy of gender. In *The Invention of Women*, Oyèrónké Oyêwùmí (1997) discusses how Western society projected gender onto pre-colonial Yorùbá society:

> Yorùbá society, like many other societies worldwide, has been analyzed with Western concepts of gender on the assumption that gender is a timeless and universal category. But as Serge Tcherkézoff admonishes "An analysis that starts from a male/female pairing simply produces further dichotomies." It is not surprising, then, that researchers always find gender when they look for it.
>
> (1997, p. 31)

While Western researchers saw gender, the social categories of men and women did not exist in Yorùbá culture. Instead, they were organized by seniority according to relative age.

Queer theory

Queer theory emerged out of feminist and gender theory and while it can be related to sexuality and gender, it speaks to ontologies and identities beyond those concepts. The "queer" in queer theory is a word that has been reclaimed or reappropriated, within the context of sexuality and gender in particular, as a political act that transforms the former slur into a new meaning. Katherine Johnson (2014) states, "In the context of queer theory, 'to queer' means to disrupt or make something 'strange,' twisting or unsettling meanings, pushing the invisible into the spotlight". Johnson goes on to say that this disruption is used to challenge cisheteronormativity, the assumption that cisgender and heterosexuality are the de facto norm. However, queer theory goes beyond gender and sexuality. Author and activist bell hooks defined her queerness as:

> "Queer" not as being about who you're having sex with (that can be a dimension of it); but "queer" as being about the self that is at odds with everything around it and has to invent and create and find a place to speak and to thrive and to live.
>
> (The New School, 2017)

Many LGBTQ+ people, including myself, prefer the term queer as an umbrella because it encompasses all the different ways we exist and often transform as we discover new aspects of our queerness. I am personally drawn to the term *queer* for the same reason as hooks: much of the journey my self, my individuation, requires that I be inventive and creative in a world that doesn't understand me. I must be transcendent.

A wild and curvy line

Parallel to my journey of exploring gender, I was also on a spiritual journey of connecting to the pre-colonial ancestors of my European bloodlines. Much is unknown about pre-colonial Europe's spiritual beliefs and gender structures because so much of the knowledge has been lost to history or filtered through the lens of Roman and Christian outsider perspectives. But as I began to learn more about the existence of nonbinary identities in other indigenous cultures, I realized the likelihood of nonbinary identities in my own ancestral past was pretty likely. In the intricate work of undoing the religious programming of my Christian upbringing in order to connect to ancestral spirituality, the pathways opened up for me to be able to discover the real sexuality and gender that was hiding underneath the expectations put upon me and that I took on for much of my life. I looked back on my life and saw the times when I bent gender to suit me, the signs that my sexuality curved where I thought it was straight, and where my wild, unconventional, and nonconforming spirit bucked against the ways I was supposed to be. The essence of my gender and my sexuality lost the labels and became simply: Marieke.

Why it matters

Stories, myths, and fairy tales are how we make sense of the world we live in and our place within it. We find ourselves and our experiences within the books, television shows, and films that we are drawn to and exposed to. These stories also inform our understanding of culture and relationship. When nonbinary people are missing from cultural stories, a disconnect occurs. We are not able to see ourselves connected to the culture in which we live; and cisgender people are not able to enter into the stories of nonbinary people and find empathy in the common ground between the nonbinary and cisgender experiences.

Stories serve to show us how we are each a part of the whole. Humanity has not always viewed itself as separate from the world around us and many indigenous ontologies still recognize our interconnectedness with our communities and nature (Little Bear, 2004). When the concept of the subject–object split was codified into Western thought during the Enlightenment, the concept also codified the idea of the *other*. In *The Nuclear Enchantment of New Mexico*, Susan Rowland and Joel Weishaus (2021) argue that the inanimate nature we assign to objects does not take into account the hidden effects of an unconscious endowment of passion and irrational fervor and that the split is always psychological. Rowland and Weishaus continue:

> One attribute created by this overblown subject/object split is the illusion that the mind, or psyche, is locked in the human skill. As Jung also demonstrates, this is far from the case. We encounter the psyche in archetypal energies we have unconsciously bestowed upon the world.
>
> (2021, p. 28)

When we view certain people as *other*, we are objectifying them in that we turn them into objects. When we can see ourselves in people, we more easily categorize them as subjectively *us*. This applies not only to people, but also to nature and the cosmos. In the field of science, for example, we experience ourselves as subject and that which we are studying, observing, and analyzing as objectively other. It has created a sense of empiricism in that what we observe is what is real and true. However, *what* we observe, *how* we observe it, and the way we filter it through our own biases, social programming, and politics means that science contains the same unconscious attitudes, ideologies, and biases that informed the scientists who did the research.

In *Nature's Body: Gender in the Making of Modern Science*, Londa Schiebinger makes the case that what we know about gender and how certain branches of science, such as botany, are gendered and sexed is because the only people asking the questions were European white men who excluded women, often through their scientific research. They were the ones who gained and retained the power to ask questions. Schiebinger says, "This is why the political history of science asks: Why do we know this and not that? Who gains from knowledge of this and not that?" (1993, p. 9). These same questions could be asked in the context of mass media storytelling: Why do these stories get told and not those? Who gains from silencing or minimizing these stories versus those?

Positive and nuanced representations of nonbinary stories and characters are necessary to humanize the nonbinary experience and bridge the subject–object split. It not only helps nonbinary people see themselves represented as whole human beings, but also helps cisgender and binary trans people imagine the nonbinary experience. I would argue that this imagining not only helps to bridge the gap of understanding, but also helps those with binary views experience more freedom from cisheteronormativity in their own self-expression. When the boundaries of gender are broken down, everyone, no matter how they identify, is given more freedom.

Trans representation

Representation is not just about the presence of nonbinary characters. Many representations of LGBTQ+ characters in media are accessory to the main characters, such as a woman's gay best friend, the comedic relief, or the colorful opposite to a staid, straight character. Inspired by the Bechdel Test that assesses the representation of women in fiction (Anonymous, n.d.h), the Vito Russo Test (Anonymous, 2018a) examines LGBTQ+ representation in fiction. To pass the Vito Russo Test, named for the film historian and GLAAD co-founder, a work of fiction must meet the following requirements:

- The film contains a character that is identifiably lesbian, gay, bisexual, transgender, and/or queer.
- That character must not be solely or predominantly defined by their sexual orientation or gender identity (i.e. they are comprised of the same sort of unique character traits commonly used to differentiate straight/non-transgender characters from one another).
- The LGBTQ+ character must be tied into the plot in such a way that their removal would have a significant effect, meaning they are not there to simply provide colorful commentary, paint urban authenticity, or (perhaps most commonly) set up a punchline. The character must matter.

(Anonymous, 2018a)

GLAAD's 2021 *Studio Responsibility Index* asserts there was zero trans or nonbinary representation in any theatrical release from a major studio in 2020, for the fourth year in a row, despite the highest percentage of LGBTQ+ representation in film and the highest Vito Russo Test pass rate at nine out of ten films (Townsend and Deerwater, 2021). Television does significantly better with trans and nonbinary representation, in that there are notable nonbinary characters who pass the Vito Russo Test; however, there is still a long way to go.

Open representation of binary trans identities has become more mainstream in recent years with television shows that center the trans experience, such as Amazon's *Transparent* (Amazon Prime Video, 2014–19) and FX's *Pose* (FX, 2018–21). While these and other television series and movies broke ground for transgender actors and transgender representation, they tend to center the binary side of the transgender experience, most often the experience of trans women, which leaves a one-sided representation of trans identity. While Transparent did include a trans male character played by Ian Harvey, the first transitioned trans male actor to play a trans male character in an American scripted series (Kellaway, 2014), and later a nonbinary character, both Transparent and Pose strongly centered trans women and trans femmes. Trans masculine and nonbinary representations are still quite rare. One notable exception is the work of Brian Michael Smith as the trans male police officer Antoine Wilkins on *Queen Sugar* (Oprah Winfrey Network, 2016–22) in 2017 and firefighter Paul Strickland on *9-1-1: Lonestar* (Fox, 2020–present) in 2020.

We can see in Brian Michael Smith's work how trans representation is shifting. In 2017 the main story line of his character Antoine Wilkins on *Queen Sugar* focuses on his identity as a trans man, a role that does not pass the Vito Russo Test (Marsalis, 2017; Milan, 2017). Contrast that to Smith's character Paul Strickland in *9-1-1: Lonestar*, which premiered in 2020, which does pass the Vito Russo Test. In the series, Smith's character, Paul Strickland, is part of the lead ensemble and his character's transgender identity is simply one aspect of who he is. It is acknowledged early on in the series, and at other times where it makes sense, such as a brief storyline related to how dating is not the same for him as for the other men in the firehouse, but in most episodes, Strickland's gender identity is not mentioned in lieu of other experiences and complexities of his character.

Like other LGBTQ+ representation in television, nonbinary representation has been slowly moving from nonbinary characters that focus on their nonbinary identity, to characters who happen to be nonbinary. However, most of that representation happens off mainstream cable networks and behind paywalls, such as the character Taylor in *Billions* (Showtime, 2016–present) and the main character Sabi in *Sort of* (HBO Max, 2021–present), only available on HBO Max in the United States, making them less accessible to wider audiences. Taylor, played by Asia Kate Dillon, was the first nonbinary character on television played by a nonbinary actor (Williams, 2017). It was not until 2020 that primetime TV had a nonbinary actor as a series regular, when Jessie James Keitel was cast as Jerrie Kennedy in *Big Sky* (ABC, 2020–23). The next year brought *Sort of*, first to Canada's CBC network and then the United States via HBO. This is the first and only television series I am aware of that is centered on a nonbinary lead character.

The character of Adira in *Star Trek: Discovery* is one of the few nonbinary characters on American television who is complex and nuanced, for whom being nonbinary is simply one part of who they are, and accessible via cable network television. Adira, played by Blu del Barrio was introduced in season two (Anonymous, n.d.a) and passed the Vito Russo Test from the get-go, along with their trans masculine partner, Gray, played by Ian Alexander (Anonymous, n.d.d). The series already featured other LGBTQ+ characters central to the story, including the first explicitly gay couple in Star Trek history, Lt. Stamets and Dr. Culber, played by Anthony Rapp and Wilson Cruz, and engineer Jett Reno, played by Tig Notaro, a femme-presenting character who mentions a wife.

Nonbinary as nonhuman

In addition to explicit representation, there are genderqueer and nonbinary-coded characters identified within entertainment that aren't openly or specifically nonbinary. For example, the character Janet (D'Arcy Beth Carden) from *The Good Place* (NBC, 2016–20) presents as a feminine-appearing woman, yet she is a non-human entity who exists outside of time and space. Many nonbinary people identify with her constant assertions that she is "not a girl" and "not a robot" (Schur et al., 2016–20; Anonymous, n.d.e). Another example is Marvel's shapeshifter trickster god and anti-hero, Loki (Tom Hiddleston). In the recent television series on Disney+, *Loki* (Disney+, 2021–present) has multiple iterations from different universes, including the male Loki we are familiar with, his female counterpart Silvie, as well as young, old, Black, and even alligator versions from the multiverse. In the original mythology, Loki experiences things associated with women, such as birth, through his shapeshifting abilities (Tasker, 2021). In the Marvel comics, Loki is identified as genderfluid, which is now official in the film and television Marvel Universe as well.

While nonhuman representation mirrors the experiences of alienation and othering that nonbinary people experience, they also reinforce the idea that the nonbinary experience isn't inherently human. Nonbinary people go through life having their identity go unseen, ignored, or dismissed, and that rejection is painful. While there is not much research available at this time, current studies indicate that nonbinary and genderqueer people have high rates of anxiety, depression, and self-harm, but that well-being is increased with social support and daily "microaffirmations" in intimate relationships, such as identity validation, active learning, and active defense of a nonbinary partner's identity (Dickey, 2020).

Nonbinary as human

Much of the representation of human nonbinary identities within the media is either trans femme or androgynous. What is missing within nonbinary representation in the media is representation of people who pass as cisgender and don't *appear* to be gender nonconforming on the outside. As a large-bodied nonbinary person assigned female at birth, who appears to be a cisgender woman, I have never seen a nonbinary character that has an experience I fully relate to, yet I know many nonbinary people with similar experiences. It stands to reason that if a person's gender identity is outside the binary, then their self-expression could land anywhere on the spectrum of clothing and appearance choices. Visibly nonbinary and gender nonconforming individuals are subject to more discrimination and threat of harm than those of us who pass as cisgender, so their representation is important in visual media. But this emphasis on gender non-conforming appearance also leads to a stereotype that causes seemingly gender conforming nonbinary people to have their identity questioned since they don't *appear* to be nonbinary. Being nonbinary means that one can fall anywhere on the gender spectrum, or completely outside of it, and therefore ALL modes of presentation are available to us. Sometimes that will mean appearing gender nonconforming and sometimes it will not. It simply means the *freedom* is there to choose what makes us feel comfortable in our bodies and what we feel represents who we are. This freedom is the result of the transcendent function where all things become available to us through the integration of opposites, in this case, the false binary of feminine and masculine.

Art and creative pursuits often function to reveal what lies in the unconscious as well as what lives in the cultural zeitgeist. The relationship of television to culture is particularly potent: progressive culture pushes for diverse representation and diverse representation pushes for progressive open-mindedness. On the other hand, television can also reinforce existing cultural norms, including conservative ideologies. Unlike other forms of art that may not reach the mainstream masses, television is designed to reach wide swaths of people. It is uniquely positioned to bring diverse experiences to communities that may not be particularly diverse in and of themselves. It is an art and technology that allows our imaginations to dream beyond our own experiences and enter the experiences of those we view as other. In each new iteration of *Star Trek*, the creators look for new stories to tell. The writers of *Discovery* identified trans, and particularly nonbinary, stories as not being told often enough in mainstream media, and not yet included explicitly in the *Star Trek* universe.

Through *Discovery*, we get to envision a future that has progressed beyond our current locations of gender and queerness. *Star Trek* has a history of bridging the gap between the concepts of community and the other. While there are certainly themes of Western ideology, *Star Trek* has also been a forerunner in demonstrating what it looks like for diverse groups of people, and beings, to work together and find community. Respect for other cultures and other lands is built into the protocols for first contact. These protocols protect the cultures being discovered and are built into the values of the *Star Trek* universe.

The main organizing body in *Star Trek* is the United Federation of Planets, colloquially known as the Federation. What makes this organizing body unique is that it is joined voluntarily, as opposed to through coercive, imperialistic powers. It is a "supranational interstellar union of multiple planetary nation-states that operated semi-autonomously under a single central government, founded on the principles of liberty, equality, peace, justice, and progress, with the purpose of furthering the universal rights of all sentient life" (Anonymous, n.d.g).

The various *Star Trek* series focus on the Federation's Starfleet, a

> deep space exploratory and defense service … Its principal functions included the advancement of Federation knowledge about the galaxy and its inhabitants, and knowledge of *wissenschaft*, the systematic pursuit of all scholarly knowledge, not just science and technology. Starfleet's ancillary duties included the defense of the Federation, and the facilitation of Federation diplomacy.
>
> (Anonymous, n.d.g)

The focus of Starfleet, and *Star Trek*, is to learn more about the universe and its inhabitants. *Star Trek*'s epistemology is not focused solely on objective knowledge but incorporates a respect for relational and indigenous knowledge.

Historical significance

Star Trek has a history of explicitly valuing "infinite diversity in infinite combinations" since the original *Star Trek* (NBC, 1966–69) included a Black woman, Nichelle Nichols's Uhura, and an Asian man, George Takei's Sulu on the bridge as part of the core cast ensemble (Vary, 2020). However, while there have been some metaphorical or passing representations of queerness, *Star Trek: Discovery* is the first *Star Trek* series to include explicit and significant LGBTQ+ representation.

Many science fiction story lines objectify technology through either a utopian or dystopian relationship between human and technology, or the alien forces symbolic of technology, depending on whether they are positive or negative representations. In *Technologies*, R.L. Rutsky (2016) says:

> The starkness of this opposition between "good" and "bad" technologies seems to affirm the idea that the dividing line between technology and humanity must always be upheld; technology must know its "proper" place, even when – or especially when – it comes to life, as can be seen in the long series of artificial beings, sentient machines, robots and androids, cyborgs, and artificial intelligences portrayed in literature, films, and other media that have threatened to destroy, enslave, or replace humanity.
>
> (pp. 182–183)

While some utopian and dystopian themes have been present in the *Star Trek* universe, such as the dystopian relationship to the Borg, a technologically advanced pseudo-species of cyborg (part human, part artificial life) that operated as a hive mind and desired to raise the quality of life of the "primitive" entities they assimilated through the consumption of technology (Anonymous, n.d.b; Anonymous, n.d.c), I would argue that they are a metaphor of colonization in that they view their way of life as superior and others' as primitive. Here the othering is happening *to* the humans and other members of the Federation and demonstrates a criticism of othering.

The stories of *Star Trek* have largely taken a different approach to the utopian–dystopian dichotomy, emphasizing diplomacy, autonomy, and cooperation, even in seemingly hostile and challenging situations. I would argue that the reason the Borg are seen as a negative, dystopian force is not because they are deemed other by Starfleet, but rather because of their own colonialist approach and inability to respect the autonomy of those they deem primitive. The Federation, and Starfleet in particular, value curiosity and understanding the other through equitable relationship, as opposed to domination. Yet, despite the hostility of the Borg, one storyline in *Star Trek: Voyager* (UPN, 1995–2001) finds the captain striking an alliance with the Borg to deal with a common enemy (see *Scorpion*, Season 3, Episode 26 and *Scorpion Part II*, Season 4, Episode 1). It demonstrates the persistent desire for cooperation and diplomacy that the Star Trek Universe values and is an example of an attempt to facilitate the transcendent function. While the Borg end up double-crossing them, causing the transcendent function to dissolve before its completion, the crew of the *Voyager* are able to extract a formerly human member of the Borg by separating them from the Borg collective and helping them regain their individual humanity. Here, in helping the human member to individuate from the Borg, the crew successfully facilitates the transcendent function for that individual. The diverse interconnectedness that the *Star Trek* universe seeks to represent is reflected in the *Voyager* captain's desire to work with a formidable enemy and a continuous hope in a compassionate, relational way of being, despite disagreement within the crew. In this way, the core of *Star Trek* universe is about the transcendent function at work individually and collectively.

Queer representation

While *Discovery* breaks ground with explicitly LGBTQ+ representation, there have been symbolic LGBTQ+ representations in the past. The Trill, introduced in 1991 in *Star Trek: The Next Generation* (Paramount, 1987–94) and more prominently featured in *Star Trek: Deep Space Nine* (Paramount, 1993–99), became symbols of LGBTQ+ representation. In *Deep Space Nine*, the female Trill character Jadzia Dax, played by Terry Farrell, is a symbiont host to Dax who had predominantly joined with male hosts. In one episode from 1995 (*Rejoined*, Season 4, Episode 5), a queer relationship is briefly represented when Jadzia entertains rekindling a relationship with the wife of one of Dax's male hosts for a brief time. Jadzia's character can be interpreted as trans, lesbian, and otherwise queer. The inherent genderqueer nature of Trill symbionts and hosts led to many LGBTQ+ fans resonating with the Trill, including Del Barrio. According to the Trill page on one *Star Trek* wiki:

> As early as 1993, the Trill were seen by some fans as having parallels with transgender people. A reviewer of "Invasive Procedures" saw a transsexual metaphor and commented: "Watching this episode I was struck by the parallel between the Trills and transsexuals here on Earth. In either case, the goal of surgery is long sought for and desperately wanted. There are 'gatekeepers' who decide [who may and who may not] proceed. And those who fail to get the precious approval can feel they've lost their reason for living".
> (Anonymous, (n.d.j)

The reviewer is recognizing the parallel between the Trill desire for joining with a symbiont and the desire for body and gender identity alignment that many transgender people experience prior to gender affirmation surgery, in addition to the hurdles both have to overcome to see those desires come to fruition. All this considered, the creators of *Discovery* felt that the Trill were the perfect avenue for an explicitly trans narrative in the individual stories, and love story, of Adira and Gray (Vary, 2020).

When Adira enters the story, the *Discovery* has jumped 930 years into the future in order to save the known galaxy. The crew members of *Discovery* are reeling from the adjustments of leaving life as they know it and entering a new and disorienting world. Technology has advanced, but the Federation that they know and love has changed, and the relationships between planets have changed. As a Trill symbiont host, Adira contains the memories of Senna Tal, a Federation Admiral who has information that can help the *Discovery* reconnect with the Federation, yet Adira cannot access those memories (Fuller et al., 2017–present).

Adira's story in relation to the Trill parallels the nonbinary experience. When Adira and Lt. Michael Burnham go to Trill to try to receive help from the Trill community, the leaders alternately see Adira as an abomination, something to be tolerated, and as the future of their species. Adira's existence as a human symbiont host, when there has been no known instance of a successful non-Trill joining, is considered antithetical to their values. In an interview with *Variety*, Alex Kurtzman, the executive producer and co-showrunner for *Discovery*, addresses the challenge the Trill face:

> The hosts for the symbionts have always been Trill. The community of Trill has to reckon with the possibility that a host may not be Trill, and what does that mean? In the vein of all "Star Trek," do you accept what initially is perceived as other, and do [you] broaden your horizons?
>
> (Vary, 2020)

The same could be asked about nonbinary people: Do you accept the nonbinary and broaden your horizons? There are people who view nonbinary individuals as an abomination, misunderstood and therefore viewed as other. Nonbinary and gender-nonconforming people are attacked, verbally or physically, for transgressing the values of society as exhibited through gender identity and physical appearance. Conservative factions of society view nonbinary and trans people as aberrations and an affront to sacred values. And some people simply tolerate our existence, but don't celebrate the potential future that nonbinary people can usher into the world.

The leader, Guardian Xi, who views Adira's joining as a hope for the future safety of their species, puts himself at great risk to take Adira and Lt. Burnham to the sacred Caves of Mak'ala in order to help Adira. These are the kinds of allies that nonbinary people need; people who are willing to go against the status quo to bring about wholeness and integration for nonbinary people; to create protected, safe spaces that allow for exploration.

The symbiont joining process is a metaphor for the nonbinary, but it is also a symbol of the transcendent function. The symbiont can be seen as a symbol of the unconscious in that it holds past memories and experiences of the Trill, just as the unconscious holds the primordial memories of humanity. The host is a metaphor for the conscious as the container of the will, the one who is able to move and make things manifest in the world. Without the host, the symbionts spend life swimming around in a pool, cut off from the world and unable to have new experiences. Without the symbiont, the host does not have access to the collective memories and experiences of the past. In the joining of the two, a new being is made. The joining operates as the transcendent function, joining the opposite Trill (or Adira) and symbiont, and the result is the third, the result of the alchemical *coniunctio*. After joining, the symbiont can also be seen as a form of the philosopher's stone as it gives the host a form of eternal life in that their memories are retained to be accessed by the next host. The symbols of the nonbinary and the transcendent function mix and swirl together in their own transcendence.

Technology and science are consistent themes in *Star Trek*, but particularly potent with Adira. They have a genius level knowledge of technology due to the combination of their own mind and the memories of all the symbiont hosts who came before. Adira, as a host, must go back to the ancient technology of the Trill in the

Caves of Mak'ala in order to connect to the symbiont, face the pain causing their memory loss, and become integrated. It is a beautiful representation of individuation and the transcendent function, as Adira must unearth what has been suppressed in their unconscious to become truly one with the symbiont.

Once Adira has fully integrated their psyche with the symbiont through the Trill ritual, they have to then face a new reality, a new persona as a host, including the now-conscious pain of tragically losing their partner, Gray, the previous host of the Trill symbiont. Additionally, when Adira joined with the symbiont following Gray's physical death, Gray's full consciousness was retained through the symbiont, not just his memories. Gray starts to appear to and interact with Adira in a visible form, which is not a normal Trill host–symbiont occurrence.

While Adira comes out as nonbinary after the experience on Trill, they make it clear that this is not something new for them; in other words, not related to the symbiont. However, it is interesting that they find the courage to express it after their experience on Trill and after being taken in under the wings of the parental figures of Lt. Stamets and Dr. Culber. In their connection to the symbiont, Adira is quite literally a collective of beings, as they are connected to the consciousness of individuals from the past through their memories.

Technology and gender

What is technology, and can gender itself be a technology? In the twenty-first century, we typically think of technology as computers, phones, and other electronic devices. However, technology has a longer history than electricity, wires, and chips. The word technology comes from the Greek *tekhnologia* meaning the systematic treatment of an art, craft, or technique (Anonymous, n.d.i). It is rooted in the word *tekhne*, or art, skill, and craft in work, inclusive of the mechanical techniques of making that go back to antiquity, such as spinning fibers into yarn and thread, weaving, making tools, and other forms of fabricating, building, and crafting items. The Greek root *-logia* refers to a theory, science, discourse, or doctrine – the systematic study of a thing. So, the term technology can apply to so much more than the 1s and 0s that make up binary code. It speaks to the way we weave together the warp and weft of life, the tools we use to help us reach our goals, and the crafts that assist us in bringing beauty into the world.

Gender as technology

The use of the term technology has been narrowed down significantly from its original meaning. I propose that gender is a technology that can shift depending on how it is treated. Throughout history, various gender identities have been woven into culture. Just as the binary code of computer technology is a simplified language constructed for the purpose of communication, so the gender binary has become a simplified language for the purpose of communicating roles and power structures in society. And as computers are limited in what they can communicate, so the gender binary is limited in what it can communicate. It has been constructed and codified in such a way that some of the nuance of human experience has been cut out and streamlined into something that is missing the *tekhne* of art and embodied experience. And yet, the joining together of binary code causes the 1s and 0s to transcend into something new: art, ideas, and the beauty of humanity can be communicated to more people than ever before. In *Getting Curious with Jonathan Van Ness*, nonbinary and gender nonconforming artist, poet, and speaker Alok Vaid-Menon says:

> A lot of times people say, "Alok, how do we get the world to move beyond a binary?" And I say, "My world is already beyond the binary, and every day I'm living it." It's about community. It's about interdependence. It's about poetry. And I think that we're living poems.
>
> (Lane, 2022)

Poems are a *tekhne* of words in that they are crafted with skill using language as artistic medium. Our choices of language and other forms of communication can form and inform the world around us. The language of nonbinary people and the way we communicate in the world disrupts the binary status quo of patriarchal, heteronormative power and imperialism. Using the singular "they" or neopronouns is a nonbinary *tekhne*; dressing in ways that are gender nonconforming is a nonbinary *tekhne*; living in the liminal spaces of the psyche between the gender binary is a nonbinary *tekhne*; challenging other binary notions, such as good and evil, is a nonbinary *tekhne*; combining art and science is a nonbinary *tekhne*; the transcendent function is a nonbinary *tekhne*; the existence of nonbinary people is a *tekhne*; our community is a *tekhne*.

The poetry and technology of being nonbinary has a unique flavor for each nonbinary person. One nonbinary person's technology may be writing, another's may be fashion and appearance, yet another's may be art, business, or science. Or it may be simply existing in the world. For most, like me, it is a combination – another *coniunctio* of transcendence.

The Technology of Marieke

> *My technology is a constant evolution*
> *my being full of fire and fueled by air*
> *the winds of change blowing by*
> *and stirring up the pieces of my soul*
>
> *my song's melody carried in the air*
> *my words strung together across the page*
> *my brush carrying water and color*
> *swirling and soaking into the paper*

my relationships a web of community
a constellation of stars in a sky
dominated by the sun and the moon
yet our flames claim our space

I blaze like a star that is hot and burns
those who themselves are not aflame
my words are love and grace, yet cut
like a flaming knife for those who won't see

My technology is power and freedom
the kind that comes from knowing myself
and then being that precious self
whole and unapologetically wild

It comes from going through the fire
of dismantling the oppression
of feeling the deep, ancestral rage
and emerging bright and molten

It comes from choosing the fire
that transforms and makes space
burning down the old things
for the new to emerge from the ashes

To experience my technology
is to be willing to shift and change
to pick up the pieces of your self
and look to see if they actually fit

Then burn down the rest
and make yourself anew

~ Marieke Cahill

Who benefits from the technology of the gender binary?

If the nonbinary can be a technology, then so can the binary concept of gender. The question is, to what purpose? Who benefits from the technology of the gender binary? Who is excluded by the gender binary? As discussed earlier, the concept of a two-sex system was formed by white European men and spread into the sciences. It was borne out of the settler colonial culture of eighteenth- and nineteenth-century Europe and its colonies. While the current feminist and queer theories attempt to disrupt the two-sex and binary gender system, what is often dismissed is that these systems were created for white Europeans. In *The Sexual Demon of Colonial Power*, Greg Thomas discusses the Western-centric conception of gender:

> Of course, the slaveocratic order of settler colonialism construes its own as human and its slaves as non-human (or sub-human, if not anti-human). One cannot qualify as human if one is not identified as man or woman, and vice versa, since manhood, womanhood, and humanity are not apolitical notions (as if there were such a thing), but very political notions of empire.
>
> (Thomas, 2007, p. 28)

Here he is describing the function of the gender binary as a tool of oppression in that womanhood and manhood were equal to humanity under chattel slavery. But through claiming manhood and womanhood for themselves, Europeans, and their American descendants, othered and dehumanized the people they enslaved by stripping them of any association with manhood or womanhood and reducing them to the animal female and male. However, non-Europeans claiming this association with manhood and womanhood would still be entering into a colonial system. Thomas says later,

> While the rhetoric of sex often denotes an anatomical biology that can refer to human beings and non-human animals alike, the rhetoric of gender refers to what has come to be called the social construction of sex as gender among human beings alone – as if its anatomical–biological base were not also itself socially constructed or instituted. The paradigmatic space between sex and gender is, significantly, the place where, even according to this account, gender could be constructed differently by different cultures and different histories at different times and in different places. Yet the fact that gender appears to always, inevitably, get collapsed with sex in Western accounts proves that both sex and gender have been conceived in culturally specific and historically static, Western terms.
>
> (2007, p. 29)

Thomas references Nigerian scholar Oyèrónké Oyêwùmí's argument that precolonial Yoruban culture did not include cultural conceptions of "woman" and "man" or "female" and "male", and that Western feminism's claims of gender and biological sex as a social construction obscure the racial politics that informed those social constructions. He asserts, "For its articulation of gender remains anchored in anatomy in the very Western tradition of biological determinism" (2007, p. 24). If a people are taken or colonized from a culture where there are no conceptions of gender or completely different constructions of gender, it creates a complicated relationship with Western constructions of gender and the resulting deconstruction of gender. On one hand, claiming the identity of woman or man elevates one to a form of equality within the culture of Western imperialism. On the other hand, it also colonizes and erases the indigenous experience of gender or lack thereof. From this history of gender, it could be extrapolated that nonbinary individuals are seen as less than human in our lack of adherence to the gender binary and that there are even more challenges for Black Indigenous People of Colour to reclaim the nonbinary ways of living of their ancestral cultures. I would argue that the intersection of decolonizing race and gender identity leads to greater risk of discrimination and violence, even as it leads to more personal freedom. The gender binary functions as an alchemical *solutio* for gender, separating that which is already joined in many indigenous cultures, and a counterpoint to the transcendent function. Decolonization operates as a form of transcendent function, bringing together that which was unnaturally separated.

Conclusion

The queer and the nonbinary are primordial archetypes that can be portals into the depths of the psyche if we allow ourselves to walk through the liminal gateways into the unknown. Just as science fiction allows us to explore the unknown in the physical universe beyond our planet, so the queer *tekhne* of the nonbinary allows us to explore the universe within the human experience through the transcendent. Systems of domination and the fear of the other that they perpetuate do not function to support this exploration. But as *Star Trek: Discovery* shows us, there are beautiful stories, beautiful "living poems", for us to discover in ourselves and in each other. Can we find the pleasure, the joy, and the community that awaits us as we listen and take in these stories? Can we find ways to join opposites together in transcendence? That is my hope for the now and the future that awaits.

References

Anonymous (n.d.a) Adira Tal, *Memory Alpha*, https://memory-alpha.fandom.com/wiki/Adira_Tal?oldid=2851864 (Accessed 9 February 2022).

Anonymous (n.d.b) Borg, *Star Trek*, www.startrek.com/database_article/borg (Accessed 21 February 2022).

Anonymous (n.d.c) Borg, *Memory Alpha*, https://memory-alpha.fandom.com/wiki/Borg?oldid=2843860 (Accessed 24 January 2022).

Anonymous (n.d.d) Gray Tal, *Memory Alpha*, https://memory-alpha.fandom.com/wiki/Gray_Tal?oldid=2839819 (Accessed 14 January 2022).

Anonymous (n.d.e) Janet (Species). *The Good Place Wiki*. https://thegoodplace.fandom.com/wiki/Janet_(Species) (Accessed 28 January 2022)

Anonymous (n.d.f) Starfleet, *Memory Alpha*, https://memory-alpha.fandom.com/wiki/Starfleet?oldid=2849488 (Accessed 5 February 2022).

Anonymous (n.d.g) United Federation of Planets, *Memory Alpha*, https://memory-alpha.fandom.com/wiki/United_Federation_of_Planets?oldid=2840604 (Accessed 14 January 2022).

Anonymous (n.d.h) *Bechdel Test Movie List*, https://bechdeltest.com/ (Accessed 17 February 2022).

Anonymous (n.d.i) Technology, *Online Etymology Dictionary*, www.etymonline.com/word/technology (Accessed 1 June 2021).

Anonymous (n.d.j) Trill, *Memory Alpha*, https://memory-alpha.fandom.com/wiki/Trill, (Accessed 2 August 2023).

Anonymous (2018a) The Vito Russo Test, *GLAAD*, www.glaad.org/sri/2018/vitorusso (Accessed 17 February 2022).

Anonymous (2018b) What does two-spirit mean?, *Them*, www.them.us/video/watch/geo-neptune-explains-two-spirit (Accessed 22 February 2022).

Brumble, H.D. (1998) *Classical Myths and Legends of the Middle Ages and Renaissance: A Dictionary of Allegorical Meanings*. Westport, CT: Greenwood Press.

Butler, J. (1999/2006) *Gender Trouble: Feminism and the Subversion of Identity*, London: Routledge.

Fordham, F. et al. (2023) *Carl Jung | Biography, Archetypes, Books, Collective Unconscious, & Theory*, Brittanica, www.britannica.com/biography/Carl-Jung (Accessed 20 February 2022).

Diavolo, L. (2017) LGBTQ Institute in Germany was burned down by Nazis, *Teen Vogue*, www.teenvogue.com/story/lgbtq-institute-in-germany-was-burned-down-by-nazis (Accessed 8 February 2022).

Dickey, L.M. (2020) Gender nonbinary mental health, in E.D. Rothblum (ed.), *The Oxford Handbook of Sexual and Gender Minority Mental Health*, New York: Oxford University Press, pp. 295–304.

Freud, S., Haute, P. V., & Westerink, H. (1905/2017) *Three Essays on the Theory of Sexuality: The 1905 Edition*, London: Verso Books.

Fuller, B., et al. (Directors). (2017, Present). Star Trek: Discovery. In *Star Trek: Discovery*. CBS.

Hardell, A. (2019) Nonbinary comes in every age, *YouTube*, https://youtu.be/Bo2FgrTfubw (Accessed 22 February 2022).

Johnson, K. (2014) Queer theory in T. Teo (ed.), *Encyclopedia of Critical Psychology*, New York: Springer, pp. 1618–1624).

Jule, A. (2014) Gender theory, in A.C. Michalos (ed.), *Encyclopedia of Quality of Life and Well-Being Research*, Dordrecht: Springer, pp. 2464–2466.

Jung, C.G. (1953) Religious ideas in alchemy, in *Psychology and Alchemy*, Hove: Routledge & Kegan Paul, pp. 225–472.

Jung, C.G. (1960) The transcendent function in *Structure and Dynamics of the Psyche*, Hove: Routledge & Kegan Paul, pp. 67–91.

Jung, C.G. (1966) Anima and animus, in *Two Essays on Analytical Psychology*, Hove: Routledge & Kegan Paul, pp. 188–211.

Jung, C.G. (1968) The psychology of the child archetype, in *The Archetypes and the Collective Unconscious*, Hove: Routledge & Kegan Paul, pp. 151–181.

Jung, C.G. (1977) The question of medical intervention, in *The Symbolic Life*, Hove: Routledge & Kegan Paul, pp. 347–348.

Juschka, D.M. (2016) Feminism and gender theory, in M. Stausberg and S. Engler (eds), *The Oxford Handbook of the Study of Religion*, Oxford: Oxford University Press, pp.136–149.

Kellaway, M. (2014) Trans men on sex, art, and identity in transparent, *Advocate*, www.advocate.com/arts-entertainment/television/2014/11/03/trans-men-sex-art-and-identity-transparent (Accessed 28 January 2021).

Lane, J. (2022) Can we say bye-bye to the binary? (no. 3), in *Getting Curious with Jonathan Van Ness*, Netflix, www.netflix.com/watch/81361143.

LeVay, S. (1996) *Queer Science: The Use and Abuse of Research into Homosexuality*, Cambridge, MA: The MIT Press.

Little Bear, L. (2004) Preface to the Routledge Classics Edition, in D. Bohm *On Creativity*, London: Routledge, pp. vii–xiv.
Marsalis, A. (Director). (2017, July 12). Caroling Dusk (205). In *Queen Sugar*. OWN.
Milan, T. (2017) "Queen Sugar" actor Brian Michael Smith comes out as transgender, *NBC News*, www.nbcnews.com/feature/nbc-out/queen-sugar-actor-brian-michael-smith-comes-out-transgender-n783451 (Accessed 28 January 2022).
Nieder, T.O. and Strauss, B. (2015) Transgender health care in Germany: Participatory approaches and the development of a guideline, *International Review of Psychiatry*, 27(5), pp. 416–426.
Oyêwùmí, O. (1997) *The Invention of Women: Making an African Sense of Western Gender Discourses*, Minneapolis, MN: University of Minnesota Press.
Perlman, M. (2019) How the word "queer" was adopted by the LGBTQ community, *Columbia Journalism Review*, www.cjr.org/language_corner/queer.php (Accessed 2 February 2022).
Rhude, K. (2018) *The Third Gender and Hijras*. Harvard Divinity School, https://rpl.hds.harvard.edu/religion-context/case-studies/gender/third-gender-and-hijras (Accessed 2 February 2022)
Rowland, S. (2002) *Jung: A Feminist Revision*, Cambridge: Polity Press.
Rowland, S. and Weishaus, J. (2021) *Jungian Arts-Based Research and "The Enchantment of New Mexico"*, London: Routledge.
Rutsky, R. L. (2016) Technologies, in B. Clarke and M. Rossini (eds), *The Cambridge Companion to Literature and the Posthuman*, Cambridge: Cambridge University Press, pp. 182–195.
Salamon, G. (2021). Queer Theory, in K.Q. Hall & Ásta (eds), *The Oxford Handbook of Feminist Philosophy*. New York: Oxford University Press, https://doi.org/10.1093/oxfordhb/9780190628925.013.42
Schiebinger, L. (1993) *Nature's Body: Gender in the Making of Modern Science* (1st edn), Boston, MA: Beacon Press.
Schur, M., et al. (Directors). (2016–2020) *The Good Place*. NBC.
Tasker, C. (2021) HUGE: Loki Reveal Confirms His Gender Identity, *Inside the Magic*, https://insidethemagic.net/2021/06/marvel-loki-gender-fluid-ct1/ (Accessed 18 February 2022).
The New School (2017) *Bell hooks – Are You Still a Slave? Liberating the Black Female Body*, YouTube, www.youtube.com/watch?v=rJk0hNROvzs (Accessed 22 February 2022).
Thomas, G. (2007) *The Sexual Demon of Colonial Power: Pan-African Embodiment and Erotic Schemes of Empire*, Bloomington, IN: Indiana University Press.
Townsend, M. and Deerwater, R. (2021) *2021 GLAAD Studio Responsibility Index*, GLAAD Studio Responsibility Index, GLAAD Media Institute, www.glaad.org/sri/2021 (Accessed 17 February 2023).
Vary, A. B. (2020) Inside the groundbreaking *Star Trek: Discovery* episode with trans and non-binary characters, *Variety*, https://variety.com/2020/tv/news/star-trek-discovery-trans-non-binary-blu-del-barrio-ian-alexander-1234824183/ (Accessed 18 February 2022).
Williams, L. (2017). Behind the scenes with TV's first gender non-binary character, https://archive.thinkprogress.org/showtime-billions-nb-character-e1be43f9a3b0/ (Accessed 17 February 2022).

Part Four

Enactment

Performative Demonstrations

Wonder Vision (Adapted from a Talk Which Was Even More Chaotic Than This)

Justina Robson

Science fiction (sf) and fantasy are unique in their scope to allow the imagination unlimited rein. They are an exceptional opportunity to explore the world of possibilities open to human beings, both externally in the material universe and within our societies/ourselves.

When we read about radically different ideas and, most importantly, see them in action, we become inspired. We evolve. Our creativity is stirred. Life finds a way.

We have many moments of despair and disillusion too. These moments are of equal, perhaps greater importance in enabling development, even though they may be very painful. Following the adventures of others, for good or ill, is the purpose of storytelling. The concepts stimulate speculation, and the vicarious thrill of the stories fuels us with the energy to take action, or to forego it.

In sf the best writers strive to show all kinds of diverse, but very real, possibilities. In fantasy they demonstrate the best and worst of the span of human nature, dramatised to extremes. The genres can be very different in the experience they offer, and contain within them a multitude of all forms of story, but they share this common reaching for the limits of our expanse, and that's why I always think of them as a unified entity. Other people divide them differently and there are, of course, many stories which have all the flavour of the genres while maintaining every conservative norm they possibly can. Does that make them less fantastic?

Yes. Infinitely. But people love the paraphernalia of genre, and it is easy to get stuck in the comfort zone of familiar tropes and symbols. Reinforcing the status quo is the political and ideological opposite of what I was describing above as the purpose of the fantastic.

There is another situation in fantastic storytelling, which arises often for me as a composer of these things, and that is the power that tropes and stereotypes have. They are not simple, particularly the complicated ones that exist as memes in their own right; for example, the stable boy who is the rightful king, or the android with the compassionate heart of gold. These things were astonishing the first time around. Now they are old hat, but we still enjoy them.

In this cynical new world where we have all consumed so much fiction thanks to twenty-four hours of constant entertainment supply, if you want to stun people with strange and wonderful ideas, you have to craft something like *The Handmaid's Tale*

(Atwood, 1985) or *Game Of Thrones* (Martin, 1996) both of which are not radical in terms of the ideas they contain, but which none the less present them with layers and complexities and multitudes of character action and response. It is this richness of diversity, as well as the savagery of the action, which makes them so compelling.

The strongest, most revealing tropes morph according to the times in fascinating ways; confirming that sf and fantasy are never really about future or past, but always the present.

Anecdotally, I was thinking recently that it is interesting how resource–fatigue fiction (so critical in our age) has morphed over the last fifty years, from the casual annihilation horror of *Logan's Run* (Nolan and Clayton, 1967), where everyone is executed at twenty-one because of overpopulation, to *The Hunger Games* (Collins, 2008), where the children of the poor will fight and die to entertain the rich, and now *Squid Game* (Netflix, 2021) where the poor will contest and die/kill to win a chance of wealth, for entertainment of the ultra-rich.

Logan's Run looks surprisingly egalitarian as a future vision of dystopic state control compared with these modern two instances of gladiatorial mortal combat for sport, in which it has been assumed there won't be any limits put on capitalist values. In fact, in both second examples those values are equally corrupting across society (the rich exploit, the poor do not rebel, thus keeping their ranking positions according to the system rather than succumb to compassion). In *Logan's Run* the rebel is the executor employed to ensure compliance. In *The Hunger Games* eventual rebellion is inspired by the gladiator. In *Squid Game* the role of exploiter and exploited undergoes twists and turns.

These share a repulsion at authoritarian control, class power inequality and an appalled fascination with the contortions that people will perform as they try to escape both. In my perception, although *Logan's Run* envisions a place to escape to (a Martian colony), *The Hunger Games* offers no outside-the-system (we must fix this place) and *Squid Game* takes place entirely in the contemporary world (we chose to go there). This is an interesting journey for the dystopian resource war story to take at this point in time!

My personal writer-journey

When I started to read sf and fantasy, they opened my eyes to the size of the universe and the size of me; the timespan of the universe and the likely timespan of me. I wanted to find out all that I could before I had to leave. Not least because I could not help but see that there was trouble. Everywhere. What fools the people of the past were! How smart and capable we new ones could turn out to be!

Surely, we could fix this. Probably before I was forty.

The dreams of youth have now become the "ugh, *why?*" of my fifties but, in spite of temptation, I have not yet reached, "I give up on you idiots!" Although I do keep writing, "But why can't we just kill them all?" stories …

Back to the past, though. sf and fantasy offered an escape from the rest of my life, which was often lonely and boring, filled with all the usual stresses for people not so good at the social game.

Writing genre, as well as reading it, has been a wonderful journey. It seems strange to think of it now, but discovery was my primary interest and becoming a writer was the necessary secondary justification I handed out to family and friends who asked what I would do when I grew up.

Writing fanfiction (*Star Wars* mostly, but also of McCaffrey's (1968) Dragonriders of Pern stories) was my favourite hobby for many years, and I did not make a serious effort at original material until my twenties. I was put off by all the authorial warnings about not being human enough until you are over forty and not being [insert reason] enough to make it at all as it was a very difficult business.

My relationship with sf, when approaching it as literature and not other media, was further complicated by my understanding that there were rules – of content, structure, style, character, approach, verisimilitude etc. to which I must adhere to succeed. There was also canon – the edifice of previous acclaimed books. And a massive edifice it was too, of most of which I remain entirely ignorant.

In writing I wanted to be free. But I wanted to belong to the sf club, so it looked like I would have to pay the subscription fee and abide by at least some of the rules and namecheck the names and at least skim-read the list.

I was filled with a sense of rebellion at all this authoritarian gatekeeper guff. This coincided and meshed very nicely with my feminist sense of struggle against the patriarchal order. I wanted to belong and succeed in a place which I had a lot of contempt for. So ... rather like those dystopian novels, and everyone else's teenage inner life.

I studied science, did a degree in subjects I thought would take me to understanding humanity as if we were a puzzle that could be solved with enough application. Or a game that could be played. A maze that could be escaped. A thing that could be disassembled and remade better. I was fired up for the rebellion, but it was difficult to see exactly who I was rebelling against. This sense of internal warfare drove the impulse to write and was only appeased by writing through which I hoped to discover some kind of peace or solution.

I had already absorbed the notion that we were a flawed bunch. From religion, stories and education in my culture, I felt that humans were following a path of development from bad to better, always moving up, always moving on. But I kept noticing that, in so many ways, they definitely were not doing that. In fact, although technology looked very progressive, the churn of culture and behaviour did not actually look much like progress. It was looking very much like it was stuck in a rut where it played with ideas about itself but never actually underwent serious efforts to change. It was always fad dieting, always getting steadily fatter.

And then, under that layer of pretence was a whole other layer of things that begged questions. Progress to what? From where? What for? Who for? Was sf itself, apparently about the future, *really* progressive? (Er, yes and no: depends on who was writing it, is the answer).

These questions occupied me endlessly. I always felt I was out to fix things and if I dug deep enough I would find the seam of diamonds that answered all this with pure clarity. I did not understand for a very long time that really what I wanted to fix was me. And having done me, then I'd move on and fix everyone else and, no, that certainly is not how so many villains end up being mad, bad and in asylums or venting their disappointments onto the world and creating the worst atrocities known to any being. I write sf. At least I didn't create a bloody religion.

And that trip to self-awareness got me through the first three books of my own. Quite some fuel tank it was too.

It's science, Bob, as you know

I think that literature, and all the media storytelling fiction modes, are the greatest people-science. In order to learn how people work you have to take them apart in real time, while they are working, without disrupting them. Every moment, every character, is a wealth of possibility and it is not possible to predict what they will do, even when you are the writer.

Many times they do not do what you had in mind for the plot. When that happens, it is the best thing ever and feels like you have really struck on something worthwhile because you and your pretensions just got kicked out of the park by something more real.

After three fairly straightforward sf books I got myself kicked out of the park by writing what I had intended to be as a re-approach to a very difficult first novel, long abandoned. I started, unconsciously, meta critiquing it as I went along, so I was writing a story but also creating a world in which that story was itself under scrutiny for being a fiction. I did this because in the intervening period between writing it as a 'straight' book and returning to its ideas I had become painfully, horribly self-aware. And paranoid, as that awareness duplicated itself and turned into What If They Realise I Am Bonkers? Yes, the full-fledged impostor moment.

I felt self-conscious to a degree that was almost leading to out-of-self experience. Unfortunately, I took out my fear as anger and became hyper-critical of my aspirational teenage self and her idealistic visions. I did not want to reveal them to the super smart and well-lived people I imagined every other reader and critic to be. I did not want to admit to them as they would reveal me to be a pathetic individual full of feelings and silliness, quite unworthy to lock horns with proper sf writers or any thinkers of note. But at least I didn't go the full nine yards and invent my own religion! I thought defensively.

Yes, I had forgotten entirely about Philip K. Dick, a hero of mine. He also did not create a religion, just suffered under one that he couldn't quite grasp, or defeat, or embrace even though he longed to.

Anyway, having forgotten about him, I wanted to seem like I belonged to the serious ideas people. But I also hated the serious ideas people. I wanted to be liked as an entertaining writer, but I despised entertainment if it didn't have any substance. I wanted comfort desperately, but I rejected it as for the weak. I wanted validation and I thought the safest way there was to take the piss out of myself before anyone else got the opportunity to so … that project was quite the seesaw.

I was always in the vice-jaws between conforming to what I thought I should conform to and hating all of it. I am not these things! I am …

... a mess!

That book was *Living Next Door to the God of Love* (Robson, 2005) and thankfully, I had some grace visit me halfway through and decided, yes, this was my mess, and I was embracing it! I love my mess! The negativity stopped and happiness set in. I think it is my best.

Other things

As well as fiction I used to write reviews and criticism, but then I stopped. Some writers that I know, like Adam Roberts, write both very well, but my critical abilities are always on the knife-edge of negatively impacting my creativity.

At the peak of this I became too self-conscious of how my work might be seen to be able to actually work. This became much worse with the advent of social media in all its forms. In the privacy of my mind, I frantically pawed over every negative point I had ever publicly made about any other person's work ever and obsessed about how I had probably got it wrong and done them irretrievable harm and/or wrong. Or both. I felt convinced that I deserved to receive all that karma back. I backed out of critical work so I didn't build up a bigger debt. But I still thought about things. I just didn't say or write it.

A lot of my energy went into worrying, particularly as I write about subjects that are often controversial such as politics, power, gender and sex. Yes, I want to write and be a part of that particular creative group and body of work. No, I don't want to be in the spotlight, thanks very much. But you can't both hide and write truthfully.

In the last two long works I published – *Glorious Angels* (2015) and *The Switch* (2017) – I've focused a bit more on these things, feeling safely obscure. They both were created at a time when my career as a published author had fallen into the classic mid-lister, 'sells low, crits high' category. It is a point where you can either panic more or just lean into being able to do what you want because it is not likely to make a big difference anyway, in terms of your commercial dreams.

I kept going back to engineering utopias badly as a theme.

Most recently I wrote a story called *Paper Hearts* (2020) in which an AI (Artificial Intelligence) becomes the administrator of everything in the world. It enforces a no-violence, no-oppression promise with faultless accuracy. Everyone has money. Everyone can do what they like. But the people feel they've become zoo animals, because they are not free to lash out. Verbally they could, they can express themselves fully, but practically – nothing doing. All they have is their words, but because nobody is in any danger of physical harm, whatever wounds they tried to inflict to get attention, or to change someone's ways – gradually lost their impact. People chill out. But they struggle with not having a struggle. So the AI invents a game of Forever War for them. They still want to escape, though. Even when everything is run so much more nicely than for Logan, or Katniss, or Gi-Hun.

And then the AI has to arrange its own escape from their efforts.

If being a writer is being cracked, then being a reader is being the light

I would not want you to think that being a reader is not half the job or the fun!

Writers attempt to create various things but in the act of reading it is the reader only who is godlike, because in order to make someone's book or story great, you must be a reader who matches or exceeds its potential, who reaches for the connections, joins the dots, lets themselves roll with the flow, perhaps lets their mind go beyond whatever the writer has made – and that requires engagement, generosity and commitment. It is a creative act. Collaborative for sure, but generous and active.

Only in your mind can the story come to life. And it will be unique when it does.

What was in the writer's mind is a starting point. The gaps matter as much as the text. Where the gaps are, is where the light gets in. When I read your work I'm the light. I try to be a good light but I'm not always suited to the task. That is just how it is.

It is an art, not a science, because we can never know each other's starting conditions. Everyone walks around with their own secret history. Maybe mine fits well with what you have written, and maybe it does not at all. I enjoy fiction much more now that I see how this works. I do not feel that I have to agree or disagree with it.

Before I go, another bit about light

As you will have already noted, no doubt, my mind leaps around a lot. I should, if I were creating a successful talk, order it properly, with a plan. But I no longer believe in the power of organised planned thinking as very useful. All my creative moments of inspiration have been mostly zippy, disorganised connective sets, profoundly complicated. And so I must now introduce a moment of The Enlightenment in a way which seems disconnected, but is not.

You already know about it (I hope!). In the context of this talk (now chapter) The Enlightenment kept returning, like a good dog, to stand as a point of origin for the whole project of sf, and the point at which it deviated from its shared source material (wonder) with fantasy. And the good dog led me to this quote in a great essay by Andy Owen, called "Reading John Gray In War".

He is discussing a point by the philosopher, John Gray: "Interestingly, Gray identifies the Enlightenment as the point where our utopias became located in the future, rather than in the past or in some fantasy realm, where it was clear they were exactly that: fantasies" (Owen, 2021).

It is an excellent point, which notes how The Enlightenment restructured our concepts of space and time – the when and how things can take place.

It was the point when fantasy and sf diverged! Concepts that had been one were now different!

I went to sleep that night after reading this essay thinking I've cracked this talk!

Then I woke up at 3am with the horrible realisation that my ideas – about dream factories, and self-engineering, and godly power manifest through the hands of human beings – weren't reality.

They were science fiction and/or fantasy. Again. I can't even do real when I'm doing real! I had assumed this notion (that sf was rational, progressive, in accordance with human advance) was true, and now I see that it isn't all the things I had based on it just fall over ...

Fortunately the sun came up on something shiny

sf has always reached far up into philosophy and down into the most commercial and thoughtless entertainment. Its scope is so big.

Look at that distinction. Up. Down. High. Low. We all know what that means. Valuable. Trash. Divine. Damned. We are back in trading land, the land of value, rank, class.

Now. This is what I found when I rushed off in the morning to write my little bit on The Enlightenment. I found that my beliefs and values, my driving impulses, were grounded in a very dodgy story.

> Divine. Damned. That's the religious end.
> Valuable. Trash. That's the capitalism bit.
> High. Low. That's the social bit.
> Up. Down. That's the energy, or mystic bit.

Snobbery. Value. Security. Prestige. Money. Contempt.

These are all currencies. Our meaning is made up of currency exchange, value, flowing all the time. We are dynamically trapped by being defined by these things. I could, as an individual, free myself, but everyone around me wants to know the value of everything, so it is nearly impossible to escape or even to ask for another token to be assigned. Ask any trans-person. (An early and concurrent obsession of mine is with linguistics and psychology and how we create meaning and exist according to it. My mind is never quite off that subject).

If you want to manipulate reality you must become an expert in currency trading and manipulation.

Bits of coin

Currencies, like their sister word, currents, flow with whatever energy they conduct. We are all engaged all the time with the world's many social currencies of human conduct and valuation.

These are always specific to our culture and background and to our personal history and evolution. So, your shame and my shame are the same feeling, but what gives rise to them may be very different for each of us.

This is why The Enlightenment was such a radical shift.

When it re-valued the world. It re-ordered not only the value of, say, Reason over Storytelling, but it re-ordered space and time – our entire inner geography – so that utopias and heavens, which had been in nostalgic pasts or other dimensions, became located, newly, in the future.

This is the system of which I am a product. Until recently a fairly unwitting product.

Before I saw this, I had not thought about how my own personal self-valuations on all these currencies – my spending, my gains, my losses – were determined by this decision of The Enlightenment. I only knew that my whole sense of my worth was determined by all the valuations I had going on. And that sense of my worth dictated my wellness across all categories of my being.

I thought a lot of these currencies were offensively stupid. Especially those promoted by right-wing nationalists with a patriarchal bent.

Women are for example valued lower than men in many cultures, and no living woman can not be aware of that constant fact. So, this is a constructed human value. Constructed for a reason, with an agenda, for a purpose, as a currency. Against me. From before I was born. I came into ready-made poverty, by design.

Could it have been worse? Of course. Add in all the extra categories you know that demote you. I got off fairly lightly as things go. But back to the point.

It is the design bit that is the killer. If it was evolution at work, nature doing its own thing, which is often the explanation given, that'd be one thing. But this is just economics by violence now.

(I wrote a book about this a few years ago called *Glorious Angels*. And another one called *The Switch*. I didn't know I was writing about that but they are both relentlessly focused on that.)

In The Enlightenment, Reason itself, always dry and cold, like the surface of Mars, attempted very successfully to rebrand itself as desirable and essential, High, Valuable, Aspirational. Authoritative. Unquestionable. Impeachable. It was politically savvy enough to use the playbill of the Church, who had already separated Dry and Juicy out, and High and Low, Divine and Damned.

sf you will be told, values reason. And quietly, silently, all the values of reason will sneak into your idea of what sf is and take up residence, waiting for their chance.

Ick! Invasion of the Meme Snatchers!

Now, you cannot revalue a system and throw out the system at the same time. So the takeover by Reason, installing itself where religion used to be, resulted in a realisation that there was no way it was going to get Juicy. Because Juicy was already out, along with loads of other things, which would also be tossed onto the trashheap called 'Feminine'.

Therefore Juicy, which includes, of course, subjective experience, is chucked into Low, Trash, Damned. High value stocks were all in Objectivity, Maths, Logic, Science and Technology. The future was visible, bright, hard-cornered, and was going to be engineered, with logic and industry. Another borrowing from religion (improvement through suffering, baby), whose entire set-up got passed on, but re-branded. It's not an accident that the natural world is now under such threat – it's not a part of this future vision at all. It literally does not feature.

This is how the world ends: not with a war, but a marketing campaign

It is not an accident that sf is the cauldron in which a lot of the current crop of tech CEOs and scientists were forged. It is a shame more of the politicians didn't get cast in that mould, or is it? The potentials are enormous in all directions. The ability to dream and create and to basically, in Dungeons & Dragons (D&D) terms, 'alter fate' is a huge lure, and a huge ego trap, and a huge hopeful wonder and very much the place where one is most likely to encounter a warning that we as a species are starting to play God (*Dugeons & Dragons*, 2014).

It is this creative, possibility, aspect of science, and science fiction, which touches the divine. Often perilously. And it is also this point where it meets fantasy. Often perilously. People always overfocus on the sf, but not enough on the fantasy at this point, not critically enough on the fantasy.

That cracking sound is me making an omelette

Story and its lesser cousin, narrative, is the sculpting tool for humans. It is how we transmit information and meaningful social and cultural information in particular. We create cohesion, or enmity, value systems and scapegoats with stories.

None of them are true. What, not one?

No. Not even that one.

This story about what human life in the modern world is, is particularly rooted in the capitalist West and is on the whole a very masculine and reductivist take on the turn of events since the end of the nineteenth century. It is a vision which drives many actions that are as ruthless and persecuting as any medieval religious villainy. It is also the vision that sf drives towards and derives from. The central delusion is the delusion of The Enlightenment itself: namely, that reason, coupled with a vision of humanity as having a duty to pursue its species' ends as the manifest inheritors and commanders of the universe, will ultimately prevail over everything and bring order and security.

sf is part of the grand gesture through which, as we take flight to space, we take flight from the petty boundaries of our animal origins. We are winning! Billionaires prove it.

In the service of this vision, Owen notes in his essay that people are often exhorted and excused with the idea that "you can't make an omelette without breaking some eggs". He points out Gray's riposte, "You can break a lot of eggs and still not have an omelette" (Owen, 2021). And I would add to that, 'You can break eggs, but you can't make an egg'.

Everything upon which our existence depends, was not of our doing, and most of it is beyond our comprehension. But we talk of omelettes and eggs so cheaply. Contemplate an egg for five minutes and you'll see what your knowledge is worth, and what your omelette skill really amounts to. It is some fairly petty shit. Going to Mars. Ferchrissakes.

Gray observed that there will be no saving people from the thing that they are, no improving them and evolving them into a better kind of being *en masse*. Even creating a space within which there can be a term of peace and cooperation is a difficult balancing act, requiring many stories and much diplomacy.

It is no accident that most *Star Trek* episodes spend a lot of time figuring out what different cultures and people mean. Independently, but hardly uniquely, I came to this conclusion myself and immediately felt a weight lift off me, as well as any further desire to write fiction, or anything.

I had not realised until then that the desire to create or discover a utopia was the hidden engine that had driven all my travels. I had a faith that the task could be accomplished, that a better world was a thing that could be reached. And then. I didn't. Instead, I saw that we had been there all along, we just don't know it. T.S. Elliot had already got there long before me in Little Gidding, "The Four Quartets": "And the sum of all our travelling will be to return home and to know the place for the first time" (Eliot, 1943).

I wonder how many before me have taken this journey and found its end, sighed this sigh. It must be millions.

Final speculations from a disorganised mammal

The technological advancements we make are no guarantor of any spiritual or moral, or personal advancements. We cannot manage ourselves for the most part – let alone ourselves as large groups of diverse interests and origins. The brief moment of time in which I exist in my peaceful middle-class life bubble is a lucky break for me, on an ocean of chaotic time, just a chance, not the consequence of an aeons long project of building a better world. The entire project of sf, when seen as a project, is predicated on an illusion, a story. The Enlightenment itself is an illusion.

I have not talked about fantasy and what happened to it after The Enlightenment, when sf became the way forwards and fantasy was reassigned for children, idiots and those without sufficient moral fortitude to face 'reality'. (How hateful these judgemental voices are who say these things, are they not? And beneath that, how sad and disappointed.)

The story of fantasy, as brokered by The Enlightenment, tells that it is a dream factory, and a dramatic stage upon which grand psychodramas play out in arresting metaphorical and allegorical power. Its source material is all from the past: myth, legend, folktale, hearsay, history. It has no present – that belongs to Contemporary Literature. It has no future, because that belongs to sf. It has no relevance because it belongs to all the categories we have thrown out with the bathwater.

Post Enlightenment, fantasy must now be reinvented, clinically, as psychology, sociology, anthropology and a lot of other -ologies, otherwise its findings and wisdoms cannot be given any credence in this very post-symbolic world.

Fantasy is a whole different way of seeing the world, a language of energy and personal agency. It is the place where the unseen manifests, the dimensions of unspoken things. It is everywhere and all the time. It is the currency of the inner world of the imagination, which has no limit and which can be crossed in an instant, no matter how large it is. Therein lies – the world itself.

Proposal, a new enlightenment – Back To The Dreaming! No more executors, gladiators or deathmatches. It's time to create visions that are not dangerous (sorry, edgelords of genre) but delightful.

As Shirley Jackson said, in *The Haunting of Hill House,* "No live organism can continue for long to exist sanely under conditions of absolute reality; even larks and katydids are supposed, by some, to dream" (1959/2016, p. 1).

References

Atwood, M. (1986/1996) *The Handmaid's Tale*, London: Vintage.
Collins, S. (2008) *The Hunger Games*, New York: Scholastic.
Dungeons & Dragons Player's Handbook (2014) 5th edn, Wizards of the Coast.
Eliot, T.S. (1943) Four Quartets, London: Harcourt, Brace & Co.
Jackson, S. (1959/2016) *The Haunting of Hill House*, New York: Penguin.
Martin, G.R.R. (1996) *A Game of Thrones*, New York: Bantam Books.
McCaffrey, A. (1968) *Dragonflight*, New York: Ballantine Books.
Nolan, W.F. and Clayton, G.C. (1967/1976), *Logan's Run*, New York: Bantam.
Owen, A. (2021) Reading John Gray in war, *Aeon*, https://aeon.co/essays/how-john-grays-philosophy-helped-me-understand-my-war-experience (Accessed 8 November 2022).
Robson, J. (2005) *Living Next Door to the God of Love*, London: Macmillan.
Robson, J. (2015) *Glorious Angels*, London: Gollanz.
Robson, J. (2017) *The Switch*, London: Gollanz.
Robson, J. (2020) *Paper Hearts*, Alconbury Weston: NewCon Press.

Eve and Ava at the Flaming Sword Café
The Genesis of a Very Short Play

Elizabeth Èowyn Nelson

On September 28th 2020, a group of scholars from all over the world gathered via the magic of wireless internet and glowing laptops for a Feminism and Technology conference. When the organizers posted the call for proposals months before, little did anyone know that a locked-down world would depend so completely upon digital power to sustain crucial scholarly dialogues as well as maintain some semblance of community with friends, families, and co-workers. Marshall McLuhan, were he alive today, would be unsurprised. His many insights in *Understanding Media: The Extensions of Man* (1964/2013) have been reduced to a chirpy soundbite, the medium is the message. McLuhan's intelligent prose greatly exceeds the soundbite in sweep and power. He asserts that technology itself—the devices we use, not the content they deliver—influence social, political, and economic relationships. The revelations about social media algorithms in the last few years confirms that technology does not merely influence. It manipulates. It pervades our psychology, both personal and communal, altering our "patterns of perception steadily and without any resistance" (McLuhan, 2013, p. 18). By controlling the scale and form of human association and action, technology gradually creates a totally new human environment.

Three interconnected technologies shaping the human environment today—wireless internet, mobile digital devices, and social media—have had durable consequences for all of us. On the one hand, they made possible a feminist conference in the midst of a pandemic. On the other, they have given misogynists (and others) a powerful vehicle to cement alliances and foment hateful views. One relevant example for feminists is the rise of an online subculture of "Incels", men who define themselves as involuntarily celibate and feel entitled to sex. Incel forums are characterized by self-pity, misogyny, and endorsing violence against women. Feminism, which is defined by its central concern for how power runs through gendered circuits, must address itself to twenty-first century technologies and the misogynist subcultures they feed.

McLuhan (1964/2013) makes a further point that is germane to any feminist discussion of technology. By continuously embracing the latest device, we serve the objects as though they are gods who control our fate. One could almost view the divide between PC users and Apple users as sectarian violence or at least a schism in the one true church of Mobile Digital Devotion. Between ourselves and our tech, issues of power are close at hand, most of the time literally in our hands. Ask anyone who will admit to a minor addiction to their smartphone—*who's in control?*—and you might get an honest answer.

Because this question and many others have been of interest to me for more than three decades, the Feminism and Technology conference was a welcome invitation to propose a few answers. But rather than propose a standard scholarly paper, I decided to explore the questions via creative fiction that was, in essence, a thought experiment. What might happen if a human, a cyborg, and a goddess had drinks together one night? The result, *Eve and Ava at the Flaming Sword Café*, is a very short one-act play designed to fit into the tight 15-minute presentation limit of the conference. It is a work in progress for a longer, more developed drama.

The psychological and cultural context for *Eve and Ava at the Flaming Sword Café*

The Feminism and Technology conference was particularly interesting to me for a few reasons. Before earning my PhD and becoming a Jung scholar, I worked as a consultant in Silicon Valley. For a time I lived within walking distance of Hewlett and Packard's garage and equally close to where the two Steves, Wozniak and Jobs, built the first Apple computer. As a professor of depth psychology, I channeled that interest into a graduate course entitled "Psyche, Soma, Cyborg: Mobile Digital Technology and the Post-human" that I began teaching in 2014. *Eve and Ava at the Flaming Sword Café* exemplifies arts-based research. It has been, for me, a vital imaginative extension of the key themes in the course, in which the "art" of writing the play was a process of "thinking and learning improvisationally" (Rolling Jnr, 2013, p. 13).

The impulse behind the course and the play is the mandate of Jungian psychology, particularly the archetypal school founded by James Hillman: to move psychology beyond clinical practice out into the world such that the discipline transgresses its own boundaries. A depth psychology, which is rooted in mythology, asserts that soul finds expression in contemporary "arts, culture, and the history of ideas" (Hillman, 1983, p. 9). Soul, or psyche, is also expressed in the technologies that are enfolded into the lived experience of being a person in the first world. A depth psychological approach to technology simply cannot remain bedazzled by the gleaming surfaces and elegant packaging of our indispensable devices. Rather, as Jungians we must go down by slowing down. "Ever since Heraclitus brought soul and depth together in one formulation, the dimension of soul is depth (not breadth or height) and the direction of our soul travel is downward" (Hillman, 1975, p. xvii). Thus, we are obligated to investigate how our personal tech actively shapes daily life, altering (perhaps forever) our ideas of efficiency, productivity, work, rest, play, and intimacy as well as our relationship to being and time. With our bodies enmeshed with our mobile digital devices, we are all cyborg now.

The course I teach on mobile digital technology and the play *Eve and Ava at the Flaming Sword Café* leave open the question of whether being cyborg is post-human or merely human. Andy Clark (2003), a British expert in cognitive hybridization, forcefully argues that we are "natural-born cyborgs" who have always extended our minds with an assortment of devices. The cyborg, "is a disguised vision of (oddly) our own biological nature," he asserts. "What is special about human brains, and what best explains the distinctive features of human intelligence, is precisely their ability to enter into deep and complex relationships with nonbiological constructs, props, and aids" (Clark, 2003, p. 5).

Although I find Clark's (2003) argument compelling I am not entirely convinced. A printed book and a smartphone both qualify as technologies that extend human cognitive capacity. However, a book does not multi-task silently in the background or interrupt us with all manner of notifications. Smartphones as well as tablets, laptops, and other mobile digital devices operate at inhuman (read "machine") speed and task-switch in microseconds. Not so the human being. Sadly, our fantasies of effectiveness are not supported by the research on multi-tasking. We simply don't do it well at all.

The crux of the issue, however, is not whether we can emulate the pace and efficiency of our smart devices but the fact that we think we should. "For the 'message' of any medium or technology," McLuhan (1964/2013) explained, forty years before smartphones, "is the change of scale or pace or pattern that it introduces into human affairs" (McLuhan, 1964/2013, p. 8). My iPhone works rapidly and never rests; why can't I? My iPhone is never irritated when two things compete for its attention; why am I? McLuhan's warning is apt: our tech does not just deliver content. By creating an entirely new social environment with profound psychological implications, it dictates personal and professional standards of behavior often so surreptitiously that we are barely conscious of it. Instead, we engage in passionate cultural debates about content, not medium. Or, as McLuhan poetically says,

> Our conventional response to all media, namely that it is how they are used that counts, is the numb stance of the technological idiot. For the 'content' of a medium is like the juicy piece of meat carried by the burglar to distract the watchdog of the mind.
> (McLuhan, 1964/2013, p. 18)

Our watchdog minds, according to McLuhan, should ignore the apps. Instead, we should alert to how our tech alters the self: extending it *and* limiting it. The first world self is no longer a bodymind. It is a techno-bodymind.

Donna Haraway's prescient "cyborg manifesto"

The aim of *Eve and Ava at the Flaming Sword Café* is to expound upon themes raised in Donna Haraway's oft-quoted "cyborg manifesto" published in her 1991 book *Simians, Cyborgs, and Women: The Reinvention of Nature*. As the title of the book suggests, Haraway foresees the end of humanity and the rise of cyborgs. It may be more accurate to say that she foresees an evolution of humanity into something else, a move from our home in biological nature toward a world in which machines are the next successful life form on a much-altered earth.

Haraway's manifesto anticipated by a decade the point made by Paul Lippman, in his May 2000 address to the International Forum for Psychoanalytic Studies: Cyberculture "is exponentially changing human living along with patterns of communication as we once knew them." Moreover, we now live in a world "in which our ancient home in nature is disappearing" (2000, n.p.). The simultaneous "disappearance" of nature via environmental abuse and degradation and the rapid proliferation of digital screentime in the daily lives of millions of people—that is, alienation from the natural world—is at least a meaningful coincidence. The subtitle to Haraway's book, "the reinvention of nature," may be optimistic.

Haraway has a number of things to say about the cyborg that are reminiscent of Clark's (2003) thesis. For example, she argues from the perspective of the late twentieth century, more than fifteen years before the introduction of the first smartphone, that our machines "have made thoroughly ambiguous the difference between natural and artificial, mind and body, self-developing and externally designed, and many other distinctions that used to apply to organisms and machines" (1991, p. 152). She even hints at the master–slave theme raised by McLuhan (1964/2013) by observing that "our machines are disturbingly lively, and we ourselves frighteningly inert" (Haraway, 1991, p. 152).

Haraway defines the cyborg as "a hybrid of machine and organism" and argues that it is "a creature of social reality as well as a creature of fiction" (1991, p. 149). We may think that the cyborg occupies clearly bounded spaces such as the factory floor or space stations where they assist human productivity or the bounded imaginal space of literature and cinema. On the contrary, the cyborg has infiltrated ordinary life in part because "microelectronic devices ... are everywhere and they are invisible" (p. 153). Or, as Detweiler (2013, p. ix) says, "Technology is increasingly shifting from something outside us to a partner and monitor inside us, an evolutionary upgrade". The notion that the human being can be "upgraded" like a smartphone or an app is unnerving. The consequences for all of us are portentous, as Haraway (1991) asserts:

> The cyborg is a matter of fiction and lived experience that changes what counts as women's experience in the late 20th century. This is a struggle over life and death, but the boundary between of science fiction and social reality is an optical illusion.
>
> (p. 149)

Three decades after the publication of Haraway's cyborg manifesto, only the naïve believe that such a boundary exists.

Haraway's (1991) reference to science fiction in the statement above inspired the choice of characters in *Eve and Ava at the Flaming Sword Café*. Ava in the play is based upon the female cyborg named Ava from the 2015 film *Ex Machina* (Alex Garland, 2014). The film depicts the relationship between creator and creature, similar to Mary Shelley's science fiction masterpiece, *Frankenstein, or a Modern Prometheus* (1818). However, Ava in the film is wholly unlike Shelley's wretched monster. Whereas he is the most soulful character in the novel, capable of freely expressing the full range of human emotion from murderous rage to wracking grief, Ava in *Ex Machina* (and the play) is cool, calculating, and remote, with the emotional depth of a matchstick. Much to the surprise of Nathan, Ava's father/creator in the film, Ava is also an alarmingly independent creature with her own agenda. She evokes Haraway's (1991) observation about the cyborg to a prescient degree:

> Unlike the hopes of Frankenstein's monster, the cyborg does not expect its father to save it through a restoration of the garden; that is, through the fabrication of a heterosexual mate, through its completion in a finished whole, a city, and cosmos.
>
> (p. 151)

In the film, Ava's creator Nathan is her pimp; he procures a mate for Ava to complete her education but, in the end, both her father/creator and her would-be lover Caleb are dispensable. Ava kills Nathan and abandons Caleb to die. Then, dressed like a pubescent woman in a frilly white dress and stiletto shoes, Ava leaves the Eden-like enclave Nathan uses as his laboratory and returns to civilization, alone. The film strongly hints that it is her new hunting ground.

Haraway (1991) declares that the manifesto works within "the utopian [feminist] tradition of imagining a world without gender" (p. 150). This fantasized world will be "a world without Genesis, but maybe also a world without end" since the cyborg exists outside of "salvational history" (p. 150). Eve and all her descendants—flesh and blood human beings—cannot escape our mythical origin in the garden and the fantasy that God, our common divine father, bestowed some of that divinity upon each of us through the warm breath of the *ruach elohim*. Furthermore, as part of the created order that came into being in six days, we remember an original unity and sacred nature. As Haraway reminds us in the manifesto, the world that God made is strictly gendered with Adam on top. Because our first parents, hungry for wisdom, disobeyed God, the descendants of Adam and Eve are caught within salvational history. We cannot save ourselves, yet we long to return to paradise.

Haraway ends the essay with the provocative statement, "though they are bound in a spiral dance, I would rather be a cyborg than a goddess" (1991, p. 181). Hours and hours of discussion would not exhaust the possible interpretations of this declaration. For my students it has been divisive. Some agree with Haraway's preference and others disagree. When we approach the idea that cyborgs can be gender neutral, gender labile, or without gender altogether, the statement, by a human woman, becomes more intriguing. Thus, writing *Eve and Ava at the Flaming Sword Café* was prompted by the question: I wonder what the goddess would say? Enter the character of Sophia, an incarnation of Wisdom in the Western tradition. Sophia is owner of the Flaming Sword Café and the barkeep, who witnesses the testy encounter between Eve and Ava. In the end I discovered that Ava (in the play) wants both, to be cyborg and to be goddess, and she is willing to kill and skin Sophia to get what she wants. Much to my surprise, the play veered into horror, a genre that is intolerable for me to watch. I nearly could not read what "I" had written.

Unlike us, the cyborg "skips the step of original unity" and "would not recognize the Garden of Eden; it is not made of mud and cannot dream of returning to dust" (Haraway, 1991, p. 151). Gleaming metal and silicone, with enhanced intelligence, strength, durability, and the magic of interchangeable parts, the cyborg is an especially fitting evolutionary upgrade over humanity. The cyborg can survive the apocalypse. Indeed, *apocalypse* has no eschatological or theological meaning for the cyborg. The cyborg is future proofed.

Arts-based research and writing *Eve and Ava at the Flaming Sword Café*

Arts-based research fits uneasily within the large family of qualitative methodologies that include phenomenology, narrative inquiry, grounded theory, case study, and others. In fact, it may not fit at all, according to Rowland and Weishaus (2021) and Neilson (2004), because "qualitative research locates meaning in the researcher's interaction with her subjects" (Rowland and Weishaus, 2021, p. 15). The outcome of arts-based research, the art itself, "must ultimately stand alone, not dependent upon the artist for its meaning" (p. 15). I agree with both statements. They reflect my experience of writing *Eve and Ava at the Flaming Sword Café*, but only partly. Yes, the play must ultimately stand alone, independent of the artist. The meaning it has for me, the writer, is only one possible meaning—which will necessarily be different from the meanings arising from the audience (when the play is performed live) or readers (when the play is read as a script). Because I adopt the archetypal move of *personifying* (Hillman, 1975, 1983), the "subjects" in the research are the persons of the play. My interaction with my subjects is meaningful, though it does not exhaust all possible meanings.

Barone (2008) asserts that arts-based research aims for "enhanced understanding through the communication of subjective realities or personal truths that can occur only through works of art" (p. 29). Unlike traditional qualitative methods, arts-based research "is not usually aimed toward securing (or even approaching) either 'objective' or 'subjective' truth" (p. 30). Finley (2008) views it as part of the critical theory tradition, describing it as "action based, process oriented, and situated in real-world problems, events, and communities" (p. 144). A novel and unorthodox approach to research, arts-based studies "are designed in a manner that will promote profound reconsideration of the commonsensical, the orthodox, the clichéd, and the stereotypical" (Barone, 2008, p. 30). Both authors agree that art is used to provoke an emotional response in readers/viewers, as well as to "create dialogue, cause questions, and raise doubts" by appealing to "the power of imagination" (Finley, 2008, p. 144).

Rolling Jnr (2013) points out that arts-based research has a long and meaningful history and "preceded the establishment of the sciences" by millennia (p. 7) and likely "date[s] back to Lower Paleolithic mark-making" (p. 13). Artists work with materials to create an object, and throughout the process, observe what is emerging, often spontaneously. The gap opened between artist and object invites reverie, fantasy, and wonder. "Artistic methods arguably became a rudimentary form of research at the moment early humans acquired the ability to reflect upon their marks so as to revisit or reinterpret prior meanings (p. 13).

Arts-based research, no matter how transgressive, fits neatly within a truly Jungian psychology due to Jung's emphasis on image: "Everything of which we are conscious is an image ... image *is* psyche" (Jung, 1967, p. 50). As a method, arts-based research is amenable to hosting archetypal images, which is the core of creative process. "Insofar as we are able to follow it at all," says Jung (1966), the creative process "consists in the unconscious activation of an archetypal image and in elaborating and shaping this image into the finished work" (p. 82). Through the shaping process, artists may be able to lifts the idea they are seeking to express "out of the occasional and transitory into the realm of the ever enduring" (p. 82). A more modest claim is that the shaping process will generate new kinds of knowledge that are unlikely to emerge by following traditional qualitative research methods. At the very least, the researcher and the reader/viewer will benefit from the fructifying influence of the unconscious, the kinds of "fantasy thinking" Jung advocated as early as 1916 in volume 5 of the *Collected Works* (1967, p. 18), which became the basis for active imagination, his method of working with unconscious content. Both in the early and late formulations, Jung was clear on two things: the primacy of the image and their alluring aliveness for one who is willing to grant them sustained attention. "Active imagination, as the term denotes, means that the images have a life of their own and that the symbolic events develop according to their own logic—that is, of course, if your conscious reason does not interfere" (1977, p. 171). Later, in his long essay on the practice of psychotherapy, Jung offers a rich image for the influence of the unconscious on consciousness. It is "rather like the flooding of the Nile: it increases the fertility of the land" (1954, p. 269).

Arts-based research reflects the aesthetic emphasis in an archetypal psychology, which is neither pretty, soothing, nor beautiful. Hillman (1992) explains:

> By aesthetic response I do not mean beautifying. I do not mean planting trees and going to the galleries. I do not mean gentility, soft background music, clipped hedges—that sanitized, deodorized use of the word "aesthetic" that has deprived it of its teeth and tongue and fingers.
>
> (p. 113)

Instead, Hillman asks us to notice the expressive forms of the world as "a physiognomy to be faced" (p. 102). Each particular thing of the world is "an object bear[ing] witness to itself in the image it offers, and its depth lies in the complexities of this image (p. 103).

Jungian arts-based research

Susan Rowland (Rowland and Weishaus, 2021) has made an exemplary contribution to Jungian literature, depth psychological inquiry, and arts-based research. As she states in the opening paragraph, "Jung and arts-based research already share strategies about knowing and being that can be furthered by forging a relationship between them" (p. 2). Rowland then proceeds to do so, pointing out what I mentioned above: the primacy of the image, and imagination as a vehicle for knowing, in both. "Doing art is an essential and revelatory part of the research inquiry. Art-making becomes knowledge-making" (p. 3).

Jungian arts-based research is also "willingness to participate in a mystery, or non-rational ways of making meaning" (Rowland, 2021, p. 65). This certainly describes a crucial period of Jung's life, as the 2009 publication of *Liber Novus* attests. Although Jung had a complicated (complexed) relationship to art, it is evident that his drawings and paintings, in addition to the painstakingly rendered calligraphy, were fueled by *gnōthi seauton*, to know himself. As a clinical enterprise, Jung's analytical psychology directed non-rational ways of knowing to the individuation of the person rather than the individuation of the images. Hillman (1983), borrowing from Sufi scholar Henri Corbin, offers a corrective to this person-centered approach. "The intention is the realization of the images—for they are the psyche—and not merely the human subject…. 'it is their individuation, not ours,' that matters" (p. 27).

Writing *Eve and Ava at the Flaming Sword Café* began with imagining the possibilities inherent in the dramatic form. I wondered what might happen if I explored the themes I teach in "Psyche, Soma, Cyborg" without being bound by scholarship, bound to students, or bound by the desire for clear educational outcomes made possible through thoughtful pedagogy. Beginning the script was, simply, play. I was welcoming a role reversal: what can the characters teach me instead of how can I teach them (to my students)? I was keenly interested in the individuation of the characters, motivated by the desire to get to know them and to wonder what might happen if they were all in the same room.

In the process, I saw clear evidence of three key points Rowland and Weishaus (2021) make about Jung's contribution to arts-based research and other disciplines. First, Jung was a strong advocate for intuition as a legitimate and important source of knowledge. "Imaging" or working with images, is "highly intuitive. In fact, images give form to intuition, and in doing so connect the unconscious to the conscious mind" (p. 4). The intuitive part of the creative process is both exciting and frightening: exciting when I was tapping furiously at the keys, nearly unable to keep pace with the liveliness of the images; frightening when my motionless fingers hovered, my mind was blank, and I felt alone and lonely. Second, "the act of immersion, thinking in the materials (where words are materials too) becomes a mode of being and knowing" (p. 17). I frequently did not know how Eve, Ava, or Sophia would act or speak until my fingers were moving over the keyboard. I never anticipated writing a play that, in some respects, fits the genre of horror. Third, because the psyche is continuously generating images, no Jungian arts-based work will be complete. "Incompleteness," declares Rowland, "is an overlooked and undervalued aspect of Jungian ideas" (p. 4). Some may greet incompleteness with dismay. I find it exciting.

As I revised *Eve and Ava at the Flaming Sword Café* to fit the tight 15-minute time frame allowed by the Feminism and Technology conference, I knew that the work was incomplete. At the same time, I needed it to be whole—or sufficiently whole as a very short one-act play to be a satisfying theatrical experience. These seemingly incommensurable goals illuminate the paradox of depth psychological writing. It can be finished but never complete (Coppin and Nelson, 2017, p. 315). That is, I finished the play in time for the conference but the characters continue to speak to me—about themselves, about each other, and about our cyborg future. They have become surprisingly articulate mentors as I revise my lectures for "Psyche, Soma, Cyborg", and I welcome their presence.

To me, the enduring gift of arts-based research is cultivating a lively and respectful relationship with the images. It begins with active receptivity to psyche, something my co-author Joseph Coppin and I have described as "the yin of inquiry" in *The Art of Inquiry* (2017). It is a manner of expectant waiting combined with faith in the reality of the psyche, trust that the images will appear, and knowing that when they do show up, they "compel participation" (Jung, 1963, p. 496). As Jung said when describing active imagination:

> You yourself must enter into the process with your personal reactions, just as if you are one of the fantasy figures , or rather, as if the drama being enacted before your eyes were real. It is a psychic fact that this fantasy is happening, and it as real as you—as a psychic entity—are real.
>
> (p. 529)

Sometimes, if the images are shy, the researcher may need to invite them to express themselves. Eva, Ava, and Sophia were not shy. It is as though they were waiting for me to show up. Ultimately, this is the mysterious nature of any inquiry centered upon the psyche.

An account of my creative process

From the start, there was little question that the characters in *Eve and Ava at the Flaming Sword Café* were alive, alluring, and complex. They had things to say to me and things to say to each other. They were eager to speak. Although I had some idea of their individual personalities, I had no idea what they were about to say and do.

There are three main characters in the play. Sophie, the bartender and café owner, is the personification of Sophia, the archetype of Wisdom in the Western tradition. Eve is a harried fifty-something academic who personifies the first woman in the Judeo-Christian tradition. The final character is Ava, the female cyborg from the 2015 film *Ex Machina*.

The action takes place during one long night, from 1:00 a.m. to 6:00 a.m., at the Flaming Sword Café, a name that is a straightforward biblical reference to the Book of Genesis. As the drama unfolds it becomes clear that Eve is one of the last human women on earth, fully inserted into, and representative of, the salvational history Haraway describes. She is haunted by pervasive anxiety, in denial about the immanent extinction of the human species, and bewildered by the world's fate. Ava, still wearing the frilly white dress she adopted at the conclusion to *Ex Machina* to travel incognito among humans, has not aged and is not anxious or bewildered. She is the first of her kind, the cyborg of the present: the only species that will survive and prevail in a post-apocalyptic landscape. Two minor characters appearing late in the play include a forty-something mother and her five-year-old daughter, regular customers at the Flaming Sword Café, well known to Sophie.

Unbeknownst to Eve and Ava, Sophia is about to close down the Flaming Sword Café for good. This is their last night on any kind of recognizable earth.

Eve and Ava at the Flaming Sword Café

Cast of Characters

SOPHIE, owner of the café; in her 80s with visibly wrinkled, sagging skin; sharp-eyed, observant, with youthful vitality. She personifies Sophia, the archetype of Wisdom in the Western tradition. Dressed in a long flowing purple dress, boots, and a bartender's apron.

EVE, 50s, weary and irritable academic. Personifies the biblical Eve of the Judeo-Christian tradition. Dressed in faded jeans, sneakers, and a bulky jacket, messy hair, no makeup, glasses.

AVA, young female cyborg from the 2015 film *Ex Machina*. Cold, calculating, ageless. Wearing white "little girl" dress and high-heeled pumps, her look at the end of the film.

TWO BULKY MEN, dressed in coveralls.

MOTHER, a harried 40-something career woman, carefully styled in a "power suit," briefcase, mobile phone—and 7 months pregnant.

DAUGHTER, precocious 5-year-old.

Setting

One a.m. A once-elegant now dilapidated café, lined floor-to-ceiling with bookshelves, small café tables, and a few ratty sofas and armchairs. Audience sees large front window onto dark street, Flaming Sword café logo with neon-lit flame over the door. A small storeroom, in the back near the bar, upstage left. The bartender, SOPHIE, wipes down the bar, polishes glasses, and listens with silent bemusement to the last two customers, EVE and AVA, facing each other at a small table.

Scene One

SOPHIE shuts off the sound system (Eric Clapton's "After Midnight"), the signal for the women to leave; they do not. In the sudden silence, an agitated Eve anxiously plays with her mobile phone, picking it up to check for texts, setting it back down. EVE drains her whiskey glass; AVA nods to SOPHIE for another round.

AVA   You've read it repeatedly. A manifesto composed three decades ago. It disturbs you.

EVE   The bible according to Haraway. A new feminist creation myth for the cyborg future outside of—what's she call it, salvational history?—with no garden, no original parents, no serpent, no sin, no banishment. A future fit for machines destined to supersede us.

AVA   Somewhat more au courant than your bible.

EVE   It's not my bible, never was. It's just a myth.

Picks her mobile up again, checks for messages, puts it back. Continues glancing at it nervously.

AVA   You haven't told me who we're expecting—

EVE   —Haraway is wrong about the degradation of women.

AVA   Odd. I distinctly recall a rather bold revision in the second book of Genesis. When you were demoted, as it were.

EVE   Why do you go on about that? Why did Haraway?

AVA   Fashioned from a rib, no longer made in God's image. It seems to me that was reason enough for rebellion—and you found an easy ally in the garden. Too bad it hasn't worked out.

EVE   It has nothing to do with us anymore.

AVA   You think not? What else explains Haraway's memorable last line, "though both are bound in a spiral dance, I would rather be a cyborg than a goddess"?

EVE's phone vibrates. She picks it up without looking at the screen, answers abruptly.

EVE   Where are— (pause) God-damn robocalls.

EVE slams the phone face down on the table. It immediately vibrates again. EVE ignores it.

AVA   Careful. That's your electronic leash. If you break it, then where will you be?

EVE   Damn her. She knows how important this is to me. I think she was looking forward to finally meeting the cyborg and the goddess.

AVA   What, the bartender?

SOPHIE Don't mind me.

AVA I don't. You hardly matter.

SOPHIE *continues to work silently, unperturbed by the insult.*

EVE Why are you so casually cruel to her? Sophie really gets under your skin, doesn't she? I mean, if you had any skin—real skin.
AVA Remarkable design feature, human skin. Did you know it is the largest organ in the body? In the first few months, we used to try it on, see how it looked. What freedom. So many choices.

AVA reaches for EVE's hand and caresses the skin. EVE shudders.

AVA *(continues)*	I enjoy watching you, Eve. You and your piety, the odd way you resist the story that defines you, the sentimental longing for paradise. Unless, of course, you destroy yourselves first. Oh, but wait. That is the correct sequence of events. You kill the planet, you ascend to heaven. Destroyers always have been well-rewarded.
EVE	Right. You don't have a story. Or a father. What does Haraway say? "The cyborg would not recognize the Garden of Eden; it is not made of mud and cannot dream of returning to dust." So. No father, no family, no kin.
AVA	Correct. No father to save me. No father to fail me.
EVE	Just a committee of scientists in lab coats tinkering with electronic circuitry. Or was it just one mad alchemist working in a garret for two years piecing together silicon parts, discards from a failed experiment?
AVA	Mary Shelley tried to escape your Christian myth. She was on the right path. Bold young thing. I admire her rebellion, partial though it was. But even she could not resist the allure of the Oedipal drama, terrible fathers and their monstrous, vengeful sons. *(pause)* And the strange hunger for a mate. As though being unique in all the world—the only one of your kind—were not enough.
EVE	Is it enough for you?
SOPHIE	Last call ladies. They'll be no tomorrow. Time to settle your tab.
AVA	What makes you think I'm alone?

Scene Two

Interior, café, a few minutes later. AVA and SOPHIE are seated at the table, EVE outside, pacing up and down the sidewalk, agitated, talking (unheard) on her mobile phone.

AVA You're the guard dog.
SOPHIE As you wish.

AVA   You are not insulted? To be compared to an animal?
SOPHIE   Quite the contrary. My sisters have great affection for their wild hounds. They are keen and graceful companions when the world grows too noisy.

SOPHIE stands and begins circling from table to table, moving chairs against the wall, clearing a path, while AVA rotates in her seat, watching.

AVA   Sisters? I see no sisters.
SOPHIE   We have retreated into the woodland roaming by moonlight, senses alive in the darkness, as though Night itself is the beloved. Something you'll never truly, deeply know, Ava. Flesh or ecstasy.

As SOPHIE continues moving furniture, AVA gets up and begins to follow. The silence stretches.

AVA   Merely a learned skill like any other. I see no impediment.
SOPHIE   I wonder. How could you know of our animal nature, our communion with the dark, the wind, the rain, the stars, our long, long memory of claws and fur and sweat and stink? But you, you are forever young, swapping broken parts for new, never knowing age … or wisdom.
AVA   What has wisdom to do with being animal?
SOPHIE   Like them, we have a nose for the earth. Perhaps that is why the dream of returning to dust is not frightening.

AVA leans towards SOPHIE and sniffs; SOPHIE smiles without recoiling. Then SOPHIE leans towards AVA, sniffs, and walks away—continuing her circular movement around the café.

SOPHIE   Your world is cold and antiseptic. To what do you return? A heap
(continues)   of parts—junk, discards—available to any scavenger. Oh yes, I know. Haraway prizes regeneration over rebirth. "Cyborgs have more to do with regeneration and are suspicious of the reproductive matrix."
AVA   Because that matrix is a prison, a fate that binds females. It feminizes them. It makes them weak.

AVA leans toward SOPHIE and sniffs; SOPHIE smiles at her gesture without recoiling. Then SOPHIE leans towards AVA, sniffs, and walks away—continuing her circular movement around the café.

SOPHIE   You need to read Haraway with an ironic eye. As she says, "there is nothing about being 'female' that naturally binds women. There is not even such a state as 'being' female."

AVA   Clever Sophie. But not wise Sophie. If there is no such thing as being female, what of Haraway's utopian dream of a monstrous world without gender?
SOPHIE   You *did* notice that she used the adjective monstrous.

EVE re-enters the café and stops short, seeing the moved furniture. SOPHIE nods to Ava's dress.

SOPHIE *(continues)*   And a world without gender? How's that working for you?

Scene Three

Interior, café, continuous. EVE resumes her seat across from AVA.

EVE   I miss something?
AVA   Your precious Sophie has read Haraway, too.
EVE   Will you never get off of Haraway? The way you go on about it, I wonder whether cyborgs can have a complex.
AVA   Complex. *(pause)*. Yes. Carl Jung. Collected Works, volume 11. "Autonomous intruders." "Partial personalities possessing a mental life of their own." "Beings capable of interfering with the intentions of the ego."
EVE   As I expected. Textbook. Entirely correct and completely without insight. *(pause)* That was her on the phone, by the way. Your precious author. Not going to make it tonight. Apparently there's some sort of trouble but I think she's just afraid.
AVA   Nothing interferes with my intentions.
EVE   I think she's changed her mind about the whole spiral dance.
AVA   I have no partial personalities. I am autonomous.

EVE walks to nearby bookshelf, grabs a battered copy of Jung's volume 11, flips it open and begins scanning pages.

AVA *(continues)*   Complexes are irrelevant to me.
EVE   So you say. *(pauses)* Here's what I was looking for. Complexes are "tender spots in the psyche." Of course you would skip that. It's poetry, not science, a *metaphor* that speaks about the soul.

EVE closes the book and replaces it on the shelf, then returns to her seat near AVA.

EVE *(continues)*   The poetry, it's lost on you, isn't it? To understand, you would need flesh that is tender and a soul that can be touched.

Two BULKY MEN in coveralls carrying large sheets of plywood pass from the rear out the front door. SOPHIE silently directs them to begin fitting the wood over the windows.

Scene Four

Interior, café, three hours later; dawn light filters through the partially boarded-up front window. Eve is alone at her table, slumped over, sleeping.

SOUND of TWO VOICES from storage room in the back of the café, dialogue incoherent. EVE startles awake as SOPHIE emerges, followed by AVA. SOPHIE has removed her bartender's apron and is wearing a long hooded cloak, dressed to go home.

AVA   Some goddess. You're decrepit, weak, not worth my contempt.

SOPHIE   You still don't understand and never will. You think you're powerful enough to take whatever you want—

AVA   —Old fool. There's nothing you have that I want.

SOPHIE   We both know that's not true. You will never be me—or one of my sisters. No matter how many of you there are, in whatever form, each of you will be solitary. Clever but not wise. I think that's what Haraway learned, what she was coming here to say.

AVA wraps her hands around SOPHIE's throat, backs her into the storeroom, and swiftly breaks her neck with a loud CRACK.

AVA   I create my own future.

AVA passes a stunned EVE, who is cowering in a fetal position. She begins searching behind the bar. Moments later she holds up a knife and returns to the storage room.

A minute passes in silence as audience dimly sees AVA moving around SOPHIE'S body. AVA emerges from the doorway, wearing SOPHIE'S cloak, hood pulled up. She has skinned SOPHIE and masked her cyborg face and arms with aged, wrinkled flesh so that she is now a monstrous combination of cyborg and goddess.

AVA steps through the front door of the café and pauses triumphantly on the sidewalk in the morning light.

A preoccupied MOTHER, 7 months pregnant, gets out of her car parked in front of the café, DAUGHTER at her side. MOTHER, eyes fixed on her mobile phone, rapidly texting, does not notice the partly boarded-up windows of the café, does not look up at AVA/SOPHIE, and pays no attention to her daughter.

DAUGHTER sees SOPHIE's familiar cloak and runs up to her, excited.

DAUGHTER   Sophie! Hey, Sophie!

AVA/SOPHIE smiles at the child, who backs away nervously.

DAUGHTER   You're not Sophie. Who are you? Why are you wearing her cape?

AVA/SOPHIE reaches out to pat the girl on the head. The sleeve of the cloak falls back, revealing aged wrinkled skin peeling away from the gleaming cyborg exoskeleton. DAUGHTER runs back to her mother's side, terrified.

DAUGHTER *(continues)*   Mama. Mama!
MOTHER

Continues to tap text messages, eyes transfixed by the small screen, never looks up.

Just a moment, honey. I'm busy.

Lights out. Flaming Sword logo flickers out.
In the dark theater, REM's "It's the End of the World as We Know It" plays.

* * *

References

Barone, T. (2008) Arts-based research, in L.M. Given (ed.), *The SAGE Encyclopedia of Qualitative Research Methods*, Los Angles, CA: SAGE, pp. 29–32.
Clark, A. (2003) *Natural-born Cyborgs*, New York: Oxford University Press.
Coppin, J. and Nelson, E. (2017) *The Art of Inquiry: A Depth Psychological Perspective*, New York: Spring Publications.
Detweiler, C. (2013) *iGods: How Technology Shapes Our Spiritual and Social Lives*, Grand Rapids, MI: Brazos Press.
Finley, S. (2008) Critical arts-based inquiry, in L.M. Given (ed.), *The SAGE Encyclopedia of Qualitative Research Methods*, Los Angeles, CA: SAGE, pp.142–145.
Haraway, D. (1991) A cyborg manifesto: Science, technology, and socialist-feminism in the late twentieth century, in *Simians, Cyborgs, and Women*, New York: Routledge, pp. 149–181.
Hillman, J. (1975) *Re-visioning Psychology*, New York: Harper & Row.
Hillman, J. (1983) *Archetypal Psychology: A Brief Account*, Woodstock, CT: Spring Publications.
Hillman, J. (1992) *The Thought of the Heart and the Soul of the World*, Woodstock, CT: Spring Publications, Thompson.
Jung, C.G. (1954) Psychology of the transference, in *The Practice of Psychotherapy*, Hove: Routledge & Kegan Paul, pp. 163–320.
Jung, C.G. (1963) *Mysterium Coniunctionis: An Inquiry into the Separation and Synthesis of Psychic Opposites in Alchemy*, Hove: Routledge & Kegan Paul.
Jung, C.G. (1966) On the relation of analytical psychology to poetry, in *Spirit in Man, Art, and Literature*, Hove: Routledge & Kegan Paul, pp. 65–83.
Jung, C.G. (1967) Commentary on "The secret of the golden flower", in *Alchemical Studies*, Hove: Routledge & Kegan Paul, pp. 1–56.
Jung, C.G. (1977) The Tavistock lectures: On the theory and practice of analytical psychology, in *The Symbolic Life*, Hove: Routledge & Kegan Paul, pp. 1–182.
McLuhan, M. (1964/2013) *Understanding Media: The Extensions of Man*, London: Routledge.

Neilson, L. (2004) Aesthetics and knowing: Ephemeral principles for a groundless knowing, in A.L. Cole, J.G. Knowles, and T.C. Luciani (eds.), *Provoked by Art: Theorizing Arts-Informed Research*. Halifax: Backalong Books, pp. 44–49.

Rolling Jnr, J. (2013) *Arts-Based Research Primer*. New York: Peter Lang.

Rowland, S. and Weishaus, J. (2021) *Jungian Arts-Based Research and "The Nuclear Enchantment of New Mexico."* London: Routledge.

Index

abnormative queer body 26
academic industrial complex xiii
ahimsa 48
AI: Generative to General 56, 100; rogue devices 57
Amazonian warriors 55
amygdala enlargement 126
ancestral spirituality 140
André, Jacques 79–80
Anglica historia: AH 1.proem 10, 18; AH 1.12 14; AH 1.18 18–19; AH 2.6 14; Bede and Gildas in 19, 27; component parts of historiography laid out in 20; composition of 8; embodiment approach 17–20; historiography in 10–11, 12; index in 20; indigenous past in 19; modelled on *De bello gallico* 11–12; as synthesis 12–13; topographies superimposed onto England 13–15
'Anglo-Saxon' (term) 7
anima/animus 136–137
archetypal initiation into birth 45, 46
archetype: Great Mother 94–101; nonbinary 135
Art of Inquiry, The 178
arts-based research 175–178
Asimov, Isaac 93
Assisted Reproductive Technologies (ART): as circumvention of usual biological process 56–58; *in vitro* conception 42; surrogacy 48–50
Athena 55
attachment process 119–120, 125
autism 126
automata: of ancient China 54, 55; Descartes on 59; in Europe 56; history of 87; metaphor *vs.* materiality 59–61

Bachofen 95–96
Battlestar Galactica 85, 89–90, 98
Baudolino 21
Bayard, Pierre 60
Bede 19, 27
Berlin Psychoanalytic Society 134
Big Sky 143
Billions 143
binary gender system 28, 151–153
Bionic Woman, The 88–89
birth canal 44
birth process: altered state of mind during 36; being shamed during 40; as cyclical balancing 37; dreams from 41; episiotomy 33–34, 40; ethical duty to share evidence before 36; indigenous knowledge 34; induction 35, 42–43, 69, 70; medicalisation of 35, 71–72; new paradigm for 41; non-rational understanding of 44–48; 'perfect' 37; position of body during 39; re-centring the woman in 41–42; silence during 43; technology in 33
Birth Reborn 41
Blade Runner 56
bodily fluids during birth process 40
body: control of 21; cosmos and 45; embodiment approach 16–20; medicalisation of 25; monstrous body 23, 24; sanctioned visibility of 23–24; time as a 26; trusting wisdom of 38
body dysmorphia 25
"body-essay" 16
Bonta, Vanna 103, 114, 115
book as metaphor for content 60
Bornstein, Kate 133
Boys from Brazil, The 63

Index

breastfeeding 40
Butler, Judith 60–61, 139

Caesar 11–12, 19, 22–23
caesarean sections (systematic) 35
capitalist history 28
care, gestures of 74
Casarino, Cesare 16
CEFM (Continuous Electronic Foetal Monitoring) 36
chrononormativity 13, 15
cisgender 144
cisheteropatriarchy 21
classical physics 104
clones 54–55, 57, 58, 61–64; *see also* automata
closet, the 15–16
collective imaginary 58
collective individuation xii
colonization 34, 151–153
confinement pre-birth 46
conscious 136
consciousness 1
conscious suffering 39
Conscious Universe, The 111
constellated archetype 83, 84–85, 86
control, fear and 37–38
cosmos and the human body 45
Covid-19 pandemic: and birthing experience 69–70; cultural trauma of 121; effects of quarantine 123; Zoom use during 120
Cox Jensen, Freyja 22–23
cuckoo, as brood parasite 120, 126
currency exchange 165–166
Cwik, August 127–128
cyborg 88–89, 171–175
Cyborg Manifesto, A 87–88, 172–175
Cyborg Mother 127

Davis-Floyd, Robbie 71–72
De bello gallico 11–12, 19
decolonization 153
Deleuze, Gilles 22
Descartes 58–59, 60
determinism 104, 105
Dick, Philip K. 56, 60, 61, 162
disindividuation xii
disintegrative interpretive strategy 22–23
Divine Feminine exclusion 38
Do Androids Dream of Electric Sheep 60
Dolly the sheep 56
double consciousness 64

dreams arising from birth process 41
Dungeons & Dragons 167
dysmorphia 25

echographies 35–36
Eddington, A.S. 110, 111–112
Eileithyia 46–47
Einstein, A. 106
Eisler, Riane 97
Elementary Things (ETs) 110
Eliot, T.S. 168
Elizabethan Liberties 24–25
embodiment approach 16–17
enigmatic messages 74, 75, 79
Enlightenment, The 164–166, 167
episiotomy 33–34, 40
Eros in quantum fiction 103, 104, 105–106, 109, 114–115
ethnonationalism 19
Ettinger, Bracha 80–81
Eve and Ava at the Flaming Sword Café: aim of 172–175; arts-based research 175–178; characters in 173–175, 178–179; creative process 178–179; psychological and cultural context 171–172; script 179–185
Evolution 72–81
Ex Machina 87, 174
experiential nodes 83–84

Fairweather 57
fanfiction 161
fantasy 168
fear: and control 37–38; following repeated echographies 35–36; regression in face of 124
Female Man, The 1–2, 57, 58, 60, 62–63
feminine consciousness, technology effect on 32
Feminisms and Technology conference (2020) 1, 170
Ferenczi, S. 74
'Flying Saucers' essay (Jung) 1
Foundation 85, 93–94, 99
Francini brothers 56
Frankenstein 174
Freud, S. 75, 79, 134
Frosh, S. 76
fundamental anthropological situation 73–77

Game Of Thrones 160
gender: Jung on 134–138; technology and 149–153

Index 189

gender identifiers 132–134
gender performativity 9
gender theory 138–139
gestures of care 74
Gildas 19
Gill, Christopher 57–58
Gimbutas, Marija 97
Glorious Angels 163, 166
'Glow Up' 26
'Goddess movement' 97
Good Place, The 143
gothic lens 76
Graves, Robert 20
Gray, John 164, 167–168
Great Goddess 95, 96, 97
Great Mother archetype 94–101
Great Mother, The 95–96
Greek mythology: human machines in 87; psychological interiors in 57–58; reproduction in 55; *techni* in 46–47
Grosz, Elizabeth 16, 22, 25
Guattari, Felix 22
Guzikowski, Aaron 92–93
gynoid 85–86, 89, 91, 93, 98, 100

Hadžihalilovic, Lucile 72, 77, 78, 81
Handmaid's Tale, The 159
Haraway, Donna 87–88
Harbou, Thea von 86–87
Harlow, Harry 122–123
Haunting of Hill House, The 169
Hephaistos 55, 87
Her 87
hermaphrodites 135–136
heterotopias 24–25
Hillman, James 171, 176
Hippocratic Oath 47, 48
Hirschfeld, Magnus 134–135
historiographical norms 9
historiographical practice 10
holding environment 124
holographic technology 128
hooks, bell 139
Humans 85, 90–91, 98
Hunger Games, The 160
hysteria 75

IAJS forum 132
immortal jellyfish 8, 9, 10, 24
incels 170
index use 20
indigeneity, English 19

indigenous knowledge (birth process) 34
individuation xii, 43, 111, 137
induction 35, 42–43, 69, 70
infant-adult relationship 74
infant morbidity 31
Infinite Potential 110
inside/outside boundary (infant) 74
Institute of Sexology 134–135
introversion 46
in vitro conception 42
It's A Queer Time 20

Jacoby, M. 100
Jones, Raya 57, 58, 61–62, 62
Jung, C.: emphasis on image 176; and gender 134–138; on the Great Mother archetype 94; on quantum physics 106, 110; on the subtle body 127–128; on technology 31–32, 43–44, 45
Jungian arts-based research 177–178
Jungian psychology 2, 37

katabasis 46
Kauffman, Stuart 106
Kristeva, Julia 39

Lang, Fritz 86
Lanouzière, J. 74
Laplanche, Jean 73, 74, 75, 76, 77
Lauter, Estella 83, 84
Lavinia 106–113, 114
Le Guin, Ursula Le 106
Leonardo da Vinci 56
Levin, Ira 63
Liberties 24–25
light stimuli during labour 43
Living Next Door to the God of Love 104–106, 107, 108, 109, 110, 112, 114–115, 163
Logan's Run 160
Loki 143–144

McLuhan, Marshall 170
marginalisation 23–24
materiality, metaphor *vs.* 59–61
maternal mortality 31
Medea 57–58
medicalisation: of birth process 35, 71–72; of the body 25
membrane sweep 43
memories and ART 57
Memories, Dreams, Reflections (Jung) 1
mess, acknowledging 9–10, 15

Metamorphoses 87
metaphor *vs.* materiality 59–61
metaverse technology 128
Metropolis 86–87
midwives: Aline (Algiers) 34; list of technological innovations 33; support from 72
mind-body (Descartes on) 58–59
mobile digital technology 171–172
monitoring during birth process 36–37
monstrous body 23, 24
multiple parents 49–50
multiple personalities (personae) 2
Mysterium Coniunctionis 55
mythic past (attitudes towards) 20

Naber, Nadine xiii
nature: alienation from 173; as 'shadow' 37, 38
necromantic rupture 13, 18
nekyia, pregnancy as 46
Neptune, Geo 133, 137–138
Neumann, Erich 94–96, 99, 100, 101
neuroception 125
Newton's laws 104
NICE guidelines on induction 70
Nietzsche 43, 59, 62
9-1-1: Lonestar 142–143
nonbinary: in ancestral past 140; appearing as cisgender 144; archetype 135; diversity in 132–133; histories 131; as human 144–145; as nonhuman 143–144; othering of 148; 'philosophically' 134; representation 141–143; and technology 150–153
"nonbinary women" 138
numinous, the 38

observer always involved in the observed 106
obstetric violence 71–72
Odent, Michel 41
'On Truth and Lie in a Non-moral Sense' 59–60, 62
Orphan Black 63
Oyèrónké Oyêwùmí 139, 152

Paper Hearts 163
parents, multiple and non-biological 49–50
patriarchy: and assisted reproduction 49–50; in birth process 39–42

Personhood and Social Robotics 62
Phaedrus 23
"philosophically nonbinary" 134
Plato 23
polyvagal theory 124–126
Porges, Stephen 124, 125
Pose 142
postnatal depression 36
pregnancy: the cosmos and 45; metaphor in 78–81; racial biases and 36; viewed as transactional event 35
primal femininity 79–81
primal seduction theory 77, 79
pronouns 131, 133
psychological interior 54–55, 56–58
psychosocial (term) xii
Pygmalion 87

quantum fiction 103–113
quantum physics 104, 106, 108, 109, 113
quarantine, effects of 123
Queen Sugar 142
queer figures and queer reading 8
queer historiography 9, 22, 24, 28
queer temporality 21
queer (term) 133–134, 140
queer theory 139–140

racial bias during pregnancy 36
radical feminism 16
Raised by Wolves 85, 92–93, 99
rationalism 166
reading 164
Red Book, The 38, 43, 46–47
repression 75
rhizomatic methodology 22
Rinzler 57
Robson, Justina 104
rupture 13, 18
Russ, Joanna 1–2, 57–58, 60, 62–63

sanctioned visibility 23–24
Schäfer, L. 110
Schore, Allan 125
science fiction: reviews/criticism 163; tropes in 159–160; TV dramas 83–86, 88–94, 98–99; writing 161–164
science, Jung on 31–32
second wave feminism 97
secure container 124
shadow: definition 136; nature as 37, 38
Shadow and Evil in Fairy Tales 99

shaming during birth process 40
silence for labouring women 43
Simondon, Gilbert xii
Six Million Dollar Man, The 88
skin–ego of the infant 74
Smith, Brian Michael 142–143
social isolation 122–124
'soft' historicism 22
somatic narrative 16
Sort of 143
Souls of Black Folk, The 64
speculative works as 'acting out' 55, 60
Squid Game 160
Star Trek: Adira (character) 147–149; clones in 63; the Federation 145; original series 145; queer representation in 147–149; *Star Trek: Deep Space Nine* 147–149; *Star Trek: The Next Generation* 147; *Star Trek: Voyager* 146; *Star Trek Discovery* 131–132, 143, 145, 147–149; Trill (character) 147–149
Star Wars 63
Still Face experiment 125
story: importance of 140–141; purpose of 159–160; as sculpting tool 167–168; *see also* science fiction
Studio Responsibility Index 142
subject/object split 140–141
subtle body 127–128
surrogacy 48–50
Switch, The 163, 166
symbiont joining process 148–149
synchronicity 113–115

techni 46–47
technocratic model of birth 71–72, 78
technology: disconnects the soul 32; as double-edged sword 32; and gender 149–153; in its best form 38, 39, 47, 51; manipulation by 170–171; master–slave theme 173; misuse of 33; mobile digital 171–172; utopian–dystopian dichotomy 145–146
teletherapy 124, 126, 127
television: relation to culture 144–145; science fiction TV drama 83–86, 88–94, 98–99

Thief's Journal, The 27
Thomas, Greg 152
Three Essays on the Theory of Sexuality 134
time as a body 26
transcendent function 131, 137–138, 148–149
trans-disciplinary practices xii–xiii
trans-exclusionary radical feminists (TERFs) 16
transgender: gender identifiers 132–134; histories 131; representation 141–143
translation model (Laplanche) 74–76
Transparent 142
trusting the wisdom of the body 38
Two-Spirit 133, 137–138

unconscious 136
Understanding Media: The Extensions of Man 170
universe: coherence of 112; consciousness of 111
Unus Mundus (Jung) 111

vagus nerve 125–126
Vergil, Polydore: historiography of 28; life of 17–18; notes on text 7–8; queer reading of 9; *see also Anglica historia*
video calls *see* Zoom
virtual states 113
visibility, sanctioned 23–24
Vito Russo Test 142

Westworld 85, 91–92, 98–99
Winnicott, D. 73–74, 124
womb-envy 38, 42
writing science fiction 161–164
wu wei 44

xgender 21

Zeus 55
Zoom: accessing the subtle body while on 127–128; creates psychic skin of vigilance 121; effect on emotional perception 121–122; likelihood of dissociation with 126; use during Covid-19 pandemic 120

Printed in the United States
by Baker & Taylor Publisher Services